Guide to America's Outdoors

Southwest

Guide to America's Outdoors
Southwest

By Mel White
Photography by George H. H. Huey

□ NATIONAL
□ GEOGRAPHIC
WASHINGTON, D.C.

Contents

Cover: View from Mather Point, Grand Canyon National Park
Page 1: Black-throated hummingbird, Arizona-Sonora Desert Museum
Pages 2-3: Three Sisters at sunrise, Monument Valley Navajo Tribal Park
Opposite: Hikers on the Mogollon Rim, Apache-Sitgreaves National Forests

Treading Lightly in the Wild

Camping, Organ Pipe National Monument

NATIONAL GEOGRAPHIC GUIDE TO AMERICA'S OUTDOORS: SOUTHWEST takes you to some of the wildest natural areas in one of the most spectacular and diverse parts of the world: the American Southwest. From the peaks of San Francisco Mountain to the depths of the Grand Canyon, from cactus-studded deserts to shaded streambeds, the incomparable land of Arizona, New Mexico, and Texas calls for special appreciation and attention.

Visitors who care about this region know they must tread lightly on the land. Ecosystems can be damaged, even destroyed, by misuse. Before embarking on a backcountry visit or a camping adventure, learn some basic conservation do's and don'ts. Leave No Trace, a national educational program, recommends the following:

Plan ahead and prepare for your trip. If you know what to expect in terms of climate, conditions, and hazards, you can pack for general needs, weather, and emergencies. The Southwest is a land of extremes: Intense summer heat can make hiking unpleasant and inadvisable, arid conditions may prohibit campfires, and sudden storms and flash floods can seriously endanger an unprepared visitor. Do yourself and the land a favor by visiting if possible during off-peak months and limiting your group to no more than four to six people. To keep trash or litter to a minimum, repackage food into reusable containers or bags. And rather than using cairns, flags, or paint cues that mar the environment to mark your way, bring a map and compass.

Travel and camp on solid, unvegetated surfaces such as rock, sand, or dry washes. Plant life in the Southwest is very delicate—even overturning a lichen-covered rock can permanently destroy its living covering. In popular areas, stay within established trails and campsites. Travel single-file in the middle of the trail to avoid trampling vegetation. When exploring off the trail in pristine, lightly traveled areas, have your group spread out to lessen impact. Good campsites are found, not made. Remember to stay at least 300 feet from waterways. After you've broken camp, leave the site as you found it.

Pack out what you pack in—and that means *everything* except human waste, which should be deposited in a cathole dug away from water, camp, and trail, and then covered and concealed. When washing dishes, clothes, or yourself, use small amounts of biodegradable soap and scatter the water away from lakes and streams. Where water is very scarce, consider using it for drinking only, and leave the washing for home.

Be sure to leave all items—plants, rocks, artifacts—as you find them.

Never touch or trace rock art. Avoid potential disaster by neither intro-
ducing nor transporting non-native species. Also, don't build or carve out
structures that will alter the environment. A don't-touch policy not only preserves resources for future generations; it also gives the next guy a crack at
the discovery experience.

Always check with local officials before building a campfire. In many
places, at many times, campfires are forbidden due to the threat of wildfires. Where they are allowed (often by permit only), they may be imprac-
tical due to the lack of firewood. When you can, try a gas-fueled camp stove
and a candle lantern. When you do build a fire, employ existing fire rings;
elsewhere, use fire pans or mound fires. Keep your fire small, use only
sticks from the ground, burn it down to ash, and don't leave until it's cold.

Respect wildlife. Watch animals from a distance (bring binoculars
or a telephoto lens for close-ups), but never approach, feed, or follow
them. Feeding weakens an animal's ability to fend for itself in the wild. If
you can't keep your pets under control, leave them at home.

Finally, be mindful of other visitors. Yield to fellow travelers on the
trail, and keep voices and noise levels low. Let natural places quiet your
mind, refresh your spirit, and remain as you found them.

MAP KEY and ABBREVIATIONS

National Park ..............................N.P.
National Historical Park ...............N.H.P.
National Historic Site .................N.H.S.
National Memorial ....NAT. MEM.
National Monument ....NAT MON.
National Preserve
National Recreation Area ............N.R.A.
National Recreation Site .............N.R.S.

National Forest ..........................N.F.
Biosphere Reserve

National Grassland .....................N.G.

National Conservation Area .........N.C.A.
National Wildlife Range
National Wildlife Refuge .............N.W.R.
Resource Conservation Area ........R.C.A.
Wildlife Area ............................W.A.

Historical State Park ..................H.S.P.
State Historical Park ..................S.H.P.
State Park ...............................S.P.

Indian Reservation .....................I.R.

Air Force Base ..........................A.F.B.
Military Reservation

National Wild & Scenic River ........N.W.& S.R.

BOUNDARIES
State or National

| FOREST | I.R. | N.P. | WILDERNESS |

POPULATION
- **PHOENIX**   above 500,000
- **Albuquerque**   50,000 to 500,000
- Casa Grande   10,000 to 50,000
- Redrock   under 10,000

U.S. Interstate
(10)

U.S. Federal or State Highway
(89) (64)

Other Road
[231]

Trail

Continental Divide

ADDITIONAL ABBREVIATIONS

BLVD.	Boulevard
C.M.A.	Cooperative Management Area
Cr.	Creek
DR.	Drive
HWY.	Highway
L.	Lake
MEM.	Memorial
Mt. s.	Mount-ain-s
N.	North
N.R.T.	National Recreational Trail
Pk.	Peak
Pt.	Point
RD.	Road
Rec.	Recreation
Res.	Reservoir
WILD.	Wilderness

□ Point of Interest   ⊬ Falls
⊛ State capital   ℓ Spring
+ Elevation   ⊁ Dam
⤸ Pass   --- Intermittent River
△ Campground   ◌ Intermittent Lake
⌓ Picnic Area   ◌ Dry Lake

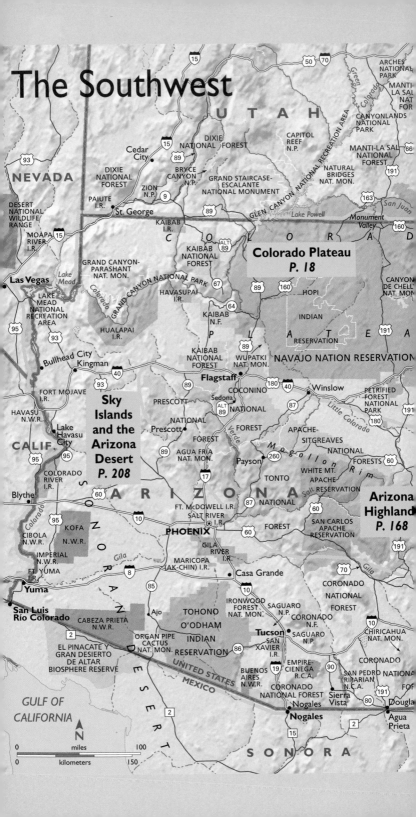

The Southwest

NEVADA

UTAH

COLORADO

Colorado Plateau
P. 18

NAVAJO NATION RESERVATION

Sky Islands and the Arizona Desert
P. 208

CALIF.

Arizona Highland
P. 168

A R I Z O N A

Las Vegas

Cedar City

St. George

Bullhead City
Kingman

Prescott

Flagstaff

Sedona

Winslow

Payson

PHOENIX

Blythe

Lake Havasu City

Yuma

San Luis Río Colorado

Casa Grande

Ajo

Tucson

Sierra Vista

Nogales

Agua Prieta

Douglas

DESERT NATIONAL WILDLIFE RANGE

MOAPA RIVER I.R.

LAKE MEAD NATIONAL RECREATION AREA

DIXIE NATIONAL FOREST

ZION N.P.

PAIUTE I.R.

KAIBAB I.R.

BRYCE CANYON N.P.

DIXIE NATIONAL FOREST

GRAND STAIRCASE-ESCALANTE NATIONAL MONUMENT

CAPITOL REEF N.P.

GLEN CANYON NATIONAL RECREATION AREA

NATURAL BRIDGES NAT. MON.

CANYONLANDS NATIONAL PARK

ARCHES NATIONAL PARK

MANTI-LA SAL NAT. FOR.

MANTI-LA SAL NATIONAL FOREST

Lake Powell

Monument Valley

CANYON DE CHELLY NAT. MON.

GRAND CANYON-PARASHANT NAT. MON.

GRAND CANYON NATIONAL PARK

HAVASUPAI I.R.

KAIBAB NATIONAL FOREST

KAIBAB N.F.

HUALAPAI I.R.

FORT MOJAVE I.R.

HAVASU N.W.R.

KAIBAB NATIONAL FOREST

WUPATKI NAT. MON.

HOPI INDIAN RESERVATION

COCONINO NATIONAL FOREST

PETRIFIED FOREST NATIONAL PARK

PRESCOTT

NATIONAL FOREST

AGUA FRIA NAT. MON.

APACHE-SITGREAVES NATIONAL FORESTS

Mogollon Rim

TONTO NATIONAL FOREST

WHITE MT. APACHE RESERVATION

Salt

COLORADO RIVER I.R.

CIBOLA N.W.R.

KOFA N.W.R.

IMPERIAL N.W.R.

FT. YUMA I.R.

CABEZA PRIETA N.W.R.

FT. McDOWELL I.R.

SALT RIVER I.R.

GILA RIVER I.R.

MARICOPA (AK-CHIN) I.R.

SAN CARLOS APACHE RESERVATION

IRONWOOD FOREST NAT. MON.

SAGUARO N.P.

CORONADO N.F.

SAGUARO N.P.

CORONADO NATIONAL FOREST

CHIRICAHUA NAT. MON.

CORONADO NATIONAL FOREST

SAN PEDRO NATIONAL RIPARIAN N.C.A.

TOHONO O'ODHAM INDIAN RESERVATION

SAN XAVIER I.R.

EMPIRE-CIENEGA R.C.A.

BUENOS AIRES N.W.R.

CORONADO NATIONAL FOREST

EL PINACATE Y GRAN DESIERTO DE ALTAR BIOSPHERE RESERVE

ORGAN PIPE CACTUS NAT. MON.

UNITED STATES
MEXICO

GULF OF CALIFORNIA

Lake Mead

Colorado

Gila

Verde

Little Colorado

Green

Colorado

San Juan

SONORA

N

miles
0   100

kilometers
0   150

Coming to Terms with Geology

I HAVE TO ADMIT THAT I USED TO BE one of those people who skip the geology sections of natural history books. I'd start the first chapter, and as soon as words like igneous and sedimentary and rhyolite and dolomite started popping up, I'd jump right ahead to the good stuff, to wit: the who, what, where, and when of flora and fauna.

Eventually, though, morning arrives even for the sleepiest among us. Just so, I came to realize that understanding the why of vegetation and wildlife required coming to terms with geology. Why do great pine forests dominate much of the Southeast? Why do waterfowl-rich prairie potholes dot North Dakota? Why is the Southwest's Llano Estacado grassland so flat? Why do the Rockies lift their snowy summits where they do? The answers lie in the Earth's transmutations over the nearly incomprehensible sweep of geologic time, a process that in the Southwest tells an especially fascinating—not to mention varied and violent—story.

I made my first trip to New Mexico and Arizona when I was seven, a kid crazy about snakes, lizards, and birds. It was an experience that would shape my life. For someone from the humid, relatively flat South, the deserts, pinyon-juniper hills, and conifer-covered mountains of the Southwest might as well have been another planet. I was infected, even then, with dreams—literal dreams—of traveling to experience new landscapes, new plants and animals.

In my twenties I started making regular trips to southern Arizona because it's the best place in the country to see birds. As my curiosity grew, I had to ask: Why? Because habitats of exceptional diversity exist in proximity. Why? Because tall mountains rise straight out of low deserts and grasslands. Why? Because the earth started pulling itself apart here more than eight million years ago.

As I traveled for this book I of course always had an eye open for the blue flash of a pinyon jay, the variegated wings of a bordered patch butterfly, the white rump of a sprinting pronghorn, but time and again I also came across intriguing and illuminating stories in the rocks, from the bizarre formations of Chiricahua National Monument in Arizona to the massive granite palisades of New Mexico's Cimarron Canyon State Park.

No matter where you go in the Southwest, I urge you not to skip over the strange words, and even stranger concepts, of the underlying geology. Understanding the why of the landscape creates a deeper appreciation for the places you'll see. The high points of Arizona, New Mexico, and Texas, for example, derive from completely different geologic processes: volcanic eruption, continental collision, and, amazingly, reef formation in an ancient tropical sea. Knowing that won't make the view any better as you stand on the summit of Wheeler or Guadalupe peaks, but it's bound to make the journey more satisfying, more complete—and more fun, too.

Mel White

Taking a breather in Oliver Lee Memorial State Park

An Ecological Crossroads

NATURE BOOKS USE THE TERMS DIVERSITY and ecological crossroads a lot
—so much so that writers often wish more synonyms existed for these
practical biological concepts. In this book, you will encounter them
frequently—for if you looked them up you might well find at the end of
their definitions a cross-reference reading "See U.S. Southwest: Arizona
and New Mexico."

When you can travel from arid desert to lush coniferous woodland and
even alpine tundra in a matter of hours, what word but diversity fits the
great range of habitats you traverse, the varied flora and fauna you can
see? The very concept of life zones—elevationally associated assemblages

Bikers, Coconino National Forest

of plants and animals corresponding with changes in latitude—was inspired by San Francisco Mountain in northern Arizona, back in 1889. Renowned biologist C. Hart Merriam noted then that traveling from the desert of the Little Colorado's canyon bottom to the tundra on Humphreys Peak, the highest point on San Francisco Mountain, was the ecological equivalent of a trip from Mexico to Canada.

Arizona and New Mexico deserve the description ecological crossroad, for they encompass parts of four major North American deserts, the southernmost Rocky Mountains, a segment of Great Plains prairie, Basin and Range fault-block peaks, semi-arid desert grasslands, critically important riparian corridors, and the world's largest contiguous ponderosa pine forest. In these two states you can see yellow-bellied marmots, blue grouse, arctic fritillary butterflies, and blue spruces, as well as antelope jackrabbits, elegant trogons, and organ pipe cactuses, just to list a few species that represent elevational and geographic extremes.

This book treats Arizona and New Mexico in six chapters corresponding to their major bioregions, with compromises for reasons of geography and travel logistics. (Otherwise, for example, the Chihuahuan Desert would be split in two by the New Mexico highlands.) We've even included a bit of Texas (the highest bit, by the way), because the same singular geologic events that led to the creation of New Mexico's Carlsbad Caverns also built the crests of nearby Guadalupe Mountains National Park, just across the state line.

The chapters follow a roughly clockwise itinerary, beginning with the Colorado Plateau, the broad, relatively flattish area of uplift centered on the Four Corners region where Arizona, New Mexico, Colorado, and Utah meet. While mountains were being pushed up and the Earth's crust was being torn apart around them, the Colorado Plateau has remained basically stable for 600 million years. "Basically" is only a comparative term, though: In that time seas have come and gone, rock have been deposited and eroded away, mammoth volcanoes have burst through the surface, and over the past six million years the Colorado River, or its ancestor, has helped carve the wonder called the Grand Canyon.

The book's smallest region comprises north-central New Mexico, where the Rocky Mountains reach their southernmost extension in the peaks around Santa Fe. The mountains currently known as the Rockies were pushed up about 70 million years ago by the collision of the North American Plate with micro plates. True alpine tundra tops a few of these summits; this stark landscape and its adjacent forest are the southernmost home for many plants and animals more commonly found in the cooler north. Bisecting the region flows the Rio Grande, here a rushing whitewater stream that provides some of the best rafting and canoeing in the Southwest.

The third chapter, covering eastern New Mexico, includes fewer conventionally scenic destinations than do the others, though the underground formations of Carlsbad Caverns National Park are a spectacular exception. The prairie of the northeastern part of the state gradually transitions southward into Chihuahuan Desert; pronghorn roam the grassland, and in winter flocks of geese and cranes offer excellent viewing at national wildlife refuges.

Chapters 4 and 5 include more Chihuahuan Desert sites, the great rift valley of the middle Rio Grande, and the rather mixed bag of highlands called the Arizona-New Mexico Mountains, which comprise their own bioregion. Partly volcanic, partly built from faulting, these more or less contiguous ranges include some of the prettiest and most rewarding destinations in the Southwest, including the White Mountains of Arizona and the rugged backcountry of New Mexico's Gila National Forest, the home of the world's first officially designated wilderness area. Also part of Chapter 5 is Arizona's famed Mogollon Rim, the escarpment that marks a portion of the southern edge of the Colorado Plateau and provides so many

Aspen on the north rim of Grand Canyon National Park

favorite summer-vacation getaway sites for desert-dwelling Arizonans, from pine-shaded campgrounds to hiking trails.

The sixth chapter is the book's longest, describing the fabulously diverse "sky island" mountains of southern Arizona, along with their surrounding desert and grassland. Many of these uplands were built by the same forces that created the Basin and Range region covering much of the West: pulling-apart movements of the Earth's crust that caused large blocks to drop and adjacent ones to tilt and lift. The result has been mountains rising like islands from arid lowlands, which isolate the forested peaks in an "ocean" of desert and scrub.

Parts of four North America deserts are included in this volume. The Sonoran Desert of southern Arizona is typified by large columnar cactuses such as the giant saguaro and benefits from two rainy seasons each year, a circumstance that contributes to its diversity of vegetation. The Mojave Desert, located mostly in California and southern Nevada, extends slightly into western Arizona. Marked in part by the presence of the Joshua tree, a multi-branched yucca, the Mojave is only marginally distinct from the Sonoran, and is even classed with it by some biologists.

The Great Basin Desert of the Colorado Plateau is the highest and coldest of the four major arid regions. Dominated by sagebrush and lacking great variety of cacti and succulents, it seems less desert-like than the others; it instead resembles an environment most people would call scrubland, though its scant rainfall qualifies it as true desert. To the east stretches the Chihuahuan Desert, reaching up from Mexico into southern New Mexico—and, depending on who's drawing the boundaries, perhaps into extreme southeastern Arizona. Boasting a notable variety of endemic plants (species found nowhere else), the Chihuahuan Desert receives more rain than other deserts and often has a grassland-like aspect.

Not all the sites covered in this book are, strictly speaking, natural areas. A few are included for their educational value, especially for travelers visiting the region for the first time. The Arizona-Sonora Desert Museum outside Tucson, Boyce Thompson Arboretum State Park east of Phoenix, the Arboretum at Flagstaff, Albuquerque's Rio Grande Nature Center, and Living Desert Zoo and Gardens State Park at Carlsbad, New Mexico, are hardly "wild," but a few hours spent enjoying them can make your explorations elsewhere more meaningful—providing you with pieces of ecological puzzles you'll put together on your hikes and drives.

Some of the most interesting and rewarding destinations in this region are in many cases among its least known. As you travel around New Mexico sampling its natural wonders, visit Oliver Lee Memorial State Park, near Alamogordo, and Valle Vidal, north of Taos. On your way to the Grand Canyon, stop at Sunset Crater Volcano National Monument, outside Flagstaff. Discover Buenos Aires National Wildlife Refuge, in south-central Arizona, and El Malpais National Monument, in northwestern New Mexico. Walk down into a volcanic crater at Capulin Volcano National Monument, east of Raton, New Mexico, and drive the auto-tour route at Bitter Lake National Wildlife Refuge, near Roswell. All will repay your attention with varied wildlife, vegetation, and scenery.

Don't be diffident, as some people are, about visiting sites carrying the designation "wilderness area." Some travelers see that label and think such places are the exclusive domain of trail-tough backpackers toting tents, sleeping bags, and a week's worth of freeze-dried food. There's no law preventing you from walking a half-hour into a wilderness area, or a half-day, turning around, and walking out. Someone who hits the trail at dawn and spends a half-day walking 2 or 3 miles, stopping often to sit quietly and look and listen, will almost always see more wildlife than the "serious" hiker who trudges along trying to rack up 20 miles a day.

Each site in this sampling of the Southwest's wonders brings its own rewards, from mountaintops to desert washes, from a multi-day hike in the Gila National Forest to a half-day float trip down the Rio Grande. As you enjoy them, take time to discover the species that make them home: Carry binoculars and field guides, and talk to naturalists and rangers about what you might see. The more you know, the more you'll appreciate the southwestern environment—and the more likely you'll be to come to its defense when it's threatened. Here as elsewhere, politicians abound who care more about logging, mining, and ranching money than about protection of natural resources. When decisions are made about the environment, you can make sure that eagles and prairie dogs and tortoises and orchids have a voice in the debate, too. ■

Climbing in Havasu Canyon, Arizona

Colorado Plateau

Hoodoo formations at Bisti/De-Na-Zin Wilderness

ALTHOUGH RELATIVELY FEW people may be familiar with the
Colorado Plateau as a geologic entity, countless millions
worldwide know very well what it looks like. The Grand
Canyon, the Painted Desert, Petrified Forest, Monument
Valley, Canyon de Chelly—all these are part of the
imagery, even iconography, of the American West, and all
are part of the Colorado Plateau.

Centered on the Four Corners region of Utah, Colorado, New Mexico, and Arizona, the plateau takes its

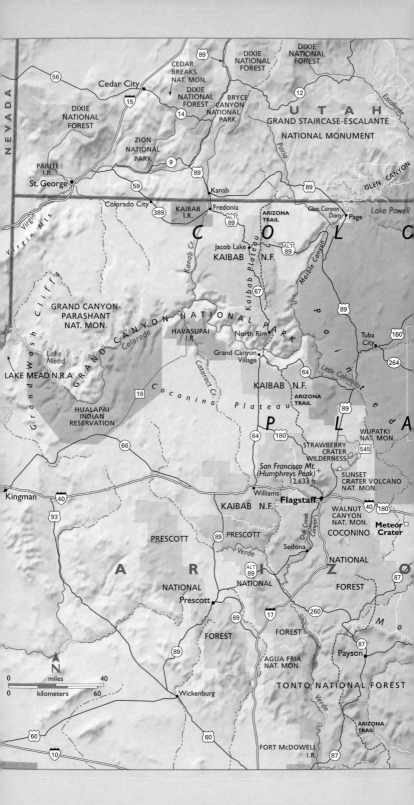

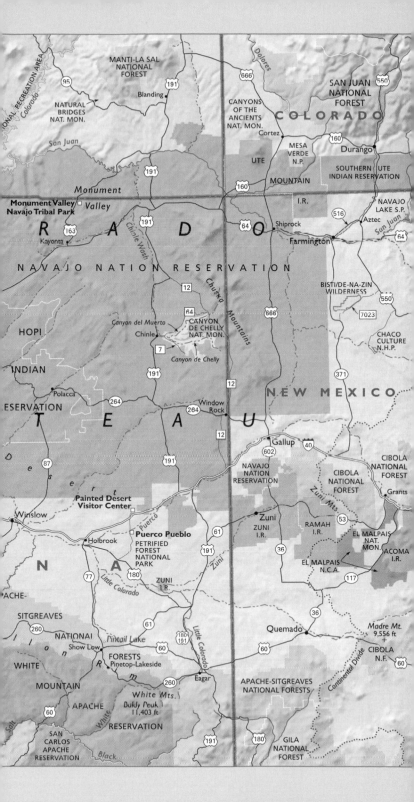

name from the great river that traverses it. The region encompasses the northwestern corner of New Mexico and most of the northern third of Arizona, where its southern edge is exceptionally well defined by the long escarpment of the Mogollon Rim. Although the Colorado Plateau has by no means remained unchanged over the vast sweep of geologic time, in comparison with the lands to its south and east it has been relatively stable for an exceedingly long period.

A succession of oceans dating back hundreds of millions of years left layers of sedimentary rock—limestone, sandstone, and shale—covering this part of the Earth as they advanced and receded. Raised as a cohesive and relatively flat whole by tectonic forces, the main plateau was later shaped by faulting, uplifting, and erosion into more or less separate units such as the Kaibab Plateau, which makes up much of the North Rim of the Grand Canyon, and the Coconino Plateau to the south.

In Canyon de Chelly and, of course, in the Grand Canyon, rivers have cut down into the soft sedimentary rock, creating deep gorges that rank among the most spectacular landscapes of North America. In Monument Valley, most of the top layers of rock have been eroded over a wide area, leaving solitary mesas and spires that themselves will disappear over succeeding eons. Many of the exposed rocks throughout the plateau contain iron-rich minerals, which oxidize to shades of deep red; iron oxides and other minerals are the "paints" that give the Painted Desert its breathtaking palette.

Portions of the Colorado Plateau have been wetlands at varying times —witness the fish and crocodile-like reptile fossils of the Petrified Forest—but at present much of it lies within the Great Basin Desert, an arid land of sparse grass, sagebrush, and scrubby junipers. In summer when heat waves shimmer or in winter when the north wind blows, it can seem a stark and uninviting landscape. But even at its starkest it can offer a kind of beauty, as at New Mexico's Bisti/De-Na-Zin Wilderness near Farmington, or in the bentonite clay badlands of the Petrified Forest.

Though the Colorado Plateau has seen relative geologic stability for several hundred million years, not all has been peace and quiet during that long period. The terrain around Flagstaff, Arizona, quite graphically shows evidence of volcanic activity, most obviously in the highlands of San Francisco Mountain, the eroded remains of a volcano that destroyed itself in a series of eruptions ending around 400,000 years ago. Not far away rises the cone of Sunset Crater. Just 750 years ago it was still pumping out ash and lava, and today you can sense the rawness of its cinders and jagged lava when you visit the national monument that protects it.

San Francisco Mountain and the Painted Desert region represent an important chapter in ecological history, for it was here that biologist C. Hart Merriam developed his theory of life zones, wherein he noted that plants and animals lived in associations based on elevation that corresponded to changes in latitude. Traveling from the arid canyon of the Little Colorado River, crossing the Painted Desert, and hiking up to the tundra at the top of Humphreys Peak, Merriam observed, was like traveling from Mexico to Arctic Canada—a journey of thousands of miles compressed into just a few dozen (see pp. 64-5).

Modern naturalists, professional and amateur, enjoy the diversity offered by the proximity of such a range of ecological zones. Pronghorn and jackrabbits inhabit grasslands; flocks of pinyon jays roam the pinyon-pine-juniper woodland; Abert's squirrels live in the ponderosa pine forest; elk and blue grouse can be found in Douglas-fir and Engel-mann spruce; and those who venture above tree line will see rare wild-flowers and alpine butterflies. All of this, and much more, exists within a half day's drive at most.

The Grand Canyon is the name that jumps out from a map of the Col-orado Plateau, and certainly it deserves every bit of fame that its awesome splendor has brought it. Of all our national parks, this surely is the most soul-stirring, in the deepest sense of that phrase. It's impossible to look into its depths without considering the nearly incomprehensible age of the Earth, the relentless movement of geology's clock, and the fragile place of human-kind on this small planet. That kind of inspiration may be the greatest reward nature study can offer us, and it's worthy of a very long journey, indeed. ■

Stream in Canyon del Muerto, Canyon de Chelly National Monument

Grand Canyon National Park

■ 1.2 million acres, including 277 miles of Colorado River ■ Northern Arizona, South Rim 90 miles north of Flagstaff ■ Best hiking spring and fall, river rafting April-Oct. Road to North Rim closed mid-Oct.–mid-May or longer, depending on weather; South Rim trails often icy and dangerous after winter snows ■ Camping, hiking, bird-watching, wildlife viewing, raft trips, mule rides ■ Adm. fee, plus additional camping and backpacking fees. Backcountry permits required ■ Reservations required for lodging, backcountry camping, river trips, and mule rides; make as far in advance as possible ■ Contact the park, P.O. Box 129, Grand Canyon, AZ 86023; phone 520-638-7888. www.nps.gov/grca

IN 1869, GEOLOGIST John Wesley Powell led the first scientific exploratory boat trip down the Colorado River, traversing a vast chasm in a region that he described as the "great unknown." A quarter century later, Powell had a different, more appreciative view of the place by then known as the Grand Canyon: He called it the "most sublime spectacle on the earth."

More than a hundred years and many thousands of adjectives have passed since then, and nobody has come up with a better way to express the emotional impact of this singular spot. People stand on the canyon rim and fall silent in awe, or shout with excitement, or laugh, or cry. They have seen pictures, of course, but nothing has prepared them for the true scale of what they find here. A mile deep, 10 miles wide, two billion years in the making—the words do their best, but they fail.

The Grand Canyon is, of course, a national park; it is also a World Heritage site, one of the Seven Natural Wonders of the World, and the place Theodore Roosevelt famously called the "one great sight every American...should see." American? Judging from the array of languages you hear on trails and at overlooks, the park has visitors from around the world. Nearly five million people a year visit the canyon—another statistic that's hard to comprehend until you've tried to find a place to park at Grand Canyon Village on a summer afternoon. The number of visitors puts tremendous pressure on park managers, who must balance the wants of eager travelers with the need to protect resources.

During peak season, private cars are banned from Hermit Road (West Rim Drive), which connects South Rim vista points west of the park hotel area; shuttle buses serve the route, cutting down on noise and congestion. At this writing, the park was in the initial stages of a far more ambitious project that would permanently take most private vehicles out of much of the South Rim area. (Most visitors complain not of too many people in the park, but of too many cars.) The plan entails using a light-rail system to bring people into the park from a transit center near Tusayan, the small town at the park's south entrance. Once at the rim, visitors will use buses and a "Greenway Trail System"—bicycle and walking paths—to get around. No doubt some people, raised on the idea of

Pinyon pines along the South Bass Trail, Grand Canyon National Park

drive-through parks, will find this inconvenient, but the result will be a quieter, cleaner, less congested park that's still accessible to everyone.

And what is this place that so many millions of people travel so far to see? On the most immediate level, there is Powell's "spectacle": a mile-deep canyon of intricately eroded, multicolored walls and buttes, a mammoth expanse of cliffs, plateaus, and side canyons laid out beneath your feet as you stand (not too close!) at the rim. Just looking, as an end in itself, could take as much time as you have to spend here.

On another level, the canyon may be the world's most comprehensive geologic textbook, displaying material down to the very bedrock of North America, nearly two billion years old. Layers of shale, sandstone, and limestone created during succeeding eras tell stories of deserts, seas, and swamps that have covered the land over hundreds of millions of years.

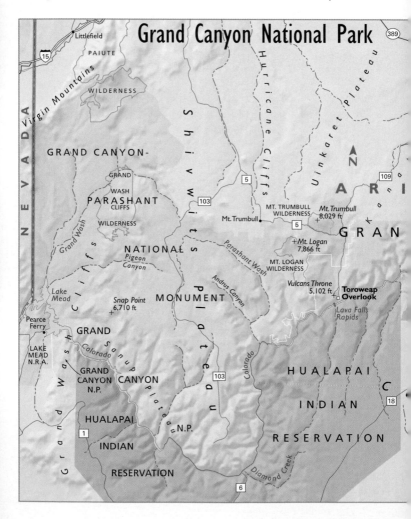

A mile below the rim runs the Colorado River, which instigated all this scenery, though it by no means created all of it. Geologists are still debating exactly how the river came to its current course. Most agree that over the past six million years the river, or its ancestor, cut down through the uplifted Colorado Plateau, giving the Grand Canyon its tremendous depth. Its width comes from erosion of the walls caused by water running off the rims; by water seeping into cracks, expanding as ice, and splitting rock; and by the combined forces of rain, temperature, and windblown dust on relatively soft sedimentary rock. Limestone and sandstone tend to erode vertically, while shale forms slopes, and it's the interbedding of differing materials that gives the canyon its stairstepped cliff-and-slope appearance. Because the Colorado Plateau tilts from north to south, water runoff is greater on the canyon's North Rim, resulting in a greater

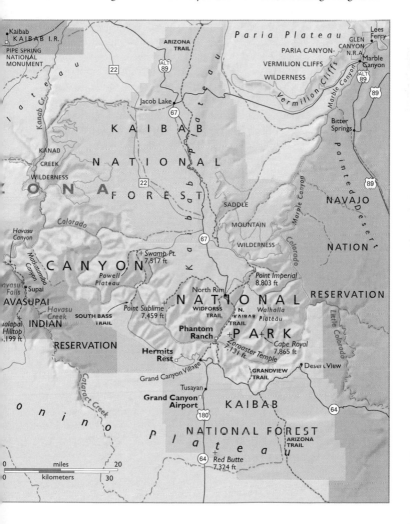

distance from river to rim on that side. This slope, too, explains why the North Rim stands 1,000 feet higher than does the South.

While some are content just to marvel at the canyon, others want to explore it, to see close-up those enormous walls, to reach that green ribbon of water at the bottom. A raft trip through the canyon provides perhaps the most intimate experience: running its ferocious rapids, camping along the Colorado, exploring side canyons that most visitors never see. Private river trips are allowed, but practically speaking, few people should plan on seeing the canyon this way: In 2000, the waiting list for such trips was more than 12 years. The alternative is commercial raft trips, which range in length from three days to three weeks. The park can provide a list of authorized outfitters, whom you should contact as far in advance as possible for details and reservations.

Advance planning is a necessity, too, for those who'd like to backpack into the canyon; visitation is limited, and many more people request permits than are granted them. No permit is needed for day hikes, but a few cautionary words are needed about any sort of trip below the rim.

Literally hundreds of times a year, visitors require help from park rangers because they underestimate the difficulty of hiking here. From a rim viewpoint, the trails below look temptingly accessible. But unlike hiking up a mountain, below-rim hikes at the Grand Canyon save the hardest part for last. Many people start down a trail in late morning in pleasant temperatures, to find themselves a few hours later hiking up an extremely steep trail without water, exhausted, suffering from the effect of altitude (the South Rim averages about 7,000 feet), in the heat of mid-afternoon—or with darkness finding them still far below the trailhead.

Remember that it takes many people at least twice as long to come up a trail as it does to descend. As a rule of thumb, you may want to turn around, no matter where you are, when you've drunk one-third of your water, unless you have confirmed that water is available along your route. Remember that when you go down into the canyon, you're traveling from a temperate woodland into a desert. Park officials strongly recommend against hiking from the rim to the river and back up in 24 hours.

What to See and Do

When planning a trip, it helps to think of Grand Canyon National Park in three parts: the South Rim, the North Rim, and the inner canyon.

The **South Rim,** with its hotels, restaurants, and shops clustered in **Grand Canyon Village** (*West Rim Drive),* attracts 90 percent of park visitors; most of the canyon's famous viewpoints are here, along with the main visitor center. Easily accessible, it's crowded from spring through fall. A day trip is possible from Flagstaff, but if you arrive midday in summer you're likely to find a long line of cars. (This situation will change when the park's light-rail transportation system opens, possibly in 2003.)

The **North Rim** is far less developed, and few park visitors

View from the South Rim, Grand Canyon National Park

head there first, or drive the 215 miles from the South Rim to reach it. Accommodations are limited, and early reservations are essential. The adjoining **Kaibab National Forest** *(North Kaibab Ranger District, Fredonia, AZ. 520-643-7395)* and its wilderness areas attract a number of campers, hikers, and backpackers.

No roads reach the **inner canyon,** accessible only by boat or via strenuous trails. Backcountry camping requires a permit, and demand is high; reserve your spot early. Rangers recommend spending at least two nights in the canyon, so you won't be hiking down one day and back the next. The only noncamping accommodation is at **Phantom Ranch,** on the Colorado River at the bottom of the Bright Angel and Kaibab Trails; reservations are required for rooms and meals. Mule trips (see sidebar p. 31) are another way to visit the inner canyon.

South Rim, West Side

Advice about many parks begins, "Stop first at the visitor center"— but you'll never make it at the Grand Canyon. If you drive in from Tusayan, you'll pull into the lookout at **Mather Point** to get your first view into the canyon. Here you'll gaze east to Yaki Point, Cedar Ridge, O'Neill Butte, beyond to Zoroaster Temple, and on to the North Rim, 8 miles and more away, depending on the direction in which you look. Below runs the **Colorado River,** which seems from this height more modest than its actual width of about 100 yards.

After taking in that first view, you'll be ready for the visitor center. After November 1, 2000, the new visitor center will be the Canyon View Information Plaza at Mather Point. If you arrive before November 1, 2000, you'll probably go to the center at Grand Canyon Village, where you can familiarize yourself with the park. Grand Canyon Village has six lodges, gift shops, restaurants and snack bars, and the **Kolb Studio,** with changing exhibits of Native American and Southwestern art. Many of the buildings in the village area are on the National Register of Historic Places. Be sure to take a look inside the 1905 **El Tovar Hotel** and the 1935 **Bright Angel Lodge,** the latter boasting a "geologic fireplace" with the rock layers of the Grand Canyon re-created in miniature. Bright Angel Lodge is the check-in point for mule trips into the canyon.

Guided Hike: Rim Trail
You're ready now to start your visit in earnest, and here's what you should do next for a good intro-duction to the canyon. Leave your car at the visitor center and take the free shuttle bus to **Yavapai Point,** one terminus of the **Rim Trail.** This easy path follows the South Rim westward from Yavapai more than 9 miles to Hermits Rest, and you couldn't ask for a better way to enjoy the wonders below. Paved for the first 3 miles, the trail stays fairly level, though some sec-tions may be too steep to be con-sidered wheelchair-accessible. You can walk as much or as little of the trail as you want; using your map and the shuttle buses, you can return to the visitor center from several points along the way. The canyon will unfold beneath you as you progress to the west, and you won't miss a single vista.

When you can take your eyes off the canyon, you'll note that you're passing through a woodland of ponderosa and pinyon pines, Utah junipers, and Gambel and shrub live oaks, intermixed with banana yuccas, Mormon teas, and cliffroses. You might spot a grizzled grayish rock squirrel or a stripe-faced cliff chipmunk, and there's no way you can miss the common ravens playing in the wind currents off the cliffs. Other birds often seen along the rim include hairy woodpeck-ers, Steller's and pinyon jays, mountain chickadees, and white-breasted nuthatches.

For some time now along the trail, you've had views of the cot-tonwoods at **Indian Garden,** 3,060 feet below the trailhead, and the side trail that leads out to **Plateau Point,** where the day mule trips go and which is a popular destination for hikers. This prominent point is part of the **Tonto Platform,** a ter-race composed largely of shale that has eroded to reveal the underly-ing stratum of sandstone. Just beyond, the canyon drops sharply into the inner gorge, where granite and schist (a metamorphic rock) date back nearly two billion years.

You'll notice how the Rim Trail climbs fairly steeply for a few hun-dred feet just west of the Bright Angel trailhead. A geologic fault runs across the canyon at this point, and slippage along its length has caused this elevation change in the otherwise flattish rim. The fault continues on the North Rim as Bright Angel Canyon. As the trail turns north you'll arrive at the **Trailview Lookout,** a good van-tage for watching hikers ascending or descending the switchbacks along the Bright Angel Trail. At about this point you'll be able to see **Red Butte,** a mesa topped by a remnant lava flow 17 miles to the south, and, on a clear day, **Humphreys Peak** 55 miles to the southeast, at 12,633 feet the tallest point in Arizona,

The paved section of the Rim Trail ends at **Maricopa Point,** 3 miles from Yavapai Point, but continues as an unmarked gravel or dirt path another 6.7 miles to Hermits Rest, a gift shop and snack bar at the end of the Hermit Road (West Rim Drive). Five shuttle-bus stops between Maricopa Point and Hermits Rest allow you to walk or ride to other wonderful overlooks such as **Hopi Point, Mohave Point,** and **Pima Point,** as well as catch a ride back to the park's visitor center.

Guided Hike: Bright Angel Trail to Plateau Point

With its trailhead just steps from the Grand Canyon Village hotels, the **Bright Angel Trail** is by far the most popular route into the canyon, used by both walkers and the famed mules. The 12.2-mile round-trip described here does not lead to the Colorado River, but it does lead to an overlook of the inner gorge. All routes into the canyon are highly strenuous, and this trail is certainly no exception; read the cautions at the beginning of this section. Water is usually available along this route from May to September.

Despite its crowds, the Bright Angel Trail is a rewarding hike—for those with the willpower to begin shortly after daybreak. Going all the way from the South Rim to Plateau Point and back usually requires from 8 to 12 hours, and getting an early start will give you time for a leisurely pace, as well as let you hike with some degree of solitude. Remember that by far the hardest part of the hike comes at the very end, as you climb the switchbacks back up to the South Rim.

As the trail angles down the canyon wall, you'll pass through two short tunnels in the first mile. Here, you're going back in time through the Kaibab and Toroweap

Mule Trips

The famous Grand Canyon mule rides make it possible to see the inner canyon without hiking down and back. (Stress on the legs is traded for soreness in a different body part.) More than a century ago, outfitters began using mules because they're less temperamental than horses, and the tradition has continued unbroken.

Seven-hour day trips down the Bright Angel Trail to Plateau Point and overnighters to Phantom Ranch are both extremely popular, and reservations (303-297-2757) ought to be made a year in advance if possible. Sometimes last-minute cancellations make spots available; check at the transportation desk in Bright Angel Lodge.

Riders must be over 4 feet 7 inches tall, weigh less than 200 pounds, not be pregnant, and understand English well enough to obey the leader's instructions. The mules are reliably surefooted, but the steepness of the trail and the vertical drops beside the switchbacks bother some people.

formations, limestone formed from the bodies of animals residing in a shallow sea more than 250 million years ago. Trailside trees are mostly pinyon pine and Utah juniper, but in moist, sheltered areas a few Douglas-firs grow, surprisingly near the desert vegetation you'll soon reach.

At the second tunnel you begin crossing Coconino sandstone, about 10 million years older than the Toroweap formation. This thick, tan layer of the canyon wall began as sand dunes in a desert environment, later compressed by overlying deposits and cemented by moisture into rock. After a series of switchbacks (they will seem endless on the way out), you reach Mile-and-a-Half Resthouse, where water is usually available May through September. At this point you have descended about 1,100 feet, and it's time to consider whether you want to go down (or rather, come up later) an even greater distance.

It's another 1,000 vertical feet down to Three-Mile Resthouse; here you've been crossing the reddish rocks of the Hermit shale and Supai formation, created by the mud of a swamp, probably a river delta, that existed here between 300 and 265 million years ago. Below this rest house, switchbacks called **Jacobs Ladder** provide a way down the tall cliffs of Redwall limestone, the legacy of another marine period 335 million years past. This stratum comprises the Grand Canyon's most noticeable rock layer, which is up to 500 feet thick in places. The surface of this naturally light-colored limestone has been stained dark red by

iron oxide washed down from the shale above.

By the bottom of Jacobs Ladder, you've left the trees of the higher canyon behind and are entering the desert environment of the Upper Sonoran life zone. The predominant plant in many places is blackbrush, a shrub in the rose family named for its bark color. Very little rain falls here, and temperatures soar in summer; only plants adapted to this demanding habitat, including yuccas, agaves, and various cactuses, can survive.

It's a different story when you reach the area around Indian Garden, with its campground, ranger station, picnic tables, mule corral, and rest rooms. Here, naturally occurring springs and precipitation gathered by the Garden Creek drainage support a variety of trees and shrubs, including Fremont cottonwoods (planted here), mesquites, ashes, and cliffroses. Native Americans once farmed this spot, and when the park was established in 1919, Havasupai Indians were still growing corn, beans, and other crops. You'll enjoy the shade, and probably settle down somewhere for a rest and a snack.

At this point you've covered 4.6 miles and descended 3,000 feet from the South Rim. The elevation change is negligible out to Plateau Point, but it's another 1.5 miles across the shadeless desert of the Tonto Platform. Look at your watch, and remember that it may take twice as long to return as it did to get here. If you decide to continue, you'll be able to look down from the point into the inner gorge of the canyon, where the dark rock dates back two bil-

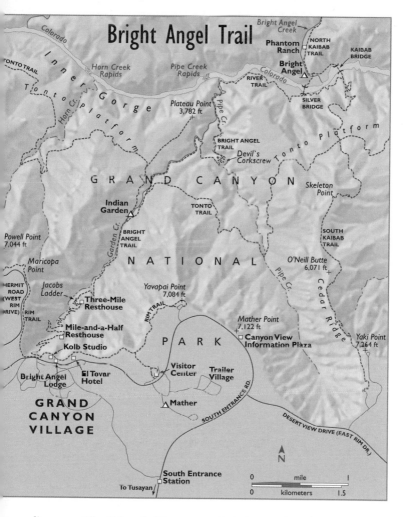

Bright Angel Trail

lion years. The Colorado River flows 1,320 feet beneath you, with Horn Creek Rapids to the west.

Turn around and look up at the buildings of Grand Canyon Village on the South Rim. Someone may be looking at you through a telescope at a Rim Trail vista. Wave, and go back up and join them.

South Rim, East Side

Back at the park entrance road, **Desert View Drive** (East Rim Drive) runs along the South Rim about 26 miles to the park boundary, but you can't drive to the next places on our tour. Take a shuttle bus to **Yaki Point** for another panoramic view, or to access the nearby South Kaibab trailhead.

The **South Kaibab Trail** leads 7.2 miles to Phantom Ranch, a trip that requires a backpacking permit or reservations at the ranch. A popular day hike entails trekking 1.5 miles to **Cedar Ridge,** a narrow rock bridge between Yaki Point and O'Neill Butte. Descending 1,460 feet (and of course ascending the same distance), this isn't an easy walk—but then there are no easy walks into the canyon. As you hike, you'll cross four of the canyon's rock layers: Kaibab limestone, which caps both rims and dates back about 250 million years; the slightly older Toroweap formation, composed of limestone and sandstone; the tall cliffs of Coconino sandstone, formed from huge sand dunes of 260 million years ago; and Hermit shale, originating as mud and silt carried by a river system about 265 million years ago. This trail is used by mule trips coming up from the river, and they have the right-of-way; if you meet a mule train, stand quietly at the side of the trail until it passes.

Another trail into the canyon begins at the parking area at

Havasu Canyon

Hikers wishing to see the spectacular waterfalls of Havasu Canyon, located outside Grand Canyon National Park on tribal land near the Havasupai village of Supai, must contact Havasupai Tourist Enterprise (520-448-2121. Fee). Reservations are needed for lodging and camping on tribal land, and hikers need permission to walk the 8-mile trail from Hualapai Hilltop (at the north end of Indian Road 18) to the village. Flash floods can be dangerous in the confined chasm.

Grandview Point, where a popular hotel stood in the 1890s. Again, the first part of the **Grandview Trail** can serve as a day hike, leading 3 miles (and 2,600 feet down) to **Horseshoe Mesa**, tiered layers of rock that truly do form a horseshoe shape. Here you'll see up close the 335-million-year-old Redwall limestone formation that comprises such a striking part of the Grand Canyon's walls. Be aware that the trail is unmaintained and steep; hiking down to Horseshoe Mesa and back in a day is strenuous. Carry plenty of water (there is none on the trail), and give this one a pass in summer. In winter the trail is often icy, and dangerous without crampons. You don't need to go all the way down, though, to get great views; there is a particularly striking panorama a couple of switchbacks down.

Continuing east on Desert View Drive, you'll pass the turns to Moran Point and Lipan Point before reaching the **Desert View** complex, where there's a general store, an information center, and a bookstore. The complex also features the 70-foot-tall **Watchtower,** a stone tower built in 1932 by architect Mary Colter of the famed Fred Harvey Company. The stunning vista from Desert View takes in a long stretch of the Colorado River, part of the gorge of the Little Colorado River (although Cape Solitude blocks a view of the actual confluence), and the Vermillion Cliffs about 50 miles to the north.

North Rim

Only 10 percent of visitors to Grand Canyon National Park take time to visit the North Rim. From

Havasu Falls, Havasu Canyon

Matkatamiba Canyon, Grand Canyon National Park

the South Rim you can see Grand Canyon Lodge at Bright Angel Point, 10 miles across the canyon, but it's 215 miles there by road, the last 65 on what is essentially a dead-end highway. Lodging is limited and usually books up long in advance. Park facilities, including lodging, restaurants, and gas stations, are closed from mid-October to mid-May; day use is permitted before or after those dates, depending on weather.

North Rim winter closure is directly related to the fact that this higher area receives far more precipitation than the South Rim, much of it in the form of snow. The rewards for those who plan ahead and make the drive here are manifold, however: splendid views, of course, with perspectives unlike the South Rim's, but also fewer crowds, a different environment, and a greater number of easy and moderate hiking possibilities. In summer, when South Rim hikes into the canyon can be

grueling desert treks, the North Rim offers above-the-canyon trails that are pleasantly temperate.

You'll see the ecological difference that higher elevation makes as you drive south along Ariz. 67 from Jacob Lake. You've left the pinyon-pine-juniper zone behind, passing instead through a ponderosa pine forest. With increased elevation, Douglas-firs, white firs, Engelmann spruces, and aspens appear, and so do birds such as blue grouse, Williamson's sapsuckers, Clark's nutcrackers, and Grace's warblers.

Drive all the way to the end of the road, to the North Rim Visitor Center (*closed mid-Oct.–mid-May*) and **Grand Canyon Lodge,** originally built in the 1920s by the Union Pacific Railroad. Walk the easy **Bright Angel Point Trail,** which runs a quarter mile to the tip of this narrow neck of North Rim sticking south into the canyon. Here you'll find one of the finest views of any park overlook.

Below are The Transept, Roaring Springs, and Bright Angel canyons, the first two side canyons of the last, a long gorge that follows a fault line running southwest to the Grand Canyon Village area on the South Rim.

Unlike the South Rim, where nearly all trails head straight down the canyon wall, the North Rim presents several less precipitous hiking possibilities. Beginning at the lodge area, the **Transept Trail** follows the western edge of the Bright Angel Point plateau 1.5 miles to the park campground; it's an easy stroll with views down into The Transept. Longer, but still an easy-to-moderate hike, the **Widforss Trail** is accessed by returning north on the main park road and turning west on a dirt road about 2 miles north of the lodge. The route follows the canyon rim before moving away from the edge into beautiful mixed coniferous forest; it ends after 5 miles at **Widforss Point,** at the canyon rim again, for more vistas.

Back south on the main road a half mile, you'll find the trailhead for the **North Kaibab Trail**, which leads 14 miles down Bright Angel Canyon to Phantom Ranch and the Colorado River. A day hike, albeit a very strenuous one, can be made by taking the trail 4.7 miles down to the water-supply facilities at **Roaring Springs;** this descends 3,400 feet, and the round-trip usually takes seven to eight hours. Of course, you don't have to go that far to sample the North Kaibab Trail; if time is short, consider a hike 0.7 mile down to **Coconino Overlook,** named for the sand-

stone formation that's such a prominent part of the canyon wall, or 2 miles to Supai Tunnel.

The North Kaibab trailhead also serves the **Uncle Jim Trail**, a 5-mile loop with tremendous views of Roaring Springs Canyon. The first mile or so of the trail is also the start of the **Ken Patrick Trail,** which leads in 10 miles to Point Imperial; at the junction, veer right to make the loop to **Uncle Jim Point.**

The Cape Royal Road winds south to the tip of the Walhalla Plateau; along the way is the north turn to **Point Imperial,** a picnic area and viewpoint at just over 8,800 feet. There's a great view here of the Little Colorado River

---

Condors Past and Future

The California condor once ranged widely across the West, but by the 1980s fewer than 30 existed in the wild and in captivity. After much debate, biologists captured the last few wild condors and added them to a captive-breeding program.

In 1996, some of these birds were released in the Vermilion Cliffs area of Arizona, north of the Grand Canyon. With additional releases, the Arizona population had increased four years later to more than 25 condors. You might spot one or more of these imposing birds along the 30 miles of Ariz. 89A west of Marble Canyon, or even in the Grand Canyon Village area.

Following pages: Yaki Point, Grand Canyon National Park

gorge, Marble Canyon, and the flat-topped Marble Platform in the distance. For those who'd like to hike the rim, the Ken Patrick Trail heads south and the **Point Imperial Trail** runs north from the lookout 3 miles to the park boundary.

The Cape Royal Road continues south to Cape Royal, where the short, easy **Cape Royal Trail** provides a view not only of the canyon and Colorado River below but of **Angel's Window**, an eroded natural arch in a wall of rock sticking out from the rim; a side trail leads out to the top of the "window." At Cape Royal you'll have a close look at the fortress-like mesas called Wotans Throne to the south. The nearby **Cliff Springs Trail** begins at the Angel's Window overlook and leads 1 mile down a wooded ravine, past a small Native American ruin. If you haven't had your fill of awesome scenery by now (and who could?), 2 miles back up the Cape Royal Road is the trailhead for the **Cape Final Trail**, which leads 2 miles east to another rim overlook stretching to the Painted Desert (see pp. 48-50).

Adjoining the national park on the north, the North Kaibab Ranger District of **Kaibab National Forest** offers campgrounds, trails, and forest roads. Trailheads into the **Saddle Mountain Wilderness,** a 40,610-acre area north of Point Imperial, are accessible via forest roads east of Ariz. 67, just north of the park boundary. With a forest road map, you can drive dirt roads to **Swamp Point,** the trailhead for the hike to **Powell Plateau.** This fairly remote part of the national park is far from the roads of Bright Angel Point, yet feasible as a challenging 10-mile round-trip day hike. Get a good map and be sure of your backcountry abilities before beginning to hike this unmaintained trail. Ask rangers about the condition of the trailhead access road before starting; a high-clearance vehicle may be needed. ■

Boaters take on the rapids of the Colorado River, Grand Canyon National Park

Monument Valley Navajo Tribal Park

■ 91,696 acres ■ Northeast Arizona, 30 miles north of Kayenta off US 163
■ Best seasons spring and fall ■ Scenic drive, horseback tours, guided tours
■ Adm. fee ■ Navajo Indian Reservation, unlike the rest of Arizona, observes
daylight savings time ■ Contact Navajo Nation Parks and Recreation Department, P.O. Box 9000, Window Rock, AZ 86515; phone 520-871-6647.
www.navajonationparks.org

NEARLY EVERYONE already, in a manner of speaking, knows Monument Valley. Having starred in such movies as *Fort Apache* and *The Searchers,* and in countless television commercials, this landscape of buttes and spires has become an icon of the American West. A visit here is, as nearly as can be, a completely visual experience. Independent hiking and backpacking are forbidden on the Navajo Indian Reservation, within which the valley lies. While guided tours and horseback tours can be arranged, the real point is simply to see this extraordinary terrain.

Though most of Monument Valley lies within Arizona, to enter you must turn south from US 163 in Utah. From here it's 4 miles to the visitor center *(435-727-3353),*

Beetle tracks, Monument Valley
Navajo Tribal Park

set above the valley, with a recognizable view of buttes called **East Mitten, West Mitten,** and **Merrick.** A 17-mile scenic loop begins here, following an unpaved road past such features as the **Three Sisters, Camel Butte,** and the slender pillar called **Totem Pole.** You can drive this route on your own, but travel away from the road is prohibited. By hiring a Navajo guide, you'll be allowed to approach some of the spires and arches for closer views and better photographs.

As hard as it may be to comprehend, this entire valley was once solid de Chelly sandstone—the same rock seen in Canyon de Chelly National Monument (see p. 42-3). Formed from dunes more than 200 million years ago, the sandstone was later uplifted and then eroded by water, wind, and ice. The bases of the buttes are composed of softer shale from an older formation, which eroded to create sloping "foundations." ■

Anasazi handprints, Canyon de Chelly National Monument

Canyon de Chelly National Monument

■ 83,840 acres ■ Northeast Arizona, just east of Chinle off U.S. 191 ■ Best seasons fall and spring. Canyon access sometimes closed by snow in winter ■ Camping, scenic drives, horseback tours, guided tours ■ Permit and fee required for hiking and guided driving tours ■ Navajo Indian Reservation, unlike the rest of Arizona, observes daylight savings time ■ Contact the monument, P.O. Box 588, Chinle, AZ 86503; phone 520-674-5500. www.nps.gov/cach

ONE OF THE MOST famously scenic landscapes in the Southwest is found within this off-the-beaten-track national monument, managed cooperatively by the National Park Service and the Navajo Nation, within whose reservation lands it lies. In this red-rock wonderland, sheer cliffs of sandstone tower hundreds of feet over broad canyon bottoms, the walls dotted with niches containing the ruins of ancient dwellings.

Dozens of Navajo families live and farm within the park, continuing a history of occupation by Native Americans dating back at least 2,000 years. Because of this unique juxtaposition of geological wonder and living culture, travel within Canyon de Chelly (pronounced "shay") is more limited than in most parks. Two roads wind along canyon rims, offering superb vistas, and one trail leads down to the canyon floor; otherwise, visitors must be accompanied by a Navajo guide, available through several local commercial firms. Vehicle tours, horseback rides, hikes, and camping trips can all be arranged, with trips ranging from a few hours to several days.

Though named for its main canyon, the park also encompasses another major canyon, **Canyon del Muerto,** and smaller side canyons. Together, the main canyons form a rough V-shape with the park **visitor center** at its point, 3 miles east of the small town of Chinle. Exhibits and a film at the visitor center will provide background on the long history of the park; you can also get information here on guided tours. Most visitors take four-wheel-drive auto tours along the canyon floor, though for those with time, horseback rides afford a quieter experience.

South Rim Drive follows the rim of Canyon de Chelly for 18 miles, passing some of the park's most famous scenes along the way. Near the beginning is **Junction Overlook,** a viewpoint of the confluence of the two major canyons. A few miles farther, turn north to the trailhead for the **White House Trail,** the only place you can enter the canyon without a guide. This 2.5-mile round-trip path leads from the canyon rim 500 feet down to a ruined dwelling occupied by Puebloan people about 1,000 years ago. The cliff that towers above you here, as elsewhere in the canyons, is formed mainly of sandstone deposited as dunes in a vast desert more than 230 million years ago. South Rim Drive ends at the amazing spectacle of **Spider Rock,** an eroded pinnacle rising 800 feet above the canyon floor.

Side roads along the 17-mile **North Rim Drive** lead to views of several ruins, including **Mummy Cave Ruin,** one of the park's largest structures, with living and ceremonial buildings flanking a central tower, all beneath an over-hanging bluff. Nearby is the over-look at **Massacre Cave,** where in 1805 Spanish soldiers killed 115 Navajo who were trapped on a ledge on the canyon wall.

At several places on the drives you'll look down at the farms and traditional hogan houses of mod-ern Navajo, with pastures beside the streams that flow intermit-tently along the canyon floors. In fall, when the Fremont cotton-woods that line the washes turn gold, the rim panoramas can be breathtaking. Though Canyon de Chelly is off main travel routes, its blend of culture and beauty makes a visit a memorable experience. ■

Canyon Cliffs

The tall cliffs of Canyon de Chelly were formed as rivers cut into sandstone rising with the uplift of the Colorado Plateau. The process began more than 60 million years ago, though the main canyon formation occurred over the past 2 million years. Canyon-cutting continues today, with erosion caused by rain, ice, and wind-carried grit. In places in the upper canyons, the walls stand 1,000 feet above their parent streams.

The dark streaks on the red cliffs are "desert varnish," created by microscopic organisms that take minerals from airborne dust particles and deposit them on the rocks.

Bisti/De-Na-Zin Wilderness

■ 43,000 acres ■ Northwest New Mexico, 32 miles south of Farmington off
N. Mex. 371 ■ Best seasons spring and fall. Very hot in summer ■ Primitive
camping, hiking ■ Contact Farmington Field Office, Bureau of Land Management, 1235 La Plata Hwy., Farmington, NM 87401; phone 505-599-8900

THIS WILDERNESS AREA isn't for everybody: There are no real trails, and the
land is harsh and dry, with only scrubby vegetation and little apparent
wildlife. But its weirdly eroded rock formations have the power to delight
hikers, especially those carrying cameras. When morning and evening
light casts shadows around the creamy buff stone, you can burn a lot of
film in a hurry capturing this scenic "badland" (the meaning of the
Navajo word from which "Bisti" derives).

Bisti and De-Na-Zin once were separate wildernesses, but in 1996
Congress designated the tract between them as wilderness, as well, creating the present contiguous area of 43,000 acres.

The wilderness lies within the **San Juan Basin,** a section of the Colorado Plateau that began sagging below the land around it more than 60
million years ago, later filling with sediments that became sandstone,
shale, and even softer rocks. The basin has seen great exploitation of
its underlying oil, gas, and coal deposits—as you'll note even on the
doorstep of the wilderness.

From Farmington, drive south on N. Mex. 371 about 37 miles and
watch for signs directing you to turn east on a gravel road, which leads in
a couple of miles to a parking area on the east side of the road. Walk up
an old road along the wash toward the east, where you're soon on your
own to enjoy the infinite shapes of the hoodoos of friable mudstone and
siltstone. Sandstone caps on softer rock create mushroom formations,
while others look like spires, miniature mountains, or Henry Moore
sculptures. You can travel as far into the wilderness as you want, but most
people are content simply to wander up the wash for a couple of miles,
exploring this geologic wonderland for a few hours. Take note of where
you are and of the direction of the parking area, and carry a compass;
there are no signs or trail markers to help you keep your bearings.

Fossils and petrified wood are common here, lying on the ground or
exposed in bluffs by continuing erosion. Because the sediments that
formed the rocks of the wilderness were laid down in part in the Jurassic
and Cretaceous periods, some of the fossils are of animals far stranger
than today's snakes and lizards. In the De-Na-Zin area, for example, a
paleontologist recently discovered the skull of a hadrosaur dinosaur, a
duck-billed plant eater that sported a fantastic 5-foot-long hollow head
crest. All such natural elements are protected, so take photos and leave
them where they are. Any fossil removed as a souvenir by a thoughtless
hiker might be a vital clue to our understanding of the curious creatures
that roamed here in the last days of the dinosaurs. ■

El Malpais National Monument and Conservation Area

■ 378,000 acres ■ Northwest New Mexico, just south of Grants off N. Mex. 117 ■ Best seasons fall and spring. Summer heat can make hiking unpleasant ■ Primitive camping, hiking, cave exploration ■ Some dirt roads impassable after rain ■ Contact the monument, 123 E. Roosevelt Ave., Grants, NM 87020; phone 505-783-4774. www.nps.gov/elma

YOU'LL FIND THE WORD "badlands" scattered all over the map of the American West, applied to places that early settlers shunned because of their rugged terrain or sparse vegetation. *El malpais* is Spanish for "the badland," and there's a special reason the phrase was used for this area of northwest New Mexico: Over a period of more than 100,000 years, ending only about 3,000 years ago, repeated volcanic eruptions left an expanse of cinder cones and lava flows covering hundreds of square miles of an intermountain plain here.

Lava tube cave, El Malpais National Monument

El Malpais, which protects much of this area, is managed cooperatively by the National Park Service (administering the 115,000-acre national monument) and the Bureau of Land Management (responsible for the adjacent 263,000-acre El Malpais National Conservation Area). These intermingled lands—including two BLM wilderness preserves, Cebolla and West Malpais—form a tract offering recreational opportunities from sight-seeing to cross-country backpacking.

What to See and Do

From I-40 just east of Grants, take N. Mex. 117 south; in 10 miles the BLM's El Malpais Ranger Station on the east side of the road can provide maps and information on the conservation area and the national monument. Just a mile or so farther south, follow a dirt road west to the **Sandstone Bluffs**

Overlook for a fine panorama of the volcanic region. Green junipers and pinyon pines dot the vast jumble of black lava immediately below this long, picturesque sandstone ridge. Off to the west rise the **Zuni Mountains,** an uplifted dome of ancient granite, stripped by erosion of the younger rocks

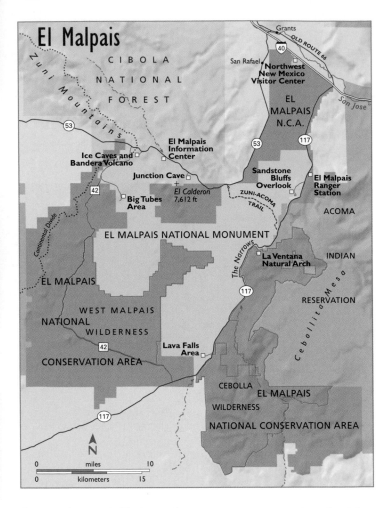

that once lay atop it. To the north stands 11,301-foot **Mount Taylor,** a volcano that may have blown apart in a violent explosion like that of Mount St. Helens in 1980.

Interpretive signs explain regional geology and identify different varieties of lava, such as rope-like *pahoehoe* and the sharp, jagged *aa.* Although there's no established trail, you can walk along the ridge—formed from the compacted dunes of a desert that existed here more than 200 million years ago—to experience its strikingly eroded contours.

Back on N. Mex. 117, continue south 5 miles to the east trailhead for the **Zuni-Acoma Trail.** This 7.5-mile route leads to N. Mex. 53 on the west side of the national monument. With a car shuttle you can hike one way; otherwise it's an out-and-back walk (which is not advised). Though this trail has little change in elevation, it's by no means easy. You'll be walking across sharp, uneven lava (very sturdy hiking boots are a must), on a route with no water and little shade; for most of its length the trail is marked by lava rock cairns that can be hard to see. With those cautions in mind, you should hike at least a little of the Zuni-Acoma Trail just to get a feel for this remarkable landscape. The trail takes its name from two Native American peoples whose pueblos were connected centuries ago by a trade route; some of the cairns and rock-fill "bridges" across lava gullies were put in place by Native Americans hundreds of years ago. Many different eruptions poured lava onto the surface at El Malpais. As you continue west, you'll cross lava flows up to 115,000 years old.

In 2.5 miles, N. Mex. 117 reaches the parking area for **La Ventana Natural Arch** in the **El Malpais National Conservation Area**. This impressive rock span is eroded from a sandstone bluff. A very short and fairly steep trail leads to the arch, but you don't have to walk all the way to enjoy this 165-foot-long formation. Continue south on N. Mex. 117 to see **The Narrows,** where the highway seems to be squeezed by lava flows on the west and 500-foot-tall sandstone bluffs to the east.

From I-40 at Grants, you can take N. Mex. 53 south 16 miles to the west trailhead for the Zuni-Acoma Trail. By hiking less than a mile east you can see both the **El Calderon Flow,** the oldest lava in El Malpais, and the much younger **Twin Craters Flow.**

Heading west 4 more miles on N. Mex. 53, you'll reach the **El Calderon Area,** where trails through ponderosa pines lead to the El Calderon cinder cone and **Junction Cave,** a quarter-mile-long lava tube. This type of structure forms when the surface of flowing lava, exposed to cooling air, hardens into a crust while liquid lava continues to flow inside. Properly prepared people (with gloves, hard hats, and three flashlights per person) are allowed to venture into the cave.

The national monument's El Malpais Information Center, a few miles west of El Calderon, offers maps and advice. Continuing west on N. Mex. 53, you'll reach the privately owned and operated **Ice Caves and Bandera Volcano** (888-ICE-CAVE. Adm. fee). Inside the main cave (another lava tube), ice formed in winter is insulated from summer heat; over time, a layer of permanent ice has built up. ∎

An Evening with Bats

In summer, rangers at El Malpais National Monument conduct a variety of programs on geology, nature, and culture. One of the most popular is the interpretive program on bats scheduled during June, July, and August.

Starting at El Calderon parking area before dusk, participants walk three-quarters of a mile to a cave to see the evening flight of bats leaving their roost to feed on insects. During the program, rangers describe the life history of these fascinating mammals. For information on the programs, call El Malpais Information Center (505-783-4774).

Petrified Forest National Park

■ 93,533 acres ■ Northeast Arizona, 25 miles east of Holbrook ■ Visit year round ■ Camping, hiking, wildlife viewing, petrified logs, petroglyphs ■ Adm. fee; back country permit required ■ Contact the park, P.O. Box 2217, Petrified Forest, AZ 86028; phone 520-524-6228. www.nps.gov/pefo

EVEN KNOWING OUR LONG human history of environmental exploitation, it's hard to imagine that anyone could look at the beautiful rainbow-colored petrified logs found in Arizona's Painted Desert and decide to crush them to make abrasive grit. Yet such an industry was contemplated in the 1890s, when people were busy dynamiting logs to get at the crystals inside and hauling off chunks to sell as souvenirs and home decor.

This abuse prompted President Theodore Roosevelt in 1906 to establish Petrified Forest as our second national monument. Since that time the site has been expanded, and in 1962 it became a national park, protecting what is almost certainly the world's finest array of petrified logs.

Though the spectacular fossilized trees here were the focus of the park, through the years scientists have found this site an immensely productive storehouse of information on the mid- to late Triassic period, about 225 million years ago. Researchers continue to discover fossil plants and animals, slowly filling in the story of life at the beginning of

Painted Desert, Petrified Forest National Park

the age of dinosaurs. In addition, the park encompasses important Native American ruins and artifacts and a small but picturesque swath of the Painted Desert, a terrain of colorfully banded hills and grassland. So, while the petrified wood is the star attraction, there's much more to enjoy here than just the famed trees.

The events that led to the formation of the petrified logs began more than 225 million years ago, when what is now northeast Arizona, then part of the supercontinent of Pangaea, lay near the Equator. Forests here and in highlands to the south were home to a tropical conifer that could reach 160 feet. As the trees died, their trunks were carried by streams to the Petrified Forest area, where they were buried by mud and sand mixed with ash from volcanic eruptions. Cut off from air, and so protected from decay, the trunks were gradually permeated by water carrying dissolved silica, which crystallized as quartz, exactly replacing the soft plant structure with hard mineral.

Not only tree trunks were buried by those Triassic streams, of course. Fossils of ferns, cycads, giant horsetails, and other plants are common in the park. Many animals have been unearthed, as well, including snails, insects, fish, and amphibians. Paleontologists have discovered several types of large reptiles here, including a few early true dinosaurs and others that resembled dinosaurs but were members of a precursor group.

The mud, sand, and ash formed a layer of sedimentary rock, now called the Chinle formation, which was itself buried by later rock. When the Colorado Plateau was uplifted, beginning about 60 million years ago, the overlying rock eroded away, exposing the Chinle formation and—as the soft rock weathered—the petrified logs it contained.

The soft clays of the Chinle formation display a wide spectrum of colors, dominated by reddish tones produced by iron oxides and including white, blue-gray, creamy buff, and near-black. It was this striking landscape that gave the Painted Desert its name. Such terrain covers a large expanse of northeastern Arizona, and the park encompasses a particularly brilliant portion.

Native Americans lived in what is now the park for about 2,000 years, and a great number of ancient villages sites and other artifacts have been located and studied. The most prominent site is Puerco Pueblo, a 100-room complex occupied from 1100 to 1200 and again from 1300 to 1400. Ancient dwellings can be visited at two sites in the park, along with petroglyphs whose ages and meanings remain uncertain.

Two notes: First, although the following account describes the park from north to south, if you're traveling along I-40 from the west you'll save time and miles by taking US 180 southeast from Holbrook and traversing the park south to north.

And second, abuse of the petrified forest didn't end with its official protection in 1906. Over the years literally tons of petrified wood have been removed—well, let's say it: stolen—by visitors, most of whom no doubt thought that "taking one little piece won't hurt anything." The park has always pleaded with visitors not to steal wood, and in recent years has begun to crack down in earnest. There are even emergency telephones at popular sites from which resource theft can be reported to rangers. Even the loss of a pebble impoverishes the park. Do your part to keep the petrified forest in Petrified Forest National Park.

What to See and Do

At the **Painted Desert Visitor Center,** just off I-40, you can view an orientation film and see models and bones of some of the large prehistoric reptiles found in the area. During the Triassic period, when park fossils originated, dinosaurs were just beginning the development that would see them dominate the later Jurassic period, so the true dinosaurs were less impressive than their relatives. Take some time to study the exhibits here, even if you're eager to get out and explore the park.

Within the first few miles of the main park road, you'll find several parking areas with interpretive signs and views of the **Painted Desert**. The best time to see the desert is early or late in the day, after a rain, when the light and colors make for the most resplendent panorama. Most of what you see are rock layers of the 200-million-year-old Chinle formation, though this part of the park also contains the harder and younger rock and lava beds of the Bida-hochi formation, just 5 to 16

Triassic Predators

The most common fossil animals found in Petrified Forest National Park are members of the phytosaur group, including *Nicrosaurus gregorii.* Some of these carnivorous giant reptiles grew up to 30 feet long and weighed five tons. They showed many of the same adaptations to an aquatic predatory lifestyle as modern crocodiles. Long, narrow jaws were lined with sharp teeth to capture fish and other prey, a long tail powered quick bursts of underwater speed, and eyes and nostrils were located atop the head, allowing *Nicrosaurus* to remain submerged as it awaited its victim.

An equally fearsome land predator, *Postosuchus* somewhat resembled a small version of the well-known *Tyrannosaurus rex,* although it, like *Nicrosaurus,* was not a true dinosaur but an earlier reptile type. Up to 13 feet long, *Postosuchus* weighed about a ton.

million years old. Rock that existed between these two periods has been removed by erosion, geologists believe.

At Tawa Point, the half-mile (one way) **Rim Trail** runs to Kachina Point, offering the chance to experience a habitat different from the desert grassland you'll pass through for much of the drive. Here in this scrubby woodland you'll see plenty of buckwheat, a distinctive plant of the park, along with many other shrubs and wildflowers, and possibly even a black-tailed jackrabbit, collared lizard, or rock wren—which, unlike the colorful trees you'll be seeing later, is not made of rock.

At Kachina Point stands the **Painted Desert Inn,** built in 1924. Now a museum and national historic landmark, the inn was redesigned in the 1940s by Mary Elizabeth Colter, the architect responsible for several buildings at Grand Canyon National Park; inside are murals of Indian traditions by Hopi artist Fred Kabotie.

Kachina Point is the trailhead for exploration of the **Painted Desert Wilderness,** covering 43,000 acres in the northern part of the park. A mile-long trail begins at the inn, but after that hikers can pick their own routes through the backcountry. Conditions can be harsh here and water is unavailable, so be sure of your own ability to cope with the desert before setting out. A permit is required for backcountry camping, but none is needed for day hikes. About 1 mile north of Kachina Point, beyond Lithodendron Wash, you'll come across the **Black Forest,** an assemblage of petrified trees of two species different from those found in the main body of the park.

The road bends south, passing more vista points, and crosses a long stretch of grassland (watch for pronghorn, golden eagles, and prairie falcons along the way) before arriving at **Puerco Pueblo,** a Native American village occupied between 900 and 600 years ago. Built of sandstone mortared

Following pages: Long Logs area, Petrified Forest National Park

with mud and featuring a central plaza, the pueblo is located along the Puerco River, a water source for the community's beans, corn, and squash. A spiral petroglyph here is one of several in the park that served as solar calendars. For one week before and one week after the summer solstice, a special program each morning demonstrates how the calendar marked this significant date. A half mile south along the main road, stop at **Newspaper Rock** to see intricate petroglyphs pecked into the dark rock varnish on large boulders. Because of past vandalism, you're no longer allowed to approach the petroglyphs closely; viewing is now through telescopes.

Back on the road, you'll soon be traversing a remarkable scene of blue-gray, cone-shaped hills in the **Blue Mesa** area. Formed of bentonite, a soft clay (easily eroded, and slippery when wet), this terrain can be explored on the paved, mile-long **Blue Mesa Trail.** Of all the landscapes in the park, this is probably the most strikingly otherworldly. The bluish color here derives from manganese oxide in the clay, while the rusty maroon color comes from iron oxide.

The next three trails along the road all access the fossil logs for which the park was named, and you should take time to walk them all. The **Crystal Forest Trail,** a 0.8-mile loop, passes through an area that once drew heavy (and destructive) commercial exploitation. In hollow logs, common here, crystals grew very large during the petrification process, creating beautiful forms of amethyst, smoky quartz, and citrine. In the late 19th century, many of these logs were dynamited to expose the gemlike crystals inside. Of the crystals that remained when the park was created, many have been taken by visitors over the years, so only small examples are left. (You can see representative specimens of these crystals at the Rainbow Forest Museum, at the end of the drive.)

The **Long Logs Trail** rates as the park's must-see stop, even for those unfortunate visitors who must rush through. What may have originated as a logjam in an ancient stream has resulted in the park's greatest concentration of petrified logs, some of them well over 100 feet long. As you walk the trail here, you're bound to marvel at the way organic material has been duplicated in rock: woodgrain, knotholes, and beetle borings, all in astonishingly fine detail. Note how logs are broken so smoothly and evenly that they seem to have been cut with a saw. It's believed that the logs fractured during the period when the Colorado Plateau was being uplifted, a process that began about 60 million years ago.

There are some huge trees along the Long Logs Trail, but the next trail is called **Giant Logs.** It begins at the **Rainbow Forest Museum,** the park's southern visitor center, which offers geology exhibits, displays of petrified wood, and models of some of the creatures that roamed here in Triassic times. On the half-mile Giant Logs loop you'll see the largest (in diameter) log in the park: "Old Faithful" measures more than 9 feet across at its base. ■

Pintail Lake

■ 57 acres ■ East-central Arizona, 4 miles north of Show Low, off Ariz. 77
■ Best seasons fall and winter ■ Hiking, bird-watching, wildlife viewing ■ Contact Lakeside Ranger District, Apache-Sitgreaves National Forests, R.R. 3, Box B-50, Pinetop-Lakeside, AZ 85929; phone 520-368-5111. www.fs.fed.us/r3/asnf

PERMANENT WETLANDS ARE FEW and far between on the Colorado Plateau, so this artificial lake and marsh area ought to be on the itinerary for bird- and wildlife-watchers in the Mogollon Rim or White Mountains area. Created in 1977 as an innovative solution for wastewater treatment, Pintail Lake now boasts a shoreline ringed with cattails, bulrushes, and sedges, as well as nesting islands that are home to variety of waterbirds.

Accessible to all by means of a barrier-free trail and viewing stations, Pintail does indeed often have northern pintail swimming across its waters, along with other ducks including mallard, cinnamon teal, gadwalls, northern shovelers, and ruddy ducks. The pied-billed grebes you'll see here resemble ducks, but belong to a completely different order; note the thoroughly unduck-like bill on this little brown diver. The black birds with white bills are American coots; again, though convergent evolution has caused them to look like ducks, they're not waterfowl, and in fact are more closely related to cranes.

Watch for other wetland loving species on or around the lake, including black-crowned night-herons, great blue herons, soras, killdeer, belted kingfishers, black phoebes, marsh wrens, and song sparrows. Shallow parts of the lake attract flocks of shorebirds in spring and fall migration—quite an unusual sight in this part of the state. Bald eagles are common winter visitors, and sometimes a peregrine falcon zooms through, hoping to pick up a quick duck dinner.

In the pinyon pines and one-seed junipers around the lake you'll find bushtits, bridled titmice, mountain chickadees, and Bewick's wrens. Out in the grassland to the east, northern harriers fly low in winter looking for rodents. Elk, mule deer, and even pronghorn might appear in this broad meadow at any time of year; the best chance of seeing these large mammals, as is usually the case in wildlife observation, comes in the early morning or late afternoon. ■

Jacques Marsh
Another good spot for close looks at wintering waterfowl is Jacques Marsh (from Ariz. 260, take Porter Rd. N 1.5 miles, turn W on Juniper Dr. for 0.6 mile), a water-treatment facility just north of the town of Pinetop-Lakeside. Dabbling and diving ducks are common here from fall through spring on seven ponds totaling 92 acres. In the fall and winter, elk come out of the surrounding ponderosa pines to graze in the grass around the ponds.

Visitors surveying Meteor Crater

Meteor Crater

■ 365 acres ■ North-central Arizona, 35 miles east of Flagstaff off I-40
■ Best months April-Oct. ■ Adm. fee ■ Contact Meteor Crater, P.O. Box 70,
Flagstaff, AZ 86002; phone 520-289-5898 or 800-289-5898

FOR ONE OF AMERICA'S natural wonders—and one of the most immediately visually accessible—Meteor Crater often has a delayed impact on the observer. At first it seems to be a big, steep-sided hole in the ground, like nature's own baseball stadium. The problem is the lack of scale. Once you grasp that it's more than 4,000 feet from one rim to the other, and that the hole is as deep as a 60-story building is tall, the mental image of the event that occurred here 50,000 years ago can be staggering.

A meteor, or a small group of them, made of iron and nickel and with a diameter of 150 feet, was traveling between 30,000 and 40,000 miles per hour when it struck this spot with a force equivalent to 20 million tons of TNT—1,000 times more powerful than the nuclear weapon dropped on Nagasaki, Japan, to end World War II. Rock at the impact area was vaporized, and 175 million tons of rock scattered to cover the surrounding plain for more than a mile in all directions. Chunks of rock were thrown for up to 24 miles. So great was the pressure that bits of graphite in the meteors—meteorites, once they hit the ground—were converted into tiny diamonds.

Thanks in part to the arid climate of the Colorado Plateau, Meteor Crater has eroded relatively little in the 50 millennia since this cataclysmic impact. For years it was thought that this was one of the volcanic craters so common around Flagstaff. An early owner of the site was convinced it was an impact crater, though; he tried unsuccessfully for 26 years to locate what he was sure would be a huge iron meteorite beneath the floor. Today scientists accept the impact theory, but believe that only minuscule fragments of the meteorite survived the collision.

Meteor Crater amply justifies a side trip off I-40, whether you simply marvel at its magnitude or take time to consider its scientific significance. Exhibits in the **visitor center** illustrate its formation, and as you visualize the impact you can't help but be awed by the forces at work—and, of course, you can't help imagining a disaster movie, as well. ■

The Arboretum at Flagstaff

■ 200 acres ■ North-central Arizona, 4 miles southwest of Flagstaff on South Woody Mountain Rd. off US 66 ■ Closed mid-Dec.–April ■ Guided walks, wildlife viewing, plant study ■ Adm. fee ■ Contact the arboretum, 4001 S. Woody Mountain Rd., Flagstaff, AZ 86001; 520-774-1442

BEFORE YOU BEGIN A journey in northern Arizona, it would be worth your time to stop by the Arboretum at Flagstaff, a botanical garden and research facility set in a ponderosa pine forest just a few miles from town. Dedicated to the native plants of the Colorado Plateau, the arboretum will give you a head start in your understanding and appreciation of regional ecology. In addition, it's a pleasant, peaceful spot where you can simply stroll through a woodland and enjoy typical wildlife of the area.

Ten acres of gardens display and identify plants you may come across on the plateau, from Douglas-firs and aspens to wildflowers such as columbines and the brilliant scarlet gilia. Rare species cultivated here include the San Francisco Peaks groundsel, an endemic of the mountains a dozen miles north, and the pink Sunset Crater beardtongue, which grows only in the volcanic soil in and around Sunset Crater (see p. 58).

With an average snowfall of 100 inches a year, Flagstaff is one of the snowiest cities in America. Its short growing season, averaging 103 days, makes gardening a challenge. Part of the Arboretum's mission is to identify plants adaptable to the region, with an emphasis on native species.

Signs along the Arboretum's 1.2-mile nature trail interpret the ecology of the ponderosa pine forest (see sidebar p. 66), the dominant habitat along the Mogollon Rim. Look beside the trail for the chewed cones and twigs that indicate the presence of the Abert's squirrel, a species closely associated with ponderosa pine. Elk, pronghorn, and mule deer might appear in the broad adjoining meadow. Steller's jays, pygmy nuthatches, and mountain chickadees are always present in the pines, and the nearby pond, wetlands, and grassland provide habitat for other birds from sparrows to hawks.

Stop, too, at the **butterfly garden** to see what's feeding on the blooms. From summer through fall the arboretum's wildflower garden will also attract several species of butterflies. ■

Sunset Crater Volcano National Monument

■ 3,040 acres ■ North-central Arizona, 15 miles northeast of Flagstaff off US 89 ■ Best months April-June; Sept.–mid-Nov. ■ Camping, hiking ■ Adm. fee ■ Contact the monument, Rt. 3, Box 149, Flagstaff, AZ 86004; phone 520-526-0502. www.nps.gov/sucr

Skyrocket gilia

SIX MILLION YEARS of volcanic activity have given the region around Flagstaff a distinctive appearance that even the most geologically oblivious find impossible to ignore. Symmetrical cones dot the landscape, revealing sites where the earth opened to discharge magma, ash, and cinders. Sunset Crater is the best place to get a close-up look at the area's turbulent past.

Sunset Crater is the youngest known volcano in Arizona. Born in 1064 or 1065, it ceased activity only about 1250, leaving a landscape that today still appears jagged, raw, and scarred. Trees, shrubs, and wildflowers grow but sparsely here, amid a terrain dominated by lava rock and cinders. NASA used the Bonito lava flow to test a lunar vehicle before the 1972 Apollo 17 mission to the moon—testament to its otherworldly look.

Late eruptions at Sunset Crater left a coating of cinders oxidized to a reddish color on its upper slopes, causing explorer John Wesley Powell (of Grand Canyon fame) to write that it "seems to glow with a light of its own." In 1928 a movie company wanted to blow up the volcano, a circumstance that led to the creation of a national monument protecting one of the Southwest's most extraordinary natural features.

As you turn east from US 89 toward Sunset Crater Volcano National Monument, you'll be on Coconino National Forest's 545 Loop. This 36-mile route passes through both Sunset Crater Volcano and nearby **Wupatki National Monument** *(520-679-2365),* which preserves ruins of a Native American pueblo occupied in the 1100s. These evocative stone buildings tell the story of a people who lived on the Colorado Plateau when Sunset Crater was active.

At the **Sunset Crater Volcano Visitor Center** *(2 miles before the western entrance on loop road),* exhibits provide an introduction to the fascinating local geology. Sunset Crater and San Francisco Mountain (see pp. 60-63 and 67) are just two of a series of volcanic features that some scientists think are the result of the movement of a tectonic plate over a hot spot. Another theory holds that the slow collision of plates along the Colorado Plateau has created volcanic activity.

At the visitor center, you'll also learn a bit about the plants and animals of the national monument. Ponderosa and pinyon pines, one-seed junipers, and aspens grow amid the black lava, and wildflowers such as Indian paintbrush, scarlet gilia, and twinpod brighten the scene. One wildflower, the pink Sunset Crater beardtongue, is endemic to the San Francisco Mountain area, blooming in June and July.

Before leaving the visitor center, buy the trail guide for the **Lava Flow Trail,** your next stop. This 1-mile path passes many distinctive volcanic features as it loops to the base of Sunset Crater. You'll see a squeeze-up (formed when molten lava oozed through a crack in a lava shell), xeno-liths (fragments of nonvolcanic rock imbedded in lava), a spatter cone (lava built up around a gas vent), and lava bubbles along the way, and you'll note the difference between jagged *aa* lava and smoother *pahoehoe* lava (both terms are Hawaiian in origin). At the far end of the loop there's a fine panorama of San Francisco Mountain to the west, with Humphreys Peak slightly asserting itself over the other summits.

From the trail you'll have a close view of the slope of Sunset Crater, spangled with the red and yellow cinders that gave it its name. No climbing is allowed on Sunset Crater; in the past, makeshift trails caused serious erosion on its slopes. The national monument will, however, allow you to climb **Lenox Crater,** just to the west. The trail begins across the road from the Bonito Flow parking area, just west of the Lava Flow Trail parking area. It takes most people about a half hour to climb the half-mile-long path to its top, and another 20 minutes to return.

Less than 2 miles east of the Lava Flow Trail parking area, take the south turn off the main park road to the **Cinder Hills Overlook,** where you'll have a good view of the rugged terrain around Sunset Crater, and of the way vegetation is spreading up its northeast slope. A few miles farther east, the **Painted Desert Vista** looks out to a line of reddish cliffs far to the north, across the sagebrush lowlands of the Colorado Plateau.

Covering 10,141 acres to the north, the **Strawberry Crater Wilderness** in **Coconino National Forest** *(Peaks Ranger District, Flagstaff, AZ. 520-526-0866. www.fs.fed.us/r3/coconino)* centers on a cone that erupted at about the same time as Sunset Crater. Hikers prepared for backcountry travel (there's no water in the wilderness) sometimes leave from the parking area here to walk 4 miles north to the crater. A shorter route to the crater can be reached by turning east onto Forest Road 546 off US 89 north of the Sunset Crater road. Drive east about 3 miles and take Forest Road 779 to the wilderness area, where a trail leads in a bit more than a mile to the crater. ∎

San Francisco Mountain

■ 69,120 acres ■ North-central Arizona, just north of Flagstaff off US 89
■ Best months April-Oct. Cross-country skiing best Jan.-Feb. High-elevation
trails snow-covered in winter ■ Camping, hiking, mountain biking, horseback
riding, bird-watching, wildlife viewing, downhill and cross-country skiing
■ Contact Peaks Ranger District, Coconino National Forest, 5075 N. Hwy. 89,
Flagstaff, AZ 86004; phone 520-526-0866. www.fs.fed.us/r3/coconino

HUNDREDS OF PEAKS, CONES, and craters dot a 2,800-square-mile region of
northern Arizona near Flagstaff, testimony to 6 million years of volcanic
eruptions. Scientists are by no means sure this activity is over: The most
recent volcano, Sunset Crater (see p. 58), erupted as recently as 1250,
practically yesterday in geologic time, and occasional minor earthquakes
remind residents that something is still going on below ground.

Towering over the other volcanic mountains—in fact towering over
all of Arizona—San Francisco Mountain rises just north of Flagstaff,
dominating the horizon for miles in all directions. Although it is, techni-

Cross-country skiers, San Francisco Mountain

cally speaking, a single mountain, its many peaks have earned it the often used name of San Francisco Peaks. Humphreys Peak, the mountain's and state's highest point at 12,633 feet, stands above neighboring Agassiz Peak, with three other crests over 11,400 feet nearby.

The peaks are eroded remnants of a once taller mountain, a volcano that may have risen more than 2,000 feet higher before it destroyed itself—either in an explosive eruption like that of Mount St. Helens in 1980, or by simply collapsing into its own empty inner magma chamber. The time of this cataclysm is not certain, but the San Francisco volcano is thought to have been active from around 1.8 million years ago up until about 400,000 years ago. Humphreys and its neighbors are eroded high points of the ancient volcano's caldera rim; an opening on the northeast side of the caldera's rim may indicate the direction of the blast that collapsed the summit.

Humphreys Peak is the heart of Coconino National Forest's Kachina Peaks Wilderness. Above tree line here, as elsewhere on San Francisco Mountain, you'll find a few square miles of true alpine tundra, a distinctive and fragile ecosystem where plants struggle to survive in a harsh environment with a short growing season. A small plant, the San Francisco Peaks groundsel—a 4-inch-tall wildflower with crinkly leaves and small yellow blooms—grows here and nowhere else in the world. Kachina Peaks takes its name from gods of the Hopi, to whom these mountains are sacred. Legend says the kachinas live on the peaks part of the year, leaving them in summer to bring rain to the arid Colorado Plateau.

Flagstaff, set at an elevation of 6,900 feet, is one of America's snowiest cities; ergo, the high-mountain hiking season is sometimes as brief as the cross-country ski season is long. Check with national forest personnel before planning a backcountry trip, and in the shoulder seasons of spring and late fall stay aware of weather forecasts no matter how blue the sky is at the moment. Even in summer, sudden severe weather can make it wiser to abort a high-mountain trip rather than continue hiking.

What to See and Do

Before heading up to the mountains, visit the excellent **Museum of Northern Arizona** *(3101 N. Fort Valley Rd . 520-774-5213. Adm. fee),* located just northwest of Flagstaff. You'll get a good grounding here in the geology of San Francisco Mountain and the Colorado Plateau, which will help you enjoy your exploration of the area.

Elden Mountain Trails

Flagstaff residents and visitors can take advantage of an extensive trail system in the hills just north of town, centered on Elden Mountain. Stop in at the **Coconino National Forest** Peaks Ranger District on US 89 just northeast of town for information; several trails begin right here. Nearby you'll also find the ruins of **Elden Pueblo,** a village occupied by the Sinagua Native American people around the 12th and 13th centuries. The public is invited to help with summer archaeological work.

If you've come here from a relatively low place and need to acclimatize to the elevation, you might want to hike some of the trails around Elden Mountain as a warm-up for higher pursuits. From the trailhead near the ranger district office on US 89 the **Elden Lookout Trail** is a strenuous 3-mile route that ascends almost 2,400 feet to the top of this 9,299-foot volcanic dome. Along the way you'll pass through the site of an extensive 1977 fire and get close views of curious lava columns. Near the top you'll have great views of Flagstaff and, to the north, **O'Leary Peak** and **Sunset Crater** (see pp. 58-59); to the south you can see famed **Oak Creek Canyon** (see pp. 174-182), near the town of Sedona.

If you need an easier warm-up walk, 2-mile **Fatman's Loop** gains only 600 feet of elevation. Both these trails are located in a transitional habitat where trees range from oaks and alligator junipers to aspens and white firs.

Inner Basin Trail

On the east side of San Francisco Mountain, the **Inner Basin Trail** makes a wonderful day hike for a couple of reasons. First, it's a beautiful walk through a tall coniferous

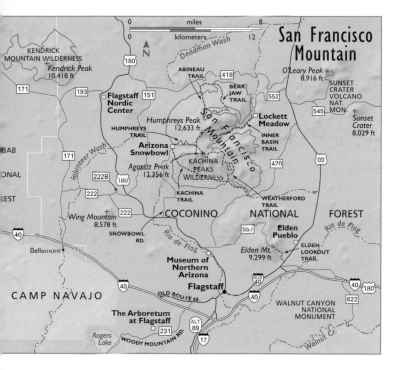

forest; and second, you'll have the thrill of knowing you're hiking into the heart of a huge volcano—even though it's been sleeping for at least 400 millennia. To reach it, drive north from Flagstaff on US 89 for 12.5 miles and turn west on Forest Road 552; in a mile, turn right at the sign for Lockett Meadow. You'll have good views of O'Leary Peak and Sunset Crater as you wind steeply up San Francisco Mountain (all these are volcanic in origin), but it's a really good idea while driving here to keep your eyes on the road.

As you follow this route, you're entering the ancient volcano through a low spot on its caldera rim, an opening that may have been blasted out by a mammoth explosive eruption. The trail begins at **Lockett Meadow,** a broad, grassy opening amid aspen groves, and ascends easily through ponderosa pines and Douglas-firs for 2 miles to the center of the volcanic caldera. There's a healthy population of elk in these mountains, and you may see porcupines, red squirrels, Steller's jays, pygmy nuthatches, Clark's nutcrackers, western tanagers, or dark-eyed juncos. Listen for the fluting whistles of the hermit thrush along the Inner Basin Trail in summer.

Hiking in Kachina Peaks Wilderness

To reach the main trailheads for the 18,960-acre **Kachina Peaks Wilderness,** drive northwest from Flagstaff 7 miles on US 180 and turn north on Snowbowl Road, which climbs 7 miles to parking lots near a downhill ski area. For

Life Zones

AN EXTRAORDINARY polymath, Clinton Hart Merriam (1855-1942) in his long career made important contributions to American ornithology, mammalogy, and ethnology. He was a medical doctor, served as chairman of the U.S. Board on Geographic Names, and was the first director of the U.S. Biological Survey, which evolved into the present U.S. Fish and Wildlife Service. In 1931 he received the Roosevelt Medal for "distinguished work in biology."

Among ecologists, Merriam is best known for pioneering work he did in 1889 in northern Arizona, where he had gone to survey plants and animals. He'd been attracted to the area because of the great diversity of life found in a relatively small area: By traveling only a few dozen miles, he and his co-workers could visit the hot hot and arid Painted Desert, scrub grasslands on the Colorado Plateau, and cool coniferous forests on San Francisco Mountain. From the top of Humphreys Peak to the canyon of the Little Colorado River, Merriam experienced an elevation difference of nearly 2 miles. As he worked, he saw similarities between differing elevations and latitudes of North America. On the canyon floor grew plants also found in Mexico; in the mountains were forests like those of Canada.

From his observations, Merriam developed his theory of "life zones"— altitudinal bands that host communities of interrelated flora and fauna. Merriam called his six life zones Lower Sonoran, Upper Sonoran, Transition, Canadian, Hudsonian, and Arctic-Alpine. Although ecologists have altered his names and refined his defining criteria, his groundbreaking concept remains dominant in scientific discussions of biotic communities.

Merriam's Lower Sonoran zone encompasses species such as creosote bush, agave, and various cactuses; the Upper Sonoran includes paloverde, scrub oaks, and yuccas. As elevation increases into the Transition and Canadian zones, vegetation includes pinyon and ponderosa pines, junipers, and Gambel oaks. Douglas-firs, aspens, and limber and ponderosa pines grow in the Canadian zone, while the Hudsonian is home to Engelmann spruces, subalpine firs, and bristlecone and limber pines. In the harsh conditions of the Arctic-Alpine zone, above tree line, only plants such as mosses, a few wildflowers, and stunted shrubs can grow.

Merriam first believed temperature was the central factor in determining life zones, but as he attempted to expand his theory to cover all of North America, he realized that it was inadequate by itself. Today, biologists know that other elements influence plant and animal communities, including precipitation, soil type, and slope. For example, north-facing slopes are usually cooler and wetter than south-facing ones; it's not unusual, as you pass through a canyon aligned east and west, to note very different plants growing on the two sides.

The pie of natural North America has been cut into more and more pieces as scientists try to understand biological diversity. The Nature Conservancy, for example, recognizes 64 ecological regions in the lower 48 states alone. Yet Merriam's life-zone theory remains the seminal idea.

In southern Arizona, the "sky islands" of such mountain ranges as the Chiricahuas and the Santa

Catalinas illustrate quite well the life-zone concept. But these southern Arizona mountains lack the alpine tundra found atop the peaks of San Francisco Mountain. With the Painted Desert just a few miles east, the Flagstaff region comprises the greatest range of life zones of any comparably sized area in the state. It's perfectly feasible that a visitor could, within two or three days, walk in both desert and tundra.

If you decide to do this, take time to observe the changes in the life-forms you'll encounter. You won't see pinyon jays in the arid desertlands or high in the mountains, but only in the pinyon-pine-juniper zone in between; the pinyon jay's cousins, Steller's jay and Clark's nutcracker, take over at higher elevations. The ponderosa pine is also an in-between species, occupying the belt between pinyon pines below and the spruce-fir forest above. Harris's antelope ground squirrels live in the desert, spotted ground squirrels live in sagebrush habitat, and red squirrels live in the high mountains.

Mule deer in pine forest, Canadian zone

Roadrunner, Lower Sonoran zone

Alpine tundra flowers, Arctic-Alpine zone

The Ubiquitous Ponderosa

A landscape of old-growth ponderosa pines, with its grassy understory and tall trunks rising skyward, creates one of the most evocative scenes of the West. This tree, which ranges from Canada to Mexico, is the most common pine in the West, and ranks behind only Douglas-fir as a commercial timber tree. Beginning around Flagstaff, North America's largest nearly pure ponderosa pine forest stretches southeast along the Mogollon Rim toward the White Mountains.

Mature ponderosa pines, which can reach heights of 180 feet, have a scaly bark that blends orange, pinkish buff, and gray; its scent reminds some people of vanilla or butterscotch. The bark of young trees (blackjacks) is furrowed into dark gray or black ridges.

Highly adapted to fire, ponderosa pines once grew naturally in open woodland with as few as 20 trees per acre; early photographs and pioneer journals testify to the striking look of vast areas of park-like forest, kept clear of brush by regularly occurring low-intensity fires. After decades of fire suppression, though, most ponderosa pines now grow in more crowded conditions, and the buildup of vegetative debris on the forest floor often fuels devastating fires. In many places, forest managers are using controlled burns to try to restore the natural density of ponderosa pine forests and lessen the chances of catastrophic wildfires.

the strenuous hike to **Humphreys Peak** (gaining 3,300 feet in 4.5 miles), park in the left (north) lot and follow the trail across the grassy meadow. (Check the weather forecast before beginning; the top portion of the hike is exposed to wind and lightning.) You'll ascend from ponderosa pines, Douglas-firs, and aspens to a forest of Engelmann spruces, subalpine firs, and limber pines as you make broad switchbacks up the mountain.

At tree line, here about 11,400 feet, the only trees that can survive the harsh conditions are bristlecone pines, stunted and contorted by fierce winds and ice. Beyond, only low shrubs, several kinds of wildflowers, and mosses grow. The Forest Service requires that hikers stay on trails above tree line to protect the very rare San Francisco Peaks groundsel and the rest of the very fragile tundra vegetation. When you reach the 12,633-foot crest (after the rocky trail tops several discouraging false summits), you'll enjoy views that stretch to the Grand Canyon and beyond.

If you'd prefer an excellent but far easier hike through woods and broad meadows, park in the south lot across Snowbowl Road from the Humphreys trailhead, and take the **Kachina Trail.** This path ascends and descends only slightly as it runs south and east around the slope for 5 miles to meet the **Weatherford Trail,** climbing from Forest Road 420. Elk are common along this route, and in forest openings you'll have good views toward Flagstaff. This is an out-and-back hike unless you arrange a shuttle at the Weatherford trailhead —or turn it into a 15-mile backpack loop using the Weatherford Trail to ascend to **Agassiz Saddle** and returning on the **Humphreys Trail.**

To experience some of the above-tree line environment of the peaks without a difficult climb, you can take the main ski lift (which operates in the summer as a scenic ride) at the Arizona Snowbowl to its terminus at 11,500 feet on the side of **Agassiz Peak.** Although the views from here are great, you'll be stuck in this spot until you ride back down; the Forest Service prohibits hiking across the tundra to protect fragile vegetation.

For a good loop day hike in the less visited northern section of the mountain, drive north from Flagstaff 14 miles on US 89 and turn west on Forest Road 418; drive 7 miles and turn south on Forest Road 9123J for 1.2 miles to a trailhead that serves the **Abineau** and **Bear Jaw Trails.** Both climb steeply through canyons to an old road that runs along a talus slope below Humphreys Peak. The road connects the two trails, making possible a 6-mile loop, ascending one trail and descending the other.

Flagstaff's snowy winters make cross-country skiing popular; the Peaks Ranger District office can provide information about the Flagstaff Nordic Center, 16 miles northwest of town off US 180, a commercial facility with 25 miles of groomed trails, and the **Wing Mountain** ski trails, a free area with over 17 miles of marked trails, 8 miles northwest of town on US 180 and 1 mile south on Forest Road 222B. ■

Southern Rocky Mountains

Truchas Peak, Pecos Wilderness

THE ROCKY MOUNTAINS, the majestic off-center backbone of North America, reach their southernmost limit in northern New Mexico: in the Sangre de Cristo Mountains, stretching from Colorado to Santa Fe, and the Sierra Nacimiento range just north of San Ysidro. Here the Rockies are bifurcated by the immense, still widening crack in the Earth's surface called the Rio Grande Rift, down which the "great river" flows. Mountains to the south, such as the Sandias near Albuquerque, share many flora and fauna species with the Rockies, but they formed from different geologic processes.

Though the Rockies seem ancient and fixed—practically eternal—in their immensity, they are in fact relatively young compared with, say, the 600-million-year-old Colorado Plateau. They were uplifted beginning at the end of the Mesozoic era, about 70 million years ago, when the collision of the North American and Pacific tectonic plates caused the Earth's crust to buckle and rise. Those early Rocky Mountains stood far higher than do today's peaks; eons of erosion have worn them down and washed their tops, now sand and gravel, into the surounding lowlands, lessening the elevation difference between mountain summits and bases.

The southern Rockies boast the highest point in New Mexico, 13,161-foot Wheeler Peak, and the second highest, 13,102-foot Truchas Peak. These and other mountains were inhospitable to early settlers, and few ventured into the high ranges except for explorers, hunters, and trappers. Today much of the region is encompassed within national forests—one of which, the Carson, is named for famed Old West scout Kit Carson, who lived and is buried in Taos.

Both Wheeler and Truchas Peaks are preserved within national forest wilderness areas, more visited today by hikers, horseback riders, and backpackers than they ever were by old-time adventurers. The Pecos Wilderness just outside Santa Fe, which includes Truchas, is easily accessible by a paved road to a ski area and offers a wonderful mountain experience to day-hikers as well as backcountry campers.

The same holds true for the Wheeler Peak Wilderness outside Taos, where the main trail to the Wheeler crest is well traveled on summer mornings by hikers who want to say they've stood on the rooftop of New Mexico.

Thick forests of fir, spruce, pine, and Douglas-fir cover these

mountains, dotted with aspen groves where past fires have created openings in the coniferous woods. Mule deer, elk, black bears, mountain lions, porcupines, Abert's and red squirrels, blue grouse, Clark's nutcrackers, gray jays, and a host of other species repay visitors who take time to stop and look and listen for wildlife.

Above tree line, where stunted, wind-contorted bristlecone pines are often the last trees growing, lie expanses of true alpine tundra, home of yellow-bellied marmots and white-tailed ptarmigan. Fragile alpine vegetation is easily destroyed and grows extremely slowly, so conscientious hikers are careful to stay on the trail when they venture into this distinctive environment. Like the New Mexico Rockies themselves, many of the

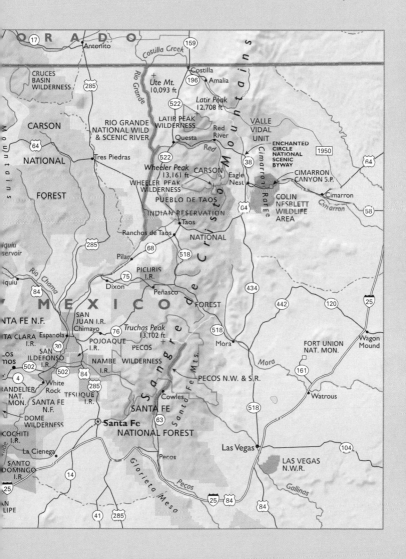

Blooming prickly pear cactus and juniper branches

species that inhabit them are at the southernmost limit of their ranges, including the pika, familiar to most high-country hikers, and the marten, seen only by the luckiest forest visitors.

Mountain trails are by no means the only paths to adventure in this region. The Rio Grande, a lazy, tamed stream in its lower reaches, rushes through spectacular canyons here, providing some of the most exciting white-water rafting, kayaking, and canoeing in the Southwest. In the renowned Taos Box, the river churns past boulders under cliffs more than 600 feet high; farther upstream the action is even more intense, with rapids up to Class VI challenged only by the most experienced and well-prepared river runners. Many rafting companies offer trips of various lengths and physical demands, so nearly everyone can enjoy the fun and thrills of floating the Rio Grande. Farther west, the Rio Chama flows past gorgeous, multicolored sandstone cliffs on a wild section between two reservoirs; its rapids aren't as formidable as the Rio Grande's, but the scenery is unsurpassed.

North almost to Colorado, Valle Vidal in Carson National Forest surely ranks among New Mexico's most underappreciated natural areas. Visited mostly by hunters and anglers in search of elk, mule deer, and the rare Rio Grande cutthroat trout, it rewards visitors with stunning mountain grassland vistas and good wildlife viewing, even for those unable to venture far from their vehicles. The entrance road is long and sometimes a little rough; persevere, though, and you'll discover a real gem set well off most travelers' intineraries.

West of the Rio Grande, a mammoth volcano emptied itself of magma more than a million years ago and then collapsed, leaving a caldera 15 miles across and a ring of peaks composing today's Jemez Mountains. In the center of this natural bowl, surrounded by Santa Fe National Forest, lay a 95,000-acre private ranch, long famed for its wildlife and other natural history attributes.

Congress has approved the purchase of the Baca Ranch (also known as Valle Grande) and its transfer to public ownership. Depending on decisions that are made (unfortunately, by politicians more than by scientists) regarding its disposition and management, this may well become one of New Mexico's finest natural areas. When traveling through this part of the state, check on the status of Valle Grande; a visit here might turn out to be a highlight of your trip. ∎

Trampas Lakes, Sangre de Cristo Mountains

Sunset over Truchas Peak and Carson National Forest

Pecos Wilderness

■ 223,667 acres ■ North-central New Mexico, northeast of Santa Fe ■ Best months July-Sept. Trails can be snow covered Nov.-May or later; some national forest campgrounds closed Sept.-May ■ Camping, hiking, fishing, bird-watching, wildlife viewing ■ Campground fee ■ Contact Santa Fe National Forest, 1474 Rodeo Rd., Santa Fe, NM 87505, phone 505-438-7840. www.fs.fed.us/ recreation/forest_descr/nm_r3_santafe.html; or Camino Real Ranger District, Carson National Forest, P.O. Box 68, Peñasco, NM 87553; phone 505-587-2255. www.fs.fed.us/recreation/forest_descr/nm_r3_carson.html

AS IF SANTA FE DIDN'T have enough distinctions—the nation's second oldest town, the oldest capital city, the highest (7,000 feet) state capital, a historic city center, great food, a renowned arts community—it also offers easy access to superb high-country hiking just a short drive from downtown. The Pecos Wilderness, located in both the Santa Fe and Carson National Forests, ranks as one of the most popular wilderness areas in the nation; while trails can be heavily used on summer weekends, weekday and fall hikes bring the kind of solitude that most wilderness visitors seek.

The mountains in the wilderness, topped by 13,103-foot Truchas Peak (the state's second highest point), compose part of the Sangre de Cristo Mountains. Geologists consider these uplands, stretching from Santa Fe north into Colorado, the southernmost limit of the Rocky Mountains; ranges to the south, such as the Sandias (see pp. 162-66) and the Sacramentos (see pp. 149-150), have geologic origins different from that of the Rockies, which were uplifted by the slow collision of tectonic plates.

The Pecos Wilderness lies mostly above 8,000 feet and so is largely covered in coniferous forest. Ponderosa pine dominates the lower slopes, blending with Douglas-fir, white fir, blue spruce, limber pine, and aspen as elevation increases. The highest woodlands are dominated by Engelmann spruce and subalpine fir; above that can be found expanses of alpine tundra, where conditions are so harsh, and the growing season so short, that only mosses, lichens, herbs, and a few stunted shrubs can exist.

What to See and Do

Santa Fe Scenic Byway

Trailheads providing access into the Pecos Wilderness are located at many points around its perimeter. Most first-time visitors approach along the **Santa Fe Scenic Byway,** a 15-mile route that runs from the city to a commercial downhill ski area, climbing from 7,000 to 10,400 feet. Even those who have no intention of hiking into the wilderness should make this drive, just to get a glimpse of the beauty of the southern Sangre de Cristos, as well as to enjoy fine roadside panoramas of the surrounding landscape.

The byway begins at Santa Fe's historic downtown plaza, winding through town to follow Artist Road, which changes to Hyde Park Road (N. Mex. 475) to the north.

About 6 miles from town, the **Chamisa Trail** (look for the trailhead on the north side of the road) makes a good introduction to ponderosa pine habitat, leading 2.5 miles to **Tesuque Creek,** where meadows can be dotted with wildflowers in summer. Here the Chamisa Trail joins the **Winsor Trail,** which climbs to the heart of the Pecos Wilderness.

A mile farther along the byway, you enter **Hyde Memorial State Park** (*740 Hyde Park Rd., Santa Fe, NM. 505-983-7175. Adm. fee),* a 350-acre area with campgrounds and picnic tables along Little Tesuque Creek. Here at 8,500 feet, Douglas-fir, blue spruce, and aspen join the ponderosa pine; birds such as Steller's jay, mountain chickadee, and western tanager enliven the forest. Several trails begin in or near the park, some connecting with the Winsor Trail.

A dozen or so switchbacks beyond the park, the byway reaches the picnic area at **Aspen Vista,** elevation 10,000 feet. All around lies a huge area of aspen, which turns brilliant gold in fall, creating one of the great natural spectacles in the Santa Fe area. An easy nearby trail follows a closed roadway several miles to the east, offering an opportunity to experience this deciduous woodland. Look for the beautiful Williamson's sapsucker here, or, with luck, a blue grouse.

Hikes

The byway ends at the ski basin, where large parking lots accommodate summer day-hikers and backpackers. Beginning near the Aspen Basin Campground, the

Following pages: Glorieta Mesa, Santa Fe National Forest

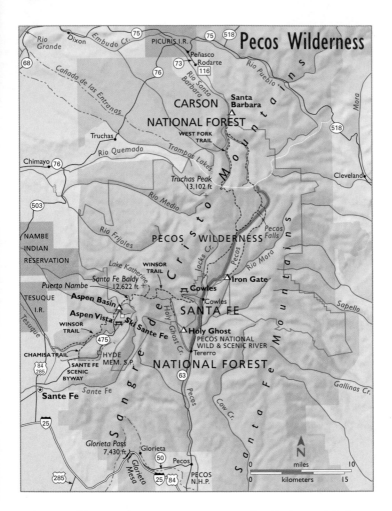

Winsor Trail is a popular route toward such wilderness destinations as Lake Katherine and adjacent 12,622-foot Santa Fe Baldy, 7.5 miles from the trailhead. In addition to the splendid views that await if you make the summit, along the way you'll have a chance to see wildlife such as elk, bighorn sheep, mule deer, Abert's squirrels, yellow-bellied marmots, and pikas; birdlife includes red-naped sapsuckers, gray jays, Clark's nutcrackers, red-breasted nuthatches, Townsend's solitaires, and dark-eyed juncos. If you don't want to hike to the lake or the peak, take the Winsor Trail about 4 miles from the trailhead to the meadows of **Puerto Nambe** for a fine day hike.

Other popular routes into the Pecos Wilderness begin north of Pecos, a small town about 25 miles east of Santa Fe (where there's a Santa Fe National Forest ranger station). Take N. Mex. 63 north from town to reach several campgrounds and trailheads. From the Holy Ghost Campground at the end of Forest Road 122, the trail up **Holy Ghost Creek** can be an excellent day hike. Farther north, past the community of Cowles at the picnic area, the Winsor Trail's east segment offers another route to Lake Katherine and Santa Fe Baldy.

A bit farther north, the Jacks Creek trailhead and Iron Gate Campground are gateways to **Pecos Falls,** a famously scenic spot on the Pecos River. A 13.5-mile stretch of the stream here is an official "wild" part of the National Wild and Scenic Rivers system; the lower 7 miles is designated as "recreational." Trout fishing is the most popular use within the latter category. Though the hike to the falls gains only moderate elevation, its 9-mile length makes it better suited for an overnight trip than a day hike.

The northern part of the Pecos Wilderness is accessed from the village of Peñasco, on N. Mex. 75 about 25 miles south of Taos. (In Peñasco you'll find the ranger office for the Camino Real District of the Carson National Forest.) Take N. Mex. 73 southeast, continuing on Forest Road 116 to the end. The Santa Barbara Campground here is closed at this writing for construction, but you can walk along the river to the trailhead from the gate if it hasn't reopened.

Trails leading up the Middle and West Forks of the Santa Barbara River offer excellent scenery as day hikes, or you can continue south on backpack trips along trails that join those from the Jacks Creek-Iron Gate area. The **West Fork Trail** provides another route

to Pecos Falls, a little longer and steeper than that from the south.

These suggestions only begin to list the possibilities for exploring the Pecos Wilderness. With a good map and advice from national forest rangers, the opportunities for day hikes and overnight trips can satisfy any traveler's desire for adventure. ■

Quaking Aspen

With its pretty white bark and leaves that turn brilliant gold in fall, quaking aspen is one of North America's most popular trees. It's also the most widely distributed, growing from northern Alaska to Mexico, and from Oregon to Newfoundland. Flattened leaf stems cause its foliage to quiver in even the gentlest breeze, hence its name.

In western mountain forests, aspens serve as a pioneer species, recolonizing areas cleared by fire, insect infestation, or other forces. Aspens grow quickly in dense stands, encouraging the successional growth of conifers such as pine, spruce, or fir.

Bandelier National Monument

■ 32,835 acres ■ North-central New Mexico, 15 miles south of Los Alamos via N. Mex. 502 and N. Mex. 4 ■ Best seasons spring and fall. Backcountry hiking can be uncomfortably hot in summer ■ Camping, hiking, cliff dwellings ■ Adm. fee. Backcountry permit required ■ Contact the monument, HCR 1, Box 1, Suite 15, Los Alamos, NM 87544; phone 505-672-0343. www.nps.gov/band

THIS FASCINATING NATIONAL MONUMENT combines natural history and Native American culture within a relatively small and very scenic area. Most visitors stay within the vicinity of the visitor center and the famed cliff dwellings, but adjoining this developed core lie more than 23,000 acres of officially designated wilderness, accessible on 70 miles of trails.

During the late 1100s, ancestors of contemporary local Pueblo Indians began settling in canyons on the Pajarito Plateau west of the Rio Grande, building houses of adobe and stone and enlarging eroded caves in the canyon walls into shelters. Over the next 500 years, a sizable community developed in the canyon now named for Frijoles Creek, with ceremonial structures, irrigated crop fields, and clusters of cliff dwellings near a central circular pueblo. For reasons not completely understood, the canyon was abandoned by the late 1500s.

The lush growth of cottonwood, ash, box elder, and ponderosa pine in Frijoles Canyon must have been as inviting to the Pueblo settlers as it seems to modern travelers. The main trail to the excavations leads up the canyon from the visitor center. You pass a large kiva (ceremonial room) and a series of cliff dwellings, including the impressive **Long House,** a condominium-style community that stretched 800 feet along the canyon wall.

The cliff dwellings loop is 1.25 miles long, but you can continue up Frijoles Creek another half-mile to **Alcove House,** a ceremonial cave reached by climbing a series of wooden ladders to a reconstructed kiva set 140 feet up on the canyon side. For a longer hike, this trail continues up the canyon more than 5 miles to a junction with a side trail; this leads 2 miles to the Ponderosa Campground on N. Mex. 4. With a car shuttle, walking down from the campground makes an easy day hike.

Another popular day hike leads downstream from the visitor center 1.5 miles to **Upper Falls,** where Frijoles Creek splashes over a ledge of hard basaltic lava below the softer volcanic tuff rock. From here it's another quarter mile to Lower Falls, and another three-quarters mile to reach the Rio Grande.

Backpacking into the **Bandelier Wilderness** requires a free permit—and preparedness to descend and ascend steep canyon walls; have a good map and plenty of water before setting out. More than 2,400 archaeological sites have been discovered in this backcountry. The chance to come across an unexpected stone wall or a petroglyph adds a dimension to hiking here not found in most natural areas. ■

Long House cliff dwelling in Frijoles Canyon, Bandelier NM

Rio Grande Wild and Scenic River

■ 68 miles long, including 4 miles of Red River above confluence with Rio Grande ■ North-central New Mexico, north and west of Taos ■ Peak river-running period May–July; some sections may be floatable into fall ■ Camping, hiking, boating, white-water rafting, fishing, mountain biking, wildlife viewing, petroglyphs ■ Camping fee; day-use fee at parking areas. Float trip permit required for some sections ■ Contact Taos Field Office, Bureau of Land Management, 226 Cruz Alta Rd., Taos, NM 87571; phone 505-758-8851 or 505-758-8148 (recorded river information); or Carson National Forest, 208 Cruz Alta Rd., Taos, NM 87571; phone 505-758-6200. www.fs.fed.us/recreation/forest_descr/nm_r3_carson.html

A PORTION OF THE Rio Grande in northern New Mexico was one of the original eight streams designated when the National Wild and Scenic Rivers system legislation was passed in 1968. If you've never seen or experienced the section of the river in question, it's pretty easy to convince yourself the honor was deserved: Simply drive northwest from Taos about 12 miles on US 64, stop at the Rio Grande High Bridge, and walk out to the center.

Once you've caught your breath, you'll understand why the Rio Grande merits preservation. Those who know the river only in its placid, irrigation-depleted incarnation downstream would hardly recognize it here, where it's carved a sheer-sided gorge 650 feet deep in the flat surrounding grassland. Not far upstream, the chasm sinks 150 feet deeper.

The Rio Grande is plenty scenic at this and many other points, but to see its wild side you can take a raft or canoe trip through some of its celebrated white water, either with your own boat or, more easily, on a commercial trip. Floating sections vary from easy stretches with beginner-level ripples to surging, boulder-choked canyons with rapids rated up to Class VI.

Some sections of the river, such as the Ute Mountain segment—beginning in Colorado and running 24 miles south into New Mexico—are remote, definitely wild, and highly restricted in the number of floaters and the times they can visit. The 9.5-mile Upper Box is so difficult that only expert kayakers venture through, and even then serious scouting and portaging are required. Anyone thinking about these segments must speak with the Taos Bureau of Land Management office in advance.

....

What to See and Do

Float Trips

The most popular trips on the Rio Grande begin at the John Dunn Bridge and run south to the Taos Junction Bridge, about 15.5 miles south of Taos. Several commercial outfitters, all of which must be approved by the BLM, offer trips on these segments; in fact, in the peak season of May through July, some stretches of the river experience conditions that on land

View south of the Rio Grande Gorge and Sangre de Cristo Mountains

might qualify as traffic.

The first 16 miles of this part of the Rio Grande compose the famed Taos Box, the most popular white water run in New Mexico. With rapids up to Class IV, it provides plenty of thrills, yet participation in a guided trip is perfectly feasible for most people in moderately good physical shape. (Raft companies have a minimum age of 12 to 14 for this trip.) A full-day journey, the Taos Box run dodges boulders and shoots rapids under cliffs hundreds of feet high.

Two easier stretches follow below the Box, both running through areas where the river canyon has widened from the deep chasm above, and the landscape is more domesticated. The **Orilla Verde** segment features only Class II rapids on its 6-mile run to the small community of Pilar. This half-day trip is excellent for kids, or anyone else unsure of how he or she feels about bouncing through white water on a rubber raft.

Beginning near the BLM's Rio Grande Gorge Visitor Center at Pilar (where you can buy maps and get information on area attractions), the 5-mile run called the **Racecourse** makes a wonderful introduction to white water rafting. With rapids that sometimes rate to Class IV, this half-day trip offers lots of excitement, yet neither its length nor its setting is intimidating. This is the end of the Rio Grande's Wild and Scenic status; here it parallels a busy highway (N. Mex. 68) as it continues to a take-out point at the Taos-Rio Arriba county line.

Hiking

You don't have to get on the water to enjoy the Rio Grande's wild beauty. Several hiking and mountain-biking trails provide the opportunity to explore its environs.

Pinyon mouse among pinyon pine branches

The **West Rim Trail** begins on the west side of the US 64 **Rio Grande High Bridge** northwest of Taos and follows the west side of the Taos Box gorge for 9 miles to N. Mex. 567, north of Pilar. Views down to the river are spectacular (and spectacularly dizzying) on this fairly level and easy walk.

Several trails begin at or near the BLM's **Wild Rivers Recreation Area** *(505-758-8851. Adm fee),* reached by turning west off N. Mex. 522 onto N. Mex. 378, 3 miles north of Questa. Even those not planning to hike or float should make the trip here, to enjoy the panorama of the confluence of the Rio Grande and Red Rivers from **La Junta Point** at the end of the road.

Though not quite as vertiginous as the view from the Rio Grande High Bridge, it's still an excellent vista down 800 feet to the rivers. A visitor center is open from Memorial Day through Labor Day, and campgrounds and picnic areas are available all year.

There are 22 miles of rim and river trails; several fairly strenuous hikes drop all the way to the Rio Grande, where you can walk alongside the river and then return to the top of the canyon on a linked trail for a loop hike (it's coming back up that's strenuous, of course).

An easy nature trail at La Junta Point remains at plateau level. From overlooks you can see bands in the canyon walls—alternating layers of gravel eroded from surrounding mountains and basaltic lava from ancient volcanoes. The nearby **Guadalupe Mountain Trail** leads 2 miles to the top of one extinct volcano, gaining 1,000 feet

to a summit with fine views of the Sangre de Cristo Mountains to the east.

In an inversion of the usual elevational distribution, vegetation in the Rio Grande Gorge grows upside down: Because the canyon bottom is cooler than the flatland at the top, pinyon pines and juniper grow here above ponderosa pine, which you'll encounter as you descend the gorge trails.

Some of those who hike down to the river have fauna, not flora, on their minds, though. There's good fishing for brown and rainbow trout in the rapids and pools of both the Rio Grande and the Red River. ∎

Rio Grande Petroglyphs

Hikers and boaters along the Rio Grande occasionally find examples of Native American rock art called petroglyphs. Unlike painted pictographs, petroglyphs were produced by carving or pecking away at the dark "desert varnish" (a mineral patina) on boulders. Because such art is difficult to date, archaeologists are often uncertain about when it was created. Though some figures are recognizable—handprints, snakes, birds, deer—the exact meanings are elusive.

To see a fabulous collection of rock art, visit **Petroglyph National Monument** *(6001 Unser Blvd., NW, Albuquerque. 505-899-0205),* located just west of town off I-40. More than 20,000 examples of petroglyphs are preserved here.

Rio Chama

Floating the Rio Chama

Although the Rio Grande's Taos Box and Racecourse are better known, New Mexico white water fans know that the Rio Chama offers its own excellent adventures for river runners.

Located west of Tierra Amarilla, the 31-mile stretch between El Vado and Abiquiu Reservoirs includes almost 25 miles of officially designated Wild and Scenic River, protected in part by a national forest wilderness.

To safeguard the river, the agencies that jointly administer it (Bureau of Land Management, U.S. Army Corps of Engineers, and Santa Fe and Carson National Forests) place strict requirements on boaters.

Permits for the most popular seasons are allocated by lottery, while other permits are given on a first-come, first-served basis. In addition, boaters must possess items ranging from first-aid kits to waste-disposal bags.

No permits are needed, though, for the 8-mile day trip from the Chavez Canyon launch site to Abiquiu Reservoir. For complete information, call the Taos BLM office (505-751-4731).

All in all, it's far easier for most people to arrange to see the Rio Chama with a commercial outfitter. River trips of from one to three days are offered, with various segments of the river featuring Class II to Class III rapids.

High canyon walls of multi-colored sandstone make the Rio Chama one of the most scenic rivers in the Southwest—and the lack of access roads and trails means that long portions will provide a true wilderness experience.

Valle Vidal

■ 100,000 acres ■ North-central New Mexico, 40 miles northeast of Taos
■ Best months July-Sept. Road closed by snow in winter; west side closed
May-June during elk calving ■ Camping, hiking, fishing, hunting, mountain biking,
horseback riding, wildlife viewing ■ Camping fee ■ Contact Questa Ranger
District, Carson National Forest, P.O. Box 110, Questa, NM 87556; phone
505-586-0520. www.fs.fed.us/recreation/forest_descr/nm_r3_carson.html

IT TAKES A LITTLE EFFORT to get to this parklike valley in the Sangre de
Cristo Mountains, but once you're here you'll enjoy one of the most scenic
spots in New Mexico. Deer and elk hunters and anglers are probably the
most numerous visitors to this multiple-use tract of Carson National Forest, but it's also popular with horseback riders; limited trails make it less of
a hiking destination than other areas of the national forest. Various regulations restrict public access at different times of year, and the one unpaved
access road can sometimes be slick or icy; it's a good idea to talk to personnel at the Questa Ranger District office when planning a visit.

To reach Valle Vidal, turn east from N. Mex. 522 at Costilla onto
N. Mex. 196; continue on Forest Road 1950. You'll pass dry hillsides with
scrubby pinyon pine, juniper, and sagebrush as the **Costilla Creek Valley**
alternately opens and narrows under tall cliffs. After 19 long miles through
private land, you reach the forest boundary.

For the next 30 miles or so, you pass through a stunning landscape of
rolling hills, with broad meadows bordered by a mixed coniferous forest
of pine, Douglas-fir, white and subalpine fir, and blue and Engelmann
spruce. Large stands of aspen cover some slopes, creating a golden spectacle in fall, and in several spots, bristlecone pines grow beside the road.

About 2,000 elk roam Valle Vidal; wild turkeys, broad-tailed hummingbirds, black-billed magpies, Clark's nutcrackers, and mountain blue-
birds can be seen along the drive. In the Rio Costilla swim Rio Grande
cutthroat trout, the only native trout species in the Rio Grande
drainage—and New Mexico's state fish. It's estimated that the cutthroat
now exists in only about 10 percent of its original range, its population
hurt by cattle grazing, dams, interbreeding with non-native trout, and
other human-caused factors.

Three miles east of the striking rocky point where Forest Road 1900
diverges north is the trailhead for the **Little Costilla Creek Trail,** one of
the area's few designated hiking routes. The trail leads north 10 miles to
Forest Road 1900; it's also the route to 12,584-foot Little Costilla Peak.
During elk calving season in May and June, the trail is closed to hikers.

Two campgrounds, Cimarron and McCrystal, offer the chance to enjoy
Valle Vidal for more than a single day. From the latter, Forest Road 1950
continues about 30 miles east and south to US 64 near the town of Cimarron. Camping is restricted to these two campgrounds; elsewhere in Valle
Vidal, you must camp at least a half mile from the road. ■

Northern Species, Southern Range

THE MOUNTAINS OF northern New Mexico provide a home for several species of animals found at or near the southern edges of their ranges. With summits ranging to 13,161-foot Wheeler Peak (the state's highest point), the uplands of the Sangre de Cristo, Jemez, and San Juan Mountains encompass tundra, mountain meadow, and spruce-fir habitats like those of the northern Rockies—or (in the case of tundra) of Arctic lands beyond tree line in Canada and Alaska.

In the last ice age, which ended only 10,000 years ago, New Mexico had a much cooler and wetter climate. "Northern" habitats, and their associated vegetation and wildlife, were more widespread, reaching down into lower elevations. As the ice retreated and the climate warmed, the distribution of these species shrank, withdrawing upward to pockets of the environments they needed to survive.

If cooler times return, the animals living in these high-country "refugia" may disperse over a wider range again; if global warming continues, they eventually may disappear from New Mexico entirely.

One such species is the snowshoe hare, also called varying hare for the twice-yearly change in its fur color from winter white to summer brown. An uncommon resident of the spruce-fir forests, it might be seen by hikers

American marten

in the Latir Peak or Wheeler Peak wilderness areas; it often freezes beside the trail when approached, hoping that its stillness and camouflage will protect it.

Two other inhabitants of the high coniferous woodland are even rarer: The marten—a large tree-climbing weasel that preys on mice and voles—needs old-growth forest to maintain a healthy population, and has declined over much of its range.

The boreal owl, a reclusive bird that nests in abandoned woodpecker holes, is often sought but seldom seen by bird-watchers; it gives its hollow *hoo* call early in the year when the mountains are often snow covered and inaccessible.

More common, but still seldom spotted, is the short-tailed weasel or ermine; like the snowshoe hare, it changes color from brown to white as summer turns to fall. This species prefers mountain meadows, as do two mammals seen much more often: the yellow-bellied marmot and pika.

The marmot can be quite common on tundra and in subalpine meadows, especially if there are rock piles near. High-country hikers always enjoy encountering marmots, which seem almost to welcome visitors to their lofty homes; curious and approachable, they're easily photographed.

The same can't be said of the pika, a chubby little mammal related to rabbits and hares. Also called cony, the pika has short, rounded ears and no visible tail; it occupies rock slides and talus slopes near or above tree line. Its habits of gathering grass for winter food and of giving sharp, loud squeaks have earned it folk names such as "rock farmer" and "calling hare."

It takes a lucky hiker to spot a white-tailed ptarmigan, a grouse of the

Boreal owl

tundra and the stunted woodland just below. Once found more widely in the northern New Mexico mountains, this species is now confined to a few peaks in the Sangre de Cristos, where transplanted birds from Colorado have bolstered the population. With plumage that molts from summer brown to winter white, the ptarmigan is well disguised, and tends to sit still and let hikers walk past instead of flying or running away.

Some less conspicuous species also make their homes in the mountain meadows. With a field guide and a bit of searching, you might come across several south-ranging "northern" butterflies, including silver-bordered fritillary, arctic fritillary, common alpine, Melissa arctic, and ruddy copper.

One species formerly common in northern New Mexico is unlikely to be found no matter how much you search or how lucky you are. The boreal toad, a subspecies of western toad, lived in the San Juan Mountains as recently as the mid-1980s. Like so many other amphibians, it has suffered grave population declines over most of its range, and is believed to have been extirpated from New Mexico. ■

Enchanted Circle Area

■ North-central New Mexico, northeast of Taos ■ Best months June-Sept.
Roads can be hazardous in winter; campgrounds closed Sept. or Oct.-May
■ Camping, hiking, fishing, mountain biking, horseback riding, downhill skiing,
cross-country skiing, wildlife viewing, scenic drive ■ Camping fee ■ Contact
Carson National Forest, P.O. Box 558, Taos, NM 87571, phone 505-758-6200.
www.fs.fed.us/recreation/forest_descr/nm_r3_carson.html; or Questa Ranger
District, Carson National Forest, P.O. Box 110, Questa, NM 87556; phone
505-586-0520

IT'S NOT TOO MUCH TO say that there's something for nearly everyone on
this route through the Sangre de Cristo Mountains. At one extreme might
be simply driving the Enchanted Circle National Scenic Byway, admiring
the views along the 84-mile loop. At the other extreme would be the strenuous hike to the top of Wheeler Peak, the highest point in New Mexico
and the focal point of the circle. The activity range in between includes
rewarding day hikes, national forest campgrounds, interesting wildlife,
and historic towns. Summer hiking and mountain biking and winter
downhill and cross-country skiing make this a year-round destination.

Sangre de Cristo Mountains from Wheeler Peak

Wheeler Peak can't be seen from Taos, the starting point of the drive; Pueblo Peak stands in the way from this western viewpoint. Once the home of explorer Kit Carson, Taos is now a famed arts community; it makes a fine base for venturing into the nearby mountains, visiting Valle Vidal (see p. 87) to the north, or floating the Rio Grande Wild and Scenic River (see p. 82-85). If you plan to do any hiking in Carson National Forest, stop by the supervisor's office here for maps and advice.

What to See and Do

From US 64 north of Taos, take N. Mex. 150 north and east toward **Taos Ski Valley resort;** the most popular trails leading into the Wheeler Peak Wilderness begin in or near here. Many day-hikers favor the 1.5-mile walk to **Williams Lake,** which in part follows a ski run as it gains about 1,600 feet to the small lake set in

a glacial cirque at 11,800 feet (trailhead and parking available near the Bavarian Lodge and the base of the Kachina chairlift). With 13,161-foot **Wheeler Peak** topping a ridge to the east and conifers struggling up to their limit of growth on the rocky slopes, the surroundings amply repay the moderate effort of the hike.

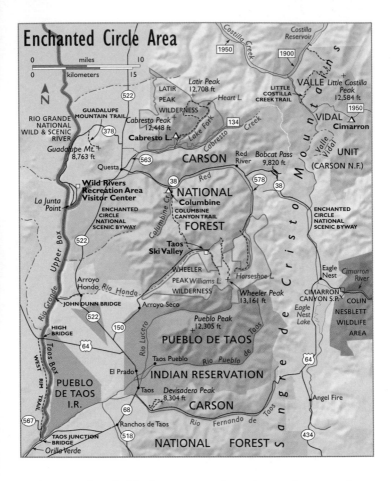

Enchanted Circle Area

0 — miles — 10
0 — kilometers — 15

N

Costilla Creek
Costilla Reservoir
1950
1900
VALLE   Little Costilla Peak 12,584 ft
Latir Peak 12,708 ft
LATIR PEAK WILDERNESS
Heart L.
LITTLE COSTILLA CREEK TRAIL
1950
VIDAL △ Cimarron
522
GUADALUPE MOUNTAIN TRAIL
Cabresto Peak 12,448 ft
134
Creek
Cabresto
Lake Fork
RIO GRANDE NATIONAL WILD & SCENIC RIVER
378
Cabresto L. △
CARSON
Red River
Bobcat Pass 9,820 ft
UNIT (CARSON N.F.)
Guadalupe Mt. 8,763 ft
563
Questa
Red
38
578
38
Wild Rivers Recreation Area Visitor Center
NATIONAL
Columbine
COLUMBINE CANYON TRAIL
La Junta Point
ENCHANTED CIRCLE NATIONAL SCENIC BYWAY
Columbine Cr.
FOREST
ENCHANTED CIRCLE NATIONAL SCENIC BYWAY
522
Taos Ski Valley
WHEELER PEAK Williams L.
Horseshoe L.
Eagle Nest
Cimarron River
Arroyo Hondo
Rio Hondo
WILDERNESS
Wheeler Peak 13,161 ft
CIMARRON CANYON S.P.
COLIN NESBLETT WILDLIFE AREA
JOHN DUNN BRIDGE
Arroyo Seco
Eagle Nest Lake
522
150
Pueblo Peak 12,305 ft
Rio Grande
HIGH BRIDGE
64
PUEBLO DE TAOS
Rio Lucero
Taos Pueblo
Rio Pueblo de Taos
84
WEST RIM TRAIL
Taos Box
El Prado
INDIAN RESERVATION
PUEBLO DE TAOS I.R.
68
Taos
Devisadero Peak 8,304 ft
CARSON
Angel Fire
567
TAOS JUNCTION BRIDGE
Orilla Verde
518
Ranchos de Taos
Rio Fernando de Taos
NATIONAL   FOREST
434
Sangre de Cristo Mountains

As you explore the lakeshore, look and listen for pikas, pudgy little mammals related to rabbits that often give sharp whistles as they scamper about the rock piles in which they live. Some of the hillocks in the vicinity are glacial moraines—debris pushed along by a glacier and then left in a heap when it melted. You might also spot an American pipit, a small, brown bird that looks something like a sparrow with a long, bobbing tail. The high mountains of New Mexico and Arizona constitute its southernmost nesting range.

It requires a serious commitment to reach Wheeler Peak, the mountain for which the 19,150-acre wilderness is named. The 8-mile trail climbs steeply from the beginning; after passing through Engelmann spruce and subalpine fir it reaches tree line, where some of the country's southernmost bristlecone pines grow. (Note the spurlike bristle on the tip of each cone scale.) Because the last part of the hike follows high, exposed ridges, you should leave early enough to reach the top before summer afternoon thunderstorms develop; if lightning threatens, turn back to below tree line immediately.

You're almost sure to see yellow-bellied marmots on the tundra, often near entrances to the burrows where they sleep through the long winters. You might see bighorn sheep in the vicinity; extirpated here, they were reintroduced in 1993. Common ravens soar overhead, while their cousins, Clark's nutcrackers and gray jays, fly through the forest below.

Driving north on N. Mex. 522, you'll reach Questa, a small town 24 miles north of Taos; a Carson National Forest ranger station here can provide maps and advice. The **Enchanted Circle National Scenic Byway** continues east on N. Mex. 38—but if you're heading toward the 20,500-acre **Latir Peak Wilderness,** turn northeast on N. Mex. 563, which becomes Forest Road 134 as it follows Cabresto Creek to the east. After 9 miles you reach Forest Road 134A, which leads north 2 miles to the campground at **Cabresto Lake,** a 15-acre impoundment with good trout fishing. This road can be very rough, and low-clearance vehicles may find it impassable; check with the Questa Ranger District office in advance. Alternatively, you can park in the lot at the road intersection and walk north to the campground.

Beginning here at 9,200 feet, a wilderness trail ascends the **Lake Fork** of **Cabresto Creek** through spruce-fir forest and streamside meadows. Most people who visit Latir Peak Wilderness head for

Near the summit of Wheeler Peak at sunset

Heart Lake, 5 miles from the trailhead. Set just below tree line at an elevation of about 11,500 feet, the lake makes a great day-hike destination; many backpackers camp near here to visit the nearby alpine peaks and glacier-sculpted ridgelines. With a wilderness map, you can make a 14-mile loop hike over the tundra ridge south of 12,708-foot **Latir Peak,** and south toward **Cabresto Peak** for a round-trip back to Cabresto Lake.

Driving east from Questa on N. Mex. 38, paralleling the Red River, the Enchanted Circle seems a little less enchanted as you pass the massive tailings from an adjacent molybdenum mine. More pleasant are several campgrounds, including Columbine. From here the popular 5.7-mile **Columbine Canyon Trail** leads south into the national forest,

Abert's Squirrel

A familiar sight among the ponderosa pine forests of southern Colorado, southern Utah, northern New Mexico, and northern Arizona, this species feeds largely on pinecones, twig bark, branch-tip buds, and a fungus that grows on the trees' roots. Where these squirrels are abundant, their feeding can "prune" the ponderosas, shaping them as if by a gardener's shears. Long tufts of hair on its ears give Abert's its nickname: tassel-eared squirrel. Chewed cones, stripped twigs, and clipped needles indicate the species' presence; when you see the clues, look up.

linking with others that connect to trailheads at Taos Ski Valley. Even a short hike up **Columbine Creek** will let you enjoy the mixed-conifer forest and see wildlife. Look for Abert's and red squirrels, least and Colorado chipmunks, porcupines, blue grouses, hairy woodpeckers, mountain chickadees, Clark's nutcrackers, Steller's jays, hermit thrushes, Townsend's solitaires, and western tanagers.

At the old mining community of Red River, now a tourist town, N. Mex. 578 leads south to trailheads for the **Wheeler Peak Wilderness,** far less used than the trails at Taos Ski Valley. Routes lead to such destinations as pretty **Horseshoe Lake,** set beside an alpine ridge below Wheeler Peak, with stunted bristlecone pines dotting the stark landscape. To get there, drive to the East Fork trailhead and hike about 5 miles on the **East Fork** and **Lost Lake Trails.**

N. Mex. 38 crosses 9,820-foot Bobcat Pass to join US 64 at Eagle Nest, from which it's a short drive east to **Cimarron Canyon State Park** (see opposite). Adjoining **Eagle Nest Lake** is a popular fishing spot, where anglers catch rainbow trout and kokanee salmon both in summer and through the ice in winter.

From Eagle Nest it's 31 miles back to Taos on US 64. Three miles east of town, the 6-mile **Devisadero Loop** trail makes a fine, moderately strenuous day hike. Beginning at El Nogal picnic area, it climbs through pinyon-pine-juniper woods to Douglas-fir, ponderosa pine, and white fir, and offers excellent views to the north and west along the way. ■

Fly-fishing, Cimarron Canyon State Park

Cimarron Canyon State Park

■ 33,000 acres ■ Northeastern New Mexico, 42 miles northeast of Taos via I-64 ■ Best months May–mid-Oct. Wildlife area is popular with hunters; check with park before hiking in fall elk or deer seasons ■ Camping, hiking, fishing, hunting, mountain biking, horseback riding, wildlife viewing ■ Camping fee ■ Contact the park, P.O. Box 185, Eagle Nest, NM 87718; phone 505-377-6271. www.emnrd.state.nm.us/nmparks/pages/parks/cimarron/cimarron.htm

A BROAD RANGE of outdoorspeople find this beautiful park an appealing destination—none more so than fly fishers, who often line the banks of the **Cimarron River** to cast for stocked brown and rainbow trout. The 8 miles of river running through the park constitute one of the best trout streams in New Mexico; US 64 parallels the river along the narrow canyon; several picnic areas and campgrounds offer parking and easy access.

Set at an elevation of 8,000 feet in the foothills of the Sangre de Cristo Mountains, the canyon is home to elk, mule deer, black bears, porcupines, and Abert's squirrels. Golden-mantled ground squirrels, often mistaken for chipmunks, scamper among the forest of Douglas-fir, white fir, ponderosa pine, and aspen. In wider areas of the canyon, beaver dams produce placid pools. Find a comfortable seat here at dusk and watch the aquatic residents begin their evening activities. Wild turkey and blue grouse walk stealthily through the forest; the latter is seldom seen, but once spotted is often absurdly approachable.

Stop at the **Palisades picnic area** to admire towering cliffs of monzonite, a granitic rock formed below the Earth's surface, now exposed and eroded into spectacular columns. To enjoy both wildlife and scenery, drive west a couple of miles and walk up the **Clear Creek Canyon Trail,** a 5-mile round-trip up a side canyon. This is one of four park trails, most of which follow old logging roads, totaling more than 30 miles. ■

Chihuahuan Desert
and Grasslands

West face of El Capitan, Guadalupe Mountains National Park

THIS REGION, a junction of desert, peaks, and prairie, has its high and low points—literally speaking. The zenith lies at the end of a hike to the top of Guadalupe Peak, at 8,749 feet the highest point in Texas. At the other extreme, you can descend more than 800 feet below ground to tour legendary Carlsbad Cavern. In between you'll find excellent wildlife viewing, extinct volcanoes, expansive grasslands, and even the old stomping grounds of a menagerie of dinosaurs.

The chapter begins where the Chihuahuan Desert meets the highlands of Guadalupe Mountains National Park, just below the New Mexico state line in western Texas. The second largest of the four major North American deserts (the Great Basin Desert, which stretches from northwestern New Mexico into Oregon, is larger), the Chihuahuan is slightly cooler and wetter than the Sonoran Desert to the west. Unlike the Sonoran, its vegetation is dominated not by cactuses, but by shrubs, agave, and yucca.

The Guadalupes occupy an exceptional position, even amid all the disparate geologic permutations in the Southwest. Fantastic as it seems, these massive peaks formed underwater as a limestone reef 250 million years ago, when a shallow sea covered this part of the Earth. Over time, tiny sea creatures built a huge, U-shaped reef around the edge of an ocean bay; while most of the reef remains buried today by newer layers of rock, in the Guadalupes geological forces have uplifted great sections of it high above the surrounding desert terrain.

So high are the summits, in fact, that forests of ponderosa pine and Douglas-fir create an "island" of northern-affinity habitat, home to species such as elk, porcupine, Steller's jay, and mountain chickadee. Linking the park's Chihuahuan Desert environment and its mountaintop woodlands, the trail up through the riparian habitat of McKittrick Canyon is renowned as one of the most beautiful walks in the Lone Star State.

Just to the north at world-famous Carlsbad Caverns National Park, you can see where water and weak acids have dissolved great interconnected chambers within the soft limestone of the same ancient reef that built the Guadalupes. Each year, millions of people walk through these underground rooms, marveling at the variety and splendor of the formations on display. Carlsbad offers a range of subterranean tours, from wheelchair-accessible paved paths to rigorous crawls through undeveloped "wild" passages. Above ground, the park protects a vast tract of Chihuahuan Desert environment as officially designated wilderness, crossed by miles of relatively little-used hiking trails.

Northward in this region, the desert gradually intergrades with the shortgrass prairie of the southern Great Plains. Covered mostly by gravels eroded from adjacent mountains, this landscape comprises broad, gently rolling expanses, where the only major topographic relief occurs at stream-cut valleys. The Pecos River drains a large part of eastern New Mexico and western Texas, providing important wetland habitat in an otherwise arid land.

Little-known Bitter Lake National Wildlife Refuge, near Roswell, offers some of the region's best wildlife viewing, especially birding. Sandhill cranes and geese are only the most conspicuous of the species found here at varying times of year; while winter brings the largest flocks, the refuge is also home to several special breeding species, including the threatened snowy plover.

Parts of the shortgrass prairie are known as the Llano Estacado (Spanish for "staked plains"), a name whose origin has been debated, but that may refer to the fencelike escarpments demarcating its

Nautiloid fossils, McKittrick Canyon Nature Trail, Guadalupe Mountains NP

boundaries. Smoothed for eons by wind and water, some areas of the Llano Estacado are among the flattest places on Earth.

This is the realm of pronghorn, prairie dogs, kit foxes, bullsnakes, burrowing owls, ferruginous hawks, and meadowlarks; of wildflowers and sweeping vistas of native grasses. Almost none of North America's native prairie has been preserved in its natural state; it was too easy to plow and (over)graze.

In the Kiowa and Rita Blanca National Grasslands near Clayton, though, you can still experience scenes reminiscent of the landscape that 19th-century pioneers crossed along the Santa Fe Trail.

Nearby, Clayton Lake State Park reveals a time far earlier than the era of stagecoaches and covered wagons. Here, at a small lake in the midst of rolling grassland, you can gaze down on the footprints of several species of dinosaur. Imprinted on a muddy shore 100 million years ago, they have been preserved by overlying layers of rock.

Evidence of volcanic activity is widespread in northeastern New Mexico. Covering some 8,000 square miles, the Raton-Clayton Volcanic Field saw a multitude of eruptions over a span of millions of years that ended only a very recent (in geologic terms) 30,000 to 40,000 years ago.

Many of the region's hills and ridges are actually volcanic cones or lava flows, creating humps and bumps on territory that otherwise would be nearly featureless. The great spreading cone of Sierra Grande, a conspicuous mountain near Des Moines (New Mexico), was formed from layers of oozing lava. At Capulin Volcano National Monument, you can drive to the top of a smaller volcano, circle its rim, and even walk down into its crater.

Other geographic regions may encompass more dramatic terrain, but none surpass eastern New Mexico in its range of natural-history experience. Whether it's exploring Carlsbad Caverns by headlamp, hiking in the high Guadalupes, or watching a herd of pronghorn through a car window, an array of discoveries await the curious and adventurous traveler. ■

McKittrick Canyon stream

Snow-dusted Texas madrone, Guadalupe Mountains NP

Guadalupe Mountains National Park

■ 86,416 acres ■ Western Texas, 110 miles east of El Paso via US 62/180
■ Best seasons fall-spring, with colorful autumn foliage in McKittrick Canyon; occasional winter storms in the high country ■ Camping, hiking, horseback riding, bird-watching, wildlife viewing ■ Camping fee; backcountry permit required ■ No food, lodging, or gasoline are available in the park; the nearest services are 35 miles away in White City, New Mexico. Bring all essential supplies with you ■ Contact the park, HC 60, P.O. Box 400, Salt Flat, TX 79847; phone 915-828-3251. www.nps.gov/gumo

EVEN WITHIN THE HONORED CIRCLE of our national parks, Guadalupe Mountains stands out for the great and fascinating diversity it offers to visitors. The park's physical features are not only visually striking, but have global geologic significance; its mountains include the four highest points in Texas, topped by 8,749-foot Guadalupe Peak; its host of plants and animals encompasses several species at the limits of their ranges, representing northern, temperate, and desert ecosystems; its human history stretches from Apache warriors and Old West pioneers to visionary 20th-century philanthropists.

Established in 1972, Guadalupe Mountains is a relatively recent addition to the national park system. Fortunately, the rugged nature of its terrain preserved it from serious alteration or abuse before the park's creation. While you'll find some fine short walks near roads, the great body of the park is still accessible only to those willing to hike into the backcountry on its 80 miles of trails. There, visitors can travel from desert habitat of creosote bush, cholla, and mesquite to mountain slopes shaded by ponderosa pine and Douglas-fir.

The great, craggy cliff called **El Capitan** has served as a traveler's landmark for as long as humans have lived in this region. Jutting from the southern edge of the mountains, it is as much a symbol of Guadalupe Mountains as Old Faithful is of Yellowstone, or Half Dome of Yosemite. And, as is so often the case in the Southwest, to comprehend its form and its natural history and that of the surrounding landscape, we must look far back in the Earth's past for a lesson in geology.

About 250 million years ago, a warm sea covered much of what is now southwestern Texas; one broad arm of the sea stretched up into southern New Mexico. Around the shores of this basin grew a roughly horseshoe-shape reef composed mainly of limestone from sponges, algae, and other tiny life forms, as well as precipitate from the ocean water itself. The reef grew to massive size before the sea retreated, leaving salt, gypsum, and other minerals on the dry floor.

Over time, new sediments buried the reef, which remained underground until parts of it were uplifted in the great phase of Basin-and-Range mountain-building that began about 15 million years ago. Most of the reef still lies below the surface, though it breaches the earth in the Guadalupes and in the Apache and Glass Mountains to the southeast.

The park's roadside geology leaflet points out evidence of reefbuilding in the Guadalupes, including horizontal layers of limestone formed on the reef's calm landward edge, eroded limestone debris on the seaward side, and bands of sandstone from interbedded beach deposits. Fossils of sea creatures can be seen in many places throughout the park. The features so prominently on display here make these mountains one of the world's finest examples of an exposed fossil reef—and the focus of decades of research by geologists.

Knowing the origin of the Guadalupes adds much to a visit here. As you hike, you can't help but imagine the scene of the reef teeming with life; and as you regard the 1,000-foot-high face of El Capitan, you try to grasp how long it must have taken to form, one speck of limestone at a time.

What to See and Do

The **visitor center,** located off US 62/180, is a mandatory stop to see geology and wildlife exhibits, learn about ranger programs, and buy maps of the backcountry.

No map is needed for the short (less than 0.4-mile) walk to **The Pinery,** the ruins of a Butter-field mail stagecoach station that operated briefly during the late 1850s. (You can also reach it from the parking lot north of the visitor center entrance on US 62/180.) Signs along the wheelchair-accessible path interpret desert vegetation.

Many of the most popular hikes begin from a trailhead at nearby Pine Springs campground. If you have only a few hours, take the 4.2-mile round-trip hike to **Devil's Hall,** a scenic, narrow canyon with high, limestone walls.

The moderately strenuous trail follows in part the dry streambed of **Pine Spring Canyon,** at one point climbing a remarkable series of rock layers called the **Hiker's Staircase.** You begin among Chihuahuan Desert vegetation, passing, as you ascend, ponderosa pine, bigtooth maple, velvet ash, and oak. You might spot a black-tailed rattlesnake along the way, but you'll more likely see a prairie or collared lizard among the rocks, or perhaps a rock squirrel.

Those prepared for an overnight backpack or a strenuous day hike can choose from several longer routes. Whenever you hike in the Guadalupes, take plenty of water (none is available away from trailheads). Also, inquire about weather conditions (especially thunderstorms where lightning is a danger) and other backcountry concerns.

The climb to **Guadalupe Peak**—the highest point in Texas at 8,749 feet—is a round-trip of 8.4 miles, gaining nearly 3,000 feet in elevation and promising dramatic views. The **El Capitan Trail** leads to the base of that mighty cliff face; many people make an 11.3-mile loop by returning on the **Salt Basin Trail.**

Wildlife

To experience the mixed coniferous forest and wildlife of the high Guadalupes, make the strenuous, 9.1-mile round-trip to **The Bowl,** a large, peak-ringed basin in the center of the mountains. Here, a beautiful forest of ponderosa pine and Douglas-fir is home to elk (introduced here in the 1920s after the original population was extirpated by hunting), mule deer, porcupine, and gray-footed chipmunk.

Birds include northern saw-whet and flammulated owls, band-tailed pigeon, hairy woodpecker, olive-sided flycatcher, plumbeous vireo, brown creeper, mountain chickadee, Steller's jay, pygmy nuthatch, western bluebird, and pine siskin, some of which nest nowhere else in Texas.

Continuing north a couple of miles up US 62/180, stop at **Frijole Ranch,** built by settlers in the 1870s to take advantage of nearby springs. Later residents raised fruit, nuts, and grain crops here, as well as livestock.

The 2.3-mile **Smith Spring Trail**, which passes two springs, is excellent for wildlife viewing. Look for elk, mule deer, scaled quail, Cassin's kingbird, western scrub-jay, Scott's oriole, and Rio Grande leopard frog as you walk. The Chihuahuan spotted whiptail, seen occasionally along this loop, is one of several related lizards with no males in the population; reproducing by parthenogenesis (virgin birth), females lay unfertilized eggs that hatch only more females.

Reef Rock

The northeastern part of the park features the popular **McKittrick Canyon Trail** (see pp. 106-107), reached by turning west off US 62/180 about 7 miles north of the visitor center. This area can get quite crowded when the bigtooth maples and other deciduous trees begin to display their fall colors; try to visit on a weekday if you arrive in October or November. The easy 0.9-mile **McKittrick Canyon Nature Trail** passes an intermittent seep; interpretive signs along the loop discuss park geology and trailside plants.

While the canyon is best known for its rich vegetation and perennial spring, its high walls illustrate well the area's reef geology. The strenuous **Permian Reef Geology Trail** climbs the canyon's north slope, gaining 2,000 feet in 4.2 miles (one way) to the top of **Wilderness Ridge,** where those who make it will have great views of the canyon and the lands to the north. A geology guide, available at the visitor center, is keyed to wayside markers.

The **Dog Canyon** area of the park, while not far from the visitor center as the raven flies, is reached by driving 12 miles northwest of Carlsbad, New Mexico, on US 285, then taking N. Mex. 137 south for 60 miles to the ranger station. Only a small percentage of visitors make it to this remote spot, with its campground and trailhead, so relative solitude is assured.

Hikes starting here connect with trails leading to The Bowl, McKittrick Canyon, and Pine Springs Campground. The short **Indian Meadow Nature Trail** interprets canyon ecology and history. A popular day hike follows the **Bush Mountain Trail** 2.3 miles to a viewpoint down West Dog Canyon.

Bigtooth maples with fall foliage, McKittrick Canyon, Guadalupe Mountains NP

McKittrick Canyon

The hike up **McKittrick Canyon** is one of the prettiest and most popular in Texas. Beginning in desert terrain, the trail follows a perennial stream up the canyon, beneath tall limestone cliffs, into mixed woodland famous for its fall foliage display (especially the bigtooth maples). Because this path is so well used, the park prohibits camping in the canyon and requires hikers to stay on the trail, out of the creek and its streamside vegetation.

You can walk as little of the route as you want, but two favorite destinations, both fine day hikes, are **Pratt Lodge** (2.4 miles up the canyon) and the picnic area called the **Grotto** (3.4 miles).

Allow plenty of time, no matter how far you go; McKittrick Canyon is definitely not a place to hurry through. Starting early in the day (as soon as the gate opens) will bring the best chance to see birds and other wildlife.

As you start your walk, note the desert vegetation—Spanish bayonet yucca, New Mexico agave, lechuguilla, sotol, ocotillo, tree cholla, and various species of prickly pear. Down here, you might spot a Texas antelope squirrel sprinting along the ground or a Texas horned lizard sunning itself.

Moving upstream, you'll begin seeing the trees that make the canyon such a shady oasis: ponderosa pine, alligator juniper (note the blocky bark for which it is named), bigtooth maple, velvet ash, chinkapin oak (an eastern species found here at the western limit of its range), gray oak, chokecherry, littleleaf walnut, and Texas madrone (distinctive with its reddish, peeling bark).

Depending on the time of year and the precipitation, wildflowers you might see along the trail include Indian paintbrush, butterfly milkweed, cardinal flower, columbine, bigleaf greeneyes (a sunflower), and dotted gayfeather (liatris). Apache plume, barberry, Mexican orange, and skunkbush are among the flowering shrubs found in the canyon.

The bird species also change as you move from desert into woodland. In the arid terrain near the trailhead, look for ash-throated flycatcher, bushtit, cactus and rock

Sitting Bull Falls

If you're heading south on N. Mex. 137 to the Dog Canyon area of Guadalupe Mountains National Park, consider a 7-mile detour along Forest Road 276 to **Sitting Bull Falls** in Lincoln National Forest (505-885-4181).

Here, a spring-fed creek cascades over a limestone bluff, dropping into a small pool; the resulting oasis of walnut, cherry, sumac, oak, and willow attracts abundant wildlife—when it's not attracting overabundant people; avoid visiting on summer weekends.

Look for mule deer, rock squirrel, white-throated swift, canyon wren, and black phoebe around the falls.

To explore further, take the adjoining trail to the top of the cascades. A mile or so from here is the spring that supplies water to the falls.

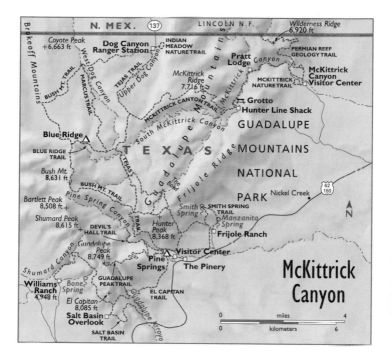

wrens, gray vireo, canyon towhee, and rufous-crowned sparrow.

Higher, you'll find broad-tailed hummingbird, band-tailed pigeon, cordilleran flycatcher, black phoebe, plumbeous vireo, canyon wren, western tanager, and black-headed grosbeak.

Partway up the canyon you'll reach Pratt Lodge, built by Wallace Pratt. The oil-company geologist, and later executive, fell in love with McKittrick Canyon's beauty and began buying land here in the 1920s. A strong advocate of the preservation of the Guadalupes, he eventually donated more than 5,000 acres to the national park.

Rest rooms and water are usually available at the lodge, but check with a ranger before counting on refilling your canteen here.

Past Pratt Lodge, you may be surprised to spot rainbow trout in the creek. Introduced here by a rancher in the 1930s, these alien fish reproduce naturally.

The riparian woods become even lusher as you ascend to the Grotto, where you'll find a shallow, cavelike overhang, complete with stalagmites and stalactites. Nearby, visit **Hunter Line Shack,** a historic structure built in the 1920s.

For those with time and stamina, the trail continues at a junction below the Grotto. It climbs 3 more steep miles to **McKittrick Ridge,** and beyond that to a backcountry camping spot more than 7 miles from the trailhead.

There are fabulous views from the ridge, but you'll probably have to take a few minutes to catch your breath before you'll be able to enjoy them. ■

Carlsbad Caverns National Park

Big Room formations, Carlsbad Caverns NP

■ 46,766 acres ■ Southeast New Mexico, 25 miles southwest of Carlsbad via US 62/180 ■ Best seasons spring and fall ■ Camping, hiking, bird-watching, cave tours, bat flight program ■ Adm. fee; additional fees for guided tours. Reservations recommended for ranger-led tours. Backcountry permit required ■ Contact the park, 3225 National Parks Hwy., Carlsbad, NM 88220; phone 505-785-2232, 800-967-2283 (reservations). www.nps.gov/cave

THE SAME GEOLOGIC forces that shaped the landscape of little-known Guadalupe Mountains National Park also set the stage for the creation of one of America's most celebrated natural places. As you stroll the main tour routes in Carlsbad Cavern or squeeze through a narrow opening of a wilder passage, you travel through the heart of a limestone reef built by plants and animals that lived in a warm, shallow sea more than 200 million years ago.

Of course, it may be hard to keep your mind on facts and figures as you gaze into spectacular underground spaces elaborately decorated with stalactites, stalagmites, columns, draperies, and other speleothems (cave formations). The immediate visual enjoyment of all this grandeur seems so much more interesting, whether you walk down through the cave's natural entrance or take an elevator from the visitor center (a portion of one tour route is wheelchair accessible).

You'll probably appreciate what you're seeing more, however, with an understanding of how the cave was created. The story begins with a Permian period ocean, when sponges, algae, bryozoans, and other living things built a gigantic, U-shaped reef along the shores of a broad bay. After the sea receded, the limestone reef was buried beneath thousands of feet of sedimentary material. About 15 million years ago, tectonic forces lifted part of it above the surface, creating the Guadalupe Mountains under which the cave lies.

Slightly acidic water seeping down through cracks began dissolving the soft limestone, a process aided by sulfuric acid formed when hydrogen sulfide gas from underlying oil and gas deposits mixed with subterranean flows. Over millions of years, the great rooms and passages of the cave were hollowed out of the limestone. For perhaps the last half million years, water continuing to filter through the cave roof carried with it calcite, the main constituent of limestone. This mineral, deposited on the ceiling, floor, or walls, sculpted the myriad formations that have so delighted visitors since famed explorer Jim Larkin White began charting the cave's passages, just after the turn of the 20th century.

It was bats that led to White's discovery of the cave. From early spring through October, hundreds of thousands of the animals roost in a passage off Carlsbad Cavern's natural entrance. At dusk, they depart in a mass flight to feed—a wildlife spectacle that each evening delights a crowd of spectators. The nightly exodus also caught the attention of White, one of the miners excavating bat guano (an excellent fertilizer) for shipment to southern California's citrus groves. He became the first to explore the cave—one of the largest and most ornate ever discovered.

Today, more than 30 miles of passages have been mapped in Carlsbad Cavern, the main cave in the national park—but not the only one. More than 85 other known caves lie within the park boundaries, including the fabled Lechuguilla Cave (see sidebar).

The national park's attractions are not all subterranean: The Chihuahuan Desert overlying the cave presents opportunities for adventure, too. More than 33,000 acres of the park have been officially designated as wilderness, where some 50 miles of trails offer backcountry solitude and the challenge of desert travel to hikers and backpackers.

For those who prefer a less challenging experience, you can explore the Guadalupe landscape by car along the winding Walnut Canyon Desert Drive (see p. 114).

While it's possible to zip down the elevator, see the Big Room, and be on your way in a couple of hours, you'll be missing a lot if that's the extent of your visit. Take the time to experience a cave tour, attend a ranger program, learn about the desert environment, and walk a trail—and you'll know why Carlsbad was designated a United Nations World Heritage Site.

Lechuguilla Cave

In 1986 explorers made one of the most astounding cave discoveries of all time when they broke through rock rubble in an old guano-mining pit in the Carlsbad Caverns National Park backcountry. More than 100 miles of passages have now been mapped within Lechuguilla Cave. Its rooms contain formations said to surpass Carlsbad's in beauty, including types never seen before—anywhere.

Already longer and deeper than its better-known neighbor, Lechuguilla continues to provide virgin passages to the experts who carefully push through its tight spaces. Access is restricted to scientists and survey teams.

Following pages: Entrance to Carlsbad Cavern, Carlsbad Caverns NP

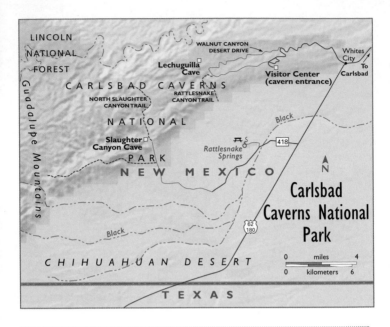

What to See and Do

At the park **visitor center,** off US 62/180 southwest of Carlsbad, you can study exhibits on cave geology and natural history, learn about optional cave tours, and check the list of ranger-led activities. These events can range from slide programs on local mammals to rope-climbing exhibitions to talks on bat-guano mining (an important early commercial use of the cave) to nature walks.

Most visitors experience the park on the major routes through Carlsbad Cavern, covering a total of about 3 miles of paved trails.

Consider renting an audio guide for your walk through the cave. This interpretive device is triggered by signals at stops along tour routes; it features illuminating commentary from geologists, cavers, and park personnel.

You have two options to see

Carlsbad Cavern: For the most complete experience, take the short walk down an amazing series of switchbacks to the natural entrance. From here, it's a 1-mile path to the lunchroom area in mid-cave; walking time is about an hour.

Alternatively, those who are less mobile or who have health problems can ride an elevator more than 750 feet down to the lunchroom, from which a fairly level path loops through the famed **Big Room.**

Whichever route you choose, remember that the temperature in the cave stays a constant 56°F; a light jacket and long pants will probably feel good.

As you descend into the cavern, leaving the sunlight behind, you pass Native American pictographs and **Bat Cave,** the side passage where the animals roost. (To prevent disturbance, no entry is allowed.) Continuing down past Devil's Den and Natural Bridge, you reach **Iceberg Rock,** a huge hunk of ceiling that fell long before anyone was around to notice.

Take a break when you reach the lunchroom before walking the mile-long **Big Room Route.** One of the largest known cave rooms in the world, the Big Room encompasses 14 acres of varied and colorful formations. This easy trail passes many of Carlsbad Cavern's most famous features, including **Giant Dome, Bottomless Pit** (not really; it's 140 feet deep), **Rock of Ages,** and **Painted Grotto.**

Guided Tours

The park calls the **Kings Palace tour** an option, but you definitely should make reservations for this 90-minute, mile-long walk through some of the cave's most scenic rooms. Moderately strenuous (you must descend and climb the equivalent of eight stories), it passes through the **Green Lake Room** (with the famous formation called the **Veiled Statue),** the elaborately decorated **Kings Palace,** and other rooms en route.

For a look at the cave off the main routes, make reservations for one of the other ranger-led tours. A three-hour tour of the **Lower Cave**'s attractions include the **Rookery,** with its beautiful "cave pearls," created when layers of calcite formed around bits of foreign material. People with a fear of heights or who are uncomfortable climbing down a ladder should probably skip this tour. The two-hour **Left Hand Tunnel tour** isn't

so intimidating. You'll pass pretty cave pools and pause to examine fossils that are more than 200 million years old.

Talk to a ranger before signing on for the **Spider Cave** or **Hall of the White Giant tours,** each four hours long. If you have even a touch of claustrophobia these aren't for you, since they require long belly-crawls through tight passages. The intrepid will see formations others don't and they'll experience something of the adventure of primitive cave exploration—in safety, with the presence of an experienced ranger.

Several miles south of the visitor center is **Slaughter Canyon Cave.** Wilder than Carlsbad, this

Rattlesnake Springs

To most visitors, Rattlesnake Springs is simply a pleasant picnic area in an outlying tract of Carlsbad Caverns National Park, where tall cottonwoods grow near historic springs. Biologists, though, recognize it as one of the most significant wetlands in New Mexico.

An oasis in the Chihuahuan Desert, Rattlesnake Springs provides a home for many species of snakes (including the plain-bellied water snake), amphibians (such as the eastern barking frog and Blanchard's cricket frog), and rare or unusual butterflies.

It's a special destination for bird-watchers; more than 300 bird species have been found around this 13-acre speck of greenery in the desert.

cave has no paved paths and no lights, only the lanterns of rangers and the flashlights of participants. On the two-hour trip, you'll pass an 89-foot-tall column called the **Monarch**, a rimstone dam known as the **Chinese Wall,** and an eerie, hooded figure dubbed the **Guardian.** Though the route involves rope-assisted climbs up slick slopes, the most difficult part is the half-mile walk up a steep desert slope to the cave entrance.

Aboveground Attractions

Just before you start down the route to the natural entrance, you'll pass two spots worth noting: One is the amphitheater from which you can watch the renowned bat flight. (Ask at visitor center for schedule.) A ranger presents a program on these much misunderstood animals before they emerge from the cave in an immense, swirling column.

More than a dozen kinds of bats have been identified in the park, but the vast majority are Mexican free-tailed bats, a migratory species that returns to the cave each spring for the females to give birth and raise their pups.

The largest bat eruptions occur during August and September, when the young begin joining their parents on the evening feeding flights; numbers fluctutate from year to year, but usually range in the hundreds of thousands. This is down from an estimated 8 million in the mid-20th century—typical of the trend elsewhere, as bat populations have suffered from loss of habitat, harassment, and pesticides.

Many visitors are confused when they see the cave swallows that nest in the natural entrance and dart in and out during the day from spring through fall. Part of the largest colony of this species in the United States, they are birds, not bats; the latter, despite their flying ability, are mammals.

You'll also pass the easy **Desert Nature Trail,** which diverges from the natural entrance path to make a half-mile loop featuring signs discussing Chihuahuan vegetation. The trail offers a quick glimpse of the park's Chihuahuan Desert environment.

For a longer look, take the 9.5-mile **Walnut Canyon Desert Drive,** a scenic loop through Guadalupe Mountains terrain with typical vegetation, such as creosote bush, sotol, ocotillo, catclaw acacia, desert willow, New Mexico agave, and lechuguilla.

An extensive trail system allows hiking and backpacking in the park's backcountry. Any of the trails can be used for day hikes, though you should be prepared for desert travel, with plenty of water, sun protection, good boots, and a map. Talk to a ranger if you have any doubts about desert hiking, and avoid such ventures in summer, when temperatures can zoom past 100°F.

One favorite short hike, the **Rattlesnake Canyon Trail,** begins at a trailhead about halfway around the Walnut Canyon Desert Drive. Descending from the road, it follows Rattlesnake Canyon (don't let the name put you off; snakes are seen here as seldom as elsewhere) south for a 3-mile walk to the park boundary, where you return along the same route to the drive. ■

Living Desert Zoo and Gardens State Park

■ 1,100 acres ■ Southeast New Mexico, just northwest of Carlsbad off
US 285 ■ Best seasons spring, fall, and winter ■Wildlife viewing ■Adm. fee
■ Contact the park, P.O. Box 100, Carlsbad, NM 88221; phone 505-887-5516.
www.emnrd.state.nm.us/nmparks/pages/parks/desert/desert.htm

STOP BY THIS nicely designed park
on the outskirts of Carlsbad for a
fine introduction to Chihuahuan
Desert ecology. Set among hills
dotted with lechuguilla and sotol
overlooking the Pecos River, Living Desert combines the features
of a zoo, a botanical garden, and
an interpretive center; after a
couple of hours here, you'll better
appreciate a visit to regional destinations such as Guadalupe
Mountains and Carlsbad Caverns
National Parks (see pp. 102-114),

Badger, Living Desert Zoo and Gardens SP

White Sands National Monument, and Bitter Lake National Wildlife
Refuge (see pp. 118-19).

Displays in the spacious **visitor center** illuminate a range of subjects, from the Permian reefs that gave birth to Carlsbad Caverns to the
adaptational features of desert flora and fauna. Outside the visitor center, a 1.3-mile **nature trail** loops past exhibits depicting varied habitats,
including an arroyo, desert uplands, and the pinyon pine-juniper zone.

In the **park aviary** you'll see birds such as bald and golden eagles,
wild turkey, burrowing owl, and greater roadrunner, as well as mountain lion and bobcat. Javelinas live in the nearby arroyo, while in the
pinyon-juniper area you'll get close-up looks at badger, porcupine, gray
fox, and the appealing little kit fox. The park also provides a home for a
few endangered Mexican gray wolves, which were extinct in the wild
until recent reintroductions (see sidebar pp. 204-205).

Continuing on the nature trail, you'll get closer looks at a few desert
snakes than you probably want to have out on a trail somewhere.
Prairie dogs populate a small village near grassy pens, where bison,
pronghorn, elk, and mule deer roam.

Like Tucson's Arizona-Sonora Desert Museum (see pp. 256-57), the
Living Desert isn't simply a zoo with a hodgepodge of animals from
around the world; it's an education-oriented park focused on its own
fascinating corner of the Southwest. A visit here is sure to be worthwhile
for everyone, from kids to hard-core adventurers. ■

Adapting to Desert Life

IN PARTS OF the Sonoran Desert in Arizona, as little as 4 inches of rain may fall in a year; in the Chihuahuan Desert of New Mexico, the average rainfall can reach around 13 inches annually—significantly more, but still paltry compared with the 30 to 60 inches that typically falls over the eastern United States.

In addition, the rain that does fall in the desert usually occurs during intense storms concentrated in brief periods, rather than in showers spread throughout the year.

In these arid lands, summer air temperatures often top 100°F, while the ground surface can soar to 150° F and higher; humidity remains about 10 percent for weeks at a time. Which brings up the question: How do animals and plants survive such severe conditions?

Adaptations to desert life are as fascinating, and nearly as varied, as the species that live in this environment. Many animals simply avoid the heat of day by living nocturnal lives. Most snakes and small mammals rest during daylight hours, often in burrows. Soil temperature drops quickly below the sun-baked surface, so a tunnel makes a cool retreat until dusk.

The threatened desert tortoise is one such creature; it needs areas where the soil is just the right texture—firm enough that its burrows won't collapse, but not too hard to dig in.

The Couch's spadefoot toad has a sharp "spade" on its hind foot with which it digs into the earth, remaining in a burrow not just overnight, but for months during the dry season; when rain falls, it quickly emerges, mates, and the females lay eggs in ephemeral pools. Because deserts can support only a relatively small population of toads, males have developed an especially loud voice to attract females that may be some distance away.

Many animals have physical characteristics that help them exist in hot, dry terrain. Scorpions can survive the loss of 40 percent of their weight in water, and endure a body temperature of 115°F. The huge ears of jackrabbits are filled with blood vessels that dissipate body heat.

Various types of desert pupfish live in alkaline lakes that expand and shrink dramatically over the course of a year; they've evolved to tolerate a vast temperature range and water that is five times saltier than seawater.

The kangaroo rat surely ranks among the top desert specialists. This little mammal never drinks, instead metabolizing water from the dry seeds it eats; its superefficient kidneys conserve water, and its nostrils condense water vapor in its breath so moisture won't be lost. The kangaroo rat also seals the entrance of its burrow to keep moisture from escaping into the dry surface air.

The adaptations of desert plants are at least as varied as those of animals. Cactuses have lost water-transferring leaves, instead evolving spines that protect and shade them, and lessen wind-caused evaporation.

Like cactuses, agaves have thick, waxy skins that hinder water loss. Candelilla, a spurge that grows in the Chihuahuan Desert, contains so much wax that it's harvested for candles, polishes, and chewing gum.

The leaves of creosote bush, an abundant plant in southwestern deserts, are coated with a resinous substance to restrict evaporation. Ocotillo leaves appear quickly after rains, then drop off when drought returns; this loss and regrowth can happen several times a year.

The green trunk and limbs of palo-verde (the name is Spanish for "green stick") contain chlorophyll and carry on photosynthesis even when the tree has shed its leaves to conserve water.

A great number of plants that would be annuals elsewhere don't necessarily renew themselves each spring in the desert. Instead, seeds can remain dormant for years until conditions are favorable, at which point they grow, flower, and set seeds in an accelerated version of the usual process. After a wet winter, dozens of species of desert wildflowers, such as brittle-bush, wallflower, and Mexican gold poppy, burst into bloom, creating a colorful spectacle that may occur only once a decade or less.

The seeds of some plants that grow along desert washes must be scarified to germinate; the "monsoon" rains (see p. 258) of summer wash the seeds along the rocky streambed, abrading them and providing moisture at the same time.

To get the water it needs to live, a mesquite tree may send roots down 175 feet. A saguaro cactus's roots go out instead of down, spreading across a circle as much as 50 feet from the plant. When rains come, the saguaro quickly grows tiny, hairlike roots that can soak up as much as 200 gallons of water; when drought returns, these rootlets die and drop off.

These are only a few examples of the methods plants and animals use to survive the harsh desert environment. The more you learn of such techniques, the more you'll appreciate the diversity of life here as you walk along a desert trail. ■

Desert tortoise eating prickly pear cactus fruit

Bitter Lake National Wildlife Refuge

■ 24,500 acres ■ Southeast New Mexico, 8 miles northeast of Roswell via
Pine Lodge Rd. ■ Best months Nov., and April-May ■ Driving tour, bird-
watching, wildlife viewing ■ Contact the refuge, P.O. Box 7, Roswell, NM 88202;
phone 505-622-6755. southwest.fws.gov/refuges/newmex/bitter.html

THOUGH IT MAY NOT BE AS well-known as some other southwestern wildlife
refuges, Bitter Lake ranks among the best regional birding destinations.
Late fall through early spring offers the greatest number of showy species
such as sandhill crane, geese, and 15 or more types of ducks, but for those
interested in natural history, there's always something worth seeing here.

To reach Bitter Lake from Roswell, drive east on US 380 from its junction with US 285 for about 3 miles; drive north on Red Bridge Road 4
miles and turn east on Pine Lodge Road to the refuge. You can stop by the
office for information, then proceed to the 8.5-mile auto-tour route.

At the viewing platform near the start of the drive, you'll get a look at
the lay of the land: The refuge comprises several shallow, man-made
impoundments in the flat meander bed of the **Pecos River,** surrounded
by scrubby grassland; to the north lies **Bitter Lake,** a seasonal playa, or
basin, that's the only natural lake on the refuge. All of these "lakes" are
fed only by springs, seeps, and rain, and so they often dry up or become
mudflats at various times of year. Refuge managers periodically lower
lake levels to allow certain species to feed or to nest (and also to provide
a fertile environment for the threatened Pecos sunflower). Scenic it may
not be, but the area provides a home for more than 350 nesting or
migratory bird species.

Bitter Lake lies at the Chihuahuan Desert's northern border, near the
western edge of the Llano Estacado's shortgrass plains. Combined with
refuge wetlands, this mix of habitats attracts not only a variety of birds,
but other wildlife as well. Look for rare spotted ground squirrels, desert
cottontail, black-tailed jackrabbit, badger, and mule deer, plus a variety of
reptiles, including collared lizard, round-tailed and Texas horned lizards,
bullsnake, and prairie and western diamondback rattlesnakes. Refuge
lakes and sinkholes are also home to several uncommon or endangered
fish, including Pecos gambusia, Pecos pupfish, greenthroat darter, and
Mexican tetra.

From fall through spring, you'll find great numbers of sandhill
cranes at Bitter Lake, along with Canada, snow, and Ross's geese, and
ducks such as northern shoveler, gadwall, American wigeon, canvasback,
redhead, and lesser scaup. American white pelicans visit in spring and
fall, and the prey found in grasslands and wetlands attracts raptors,
including northern harrier, Swainson's, red-tailed, and ferruginous
hawks, American kestrel, and prairie falcon.

Sinkhole Lakes

The limestone underlying the Roswell region contains large amounts of water-soluble gypsum. In places, underground pockets of gypsum have dissolved and the overlying rock has collapsed, creating sinkholes. To see a group of eight sinkholes, drive southeast of Roswell to **Bottomless Lakes State Park** *(N. Mex. 409, a few miles S of US 380. 505-624-6058)* The lakes here aren't actually bottomless, of course; the deepest is about 90 feet.

Rare fish, including Pecos pupfish and Pecos gambusia, survive in a few of the lakes. The park is also home to the barking frog, a rarely seen species that inhabits limestone caves and rock fissures. Males emerge at night after rains to give their call, which sounds like the bark of a small dog.

Mudflats and shallow-water areas offer feeding grounds for a variety of shorebirds and waders; several species remain to nest on the refuge, among them American bittern, snowy egret, black-crowned night-heron, snowy plover, black-necked stilt, and American avocet. Small numbers of least terns, an endangered species in many areas, also breed at Bitter Lake.

Among the other common birds you're likely to see are ring-necked pheasant, scaled quail, American coot, greater roadrunner, ladder-backed woodpecker, Say's phoebe, Chihuahuan raven, red-winged blackbird, and both eastern and western meadowlarks.

Some sinkholes (see sidebar) are home to rare endemic species: Noel's amphipod, a tiny crustacean, and Roswell spring snail, an even tinier snail, can be found nowhere else in the world. Refuge personnel sometimes offer tours to restricted areas to allow viewing of these and other species; ask at the refuge office for details. ■

Mirror Lake, Bottomless Lakes State Park

Maxwell National Wildlife Refuge

■ 3,700 acres ■ Northeast New Mexico, 25 miles south of Raton via
N. Mex. 445 and N. Mex. 505 ■ Best months Nov.-March. Winter can
bring snow and slick roads ■ Bird-watching, wildlife viewing ■ Contact the
refuge, P.O. Box 276, Maxwell, NM 87728; phone 505-375-2331.
southwest.fws.gov/refuges/newmex/maxwell.html

Early spring at Maxwell NWR

JUST MINUTES OFF I-25, this small,
drive-through refuge makes a
quick, easy detour to enjoy a range
of wildlife: waterfowl, raptors,
grassland birds, and an accessible
"town" of the entertaining little
rodents known as prairie dogs.
Most of the refuge consists of
grassland, but three lakes (called
12, 13, and 14) totaling several
hundred acres serve as focal points
for much of the bird-watching.

As you drive north into the
refuge from N. Mex. 505, you'll
pass **Lake 12** to the west, with the tall peaks of the Sangre de Cristo Mountains looming in the distance. The lake can be covered with grebes, pelicans, and ducks, but close approach is prohibited; a spotting scope helps,
as does morning light. A short distance north is the refuge office, where
you can pick up a map and a bird list.

Continue north to **Lake 13,** partially bordered by a levee road that
offers great viewing. Waterfowl are common here from fall through
spring; in winter, bald eagles perch in the tall, lakeside cottonwoods,
occasionally taking flight to pick up a meal. Golden eagles are seen here
much less commonly; remember that bald eagles don't acquire their distinctive white head and tail until they're several years old—so not every
dark eagle is a golden. The long-winged hawk with a white rump that you
see cruising slowly, a few feet off the ground, is a northern harrier, a
grassland specialist. Sandhill cranes are common in fall migration;
depending on the severity of the weather, they may winter here as well.

Return south past the headquarters and turn east. Stop here and there
to scan fields and trees for nesting birds, including American kestrel; eastern, Cassin's, and western kingbirds; black-billed magpie; loggerhead
shrike; blue grosbeak; vesper and grasshopper sparrows; and lark bunting.

Turn south at the first road to drive past the refuge's black-tailed prairie
dog colony. Ranchers find the rodents more pesky than cute; after decades
of efforts to eliminate them in the West, today they exist in scattered populations in only a fraction of their former abundance. Watch for burrowing
owl, an occasional visitor here. The eastern refuge boundary road leads to
Lake 14, another good spot for viewing waterbirds of various species. ■

Capulin Mountain, Capulin Volcano National Monument

Capulin Volcano National Monument

■ 792 acres ■ Northeast New Mexico, 33 miles southeast of Raton via US 64/87 and N. Mex. 325 ■ Best seasons spring-fall. Entrance road may be closed occasionally by winter snows or summer thunderstorms ■ Hiking ■ Adm. fee ■ Contact the monument, P.O. Box 40, Capulin, NM 88414; phone 505-278-2201. www.nps.gov/cavo

THE WEST HAS AN abundance of volcanoes that don't look like volcanoes. US 64/87, on its way from Raton to Clayton, makes a detour around one such feature: Sierra Grande, a massive volcanic peak, is probably seen by the average traveler simply as a generic mountain. But just to the north rises a summit about which no one could have any doubt.

The graceful and symmetrical—even beautiful—truncated cone of Capulin Mountain looks like every child's drawing of a volcano, lacking only bright red flames and dark ash clouds. But even though Capulin is the result of a relatively recent (in geologic time) eruption, no one saw such a show; it was active long before humans reached North America.

A great portion of northeastern New Mexico displays evidence of volcanic activity, the result of millions of years of eruptions in what is known as the Raton-Clayton Volcanic Field. The field covers about 8,000 square miles and its last activity is believed to have occurred around 30,000 to 40,000 years ago.

Cinder cones and lava flows may be seen in many places; one flow surged east to create Black Mesa, the highest point in Oklahoma.

Sierra Grande is an unusual shield volcano, formed when great amounts of thick lava piled up to form a broad, gently sloped peak.

About 60,000 years ago, a small vent opened in the ground 10 miles northwest of Sierra Grande, shooting cinders and ash into the air. When they fell, they formed a ring around the vent, growing taller as more material spewed from the earth. As the resulting cone rose, cinders slipped down the sides until they found their angle of repose, creating an evenly sloped peak—although prevailing winds from the west caused the eastern rim to rise higher than the rest.

At various times during the eruption, lava oozed out from vents in the cone, eventually spreading almost 16 square miles around the volcano. The eruption might have lasted several months or many years; scientists have been unable to determine its duration. The result of all this activity was Capulin Mountain, which today rises 1,300 feet above the surrounding grassland, its handsome form and geological history protected since 1916 within Capulin Volcano National Monument.

Flannel mullen between lichened volcanic rock, Capulin Volcano NM

What to See and Do

Even before you turn north on N. Mex. 325 from the small town of Capulin toward the mountain, you'll notice distinctive features—jagged black lava fields and oddly shaped cones and domes—dotting the landscape. On Capulin's smooth slope, the access road spirals enticingly up toward the rim.

At the park **visitor center,** a short film illustrates volcanic geology, focusing on Parícutin, a volcano in Mexico. Scientists believe that its eruption was very similar to that of Capulin's.

Both the visitor center and the nearby picnic area at Capulin sit on lava flows, allowing close-up looks at this igneous material, especially along the 1-mile **Lava Flow Trail.** In summer, park interpreters present short programs on volcanoes.

By the time Capulin's eruption ended, plant life had probably been killed for miles around by heat, gas, and ash. In the millennia since, vegetation has reclaimed the sides of the cone. As you drive to the top, you pass through scrubby woodland of pinyon and ponderosa pine, juniper, oak, mountain mahogany, skunkbush, and other trees and shrubs—including chokecherry, from whose Spanish name Capulin takes its own.

Wildflowers such as Indian paintbrush, penstemon, lupine, and verbena brighten open areas in spring and summer.

The access road reaches a parking area at a low point on the rim's west side, with a view down into the now shallow crater, partly filled with eroded cinders. Two fine trails begin here: The 0.2-mile **Crater Vent Trail** leads down into the crater to the vent area; few places in the world allow such easy access into the heart of a volcano. You shouldn't worry about being at ground zero in case Capulin wakes again: Volcanologists say that this type of cinder cone is monogenetic, meaning that it erupts only once. While another eruption in this general area is possible, it won't be at Capulin.

The **Crater Rim Trail,** as its name implies, follows the top of the crater for a 1-mile circle, with wonderful views in all directions. On a clear day you can see four states—New Mexico, Colorado, Oklahoma and Texas—from here.

Sierra Grande dominates the scene to the southeast; as a geographic footnote, there is no higher point than this 8,720-foot mountain between here and the Atlantic Ocean. To the east rise the summits of the Sangre de Cristos, the southernmost range of the Rocky Mountains. And all around you are smaller cones (including one to the northeast called Baby Capulin) and mesas formed as lava protected the softer, underlying rock from erosion.

Although geology is the main attraction in the national monument, you might spy a mule deer, a porcupine, a thirteen-lined ground squirrel, or a western rattlesnake as you hike. Birds that nest in the Capulin area include wild turkey, ferruginous hawk, pinyon jay, black-headed grosbeak, lesser goldfinch, and the beautiful mountain bluebird—its color like a bit of the sky fallen to earth. ∎

Clayton Lake State Park

■ 570 acres ■ Northeast New Mexico, 12 miles northwest of Clayton
■ Best months April-Oct. ■ Camping, fishing, bird-watching, wildlife viewing,
dinosaur tracks ■ Adm. fee ■ Contact the park, RR Box 20, Seneca, NM
88437; phone 505-374-8808

Fishing on Clayton Lake

AS YOU FOLLOW N. Mex. 370 and N. Mex. 455 from Clayton out to this state park, you have wonderful sweeping views of rolling grassland where pronghorn and mule deer roam. You may spot a ferruginous hawk (a threatened prairie raptor) soaring overhead. And at the lake itself, a variety of waterbirds—and perhaps even a bald eagle—may be present in winter. But the wildlife for which Clayton Lake is known is of a far more exotic type.

One hundred million years ago, this area was on the edge of a warm sea that covered much of what is now North America. Dinosaurs walked along the shoreline—some browsing on plants, others hunting the plant-eaters. They left tracks that hardened in the mud and eventually were preserved as impressions in sandstone. Covered for eons by layers of sedimentary rock, many of them are now exposed on the surface, delighting the two-legged mammals who come to gaze in wonder at one of the most extensive collections of dinosaur footprints on the continent. More than 500 separate prints, representing eight different kinds of dinosaurs, have been discovered here.

Take the short trail beside the lake and cross the dam to reach the **area of dinosaur tracks,** where an interpretive display provides information and a walkway allows close looks.

Early morning and late afternoon, when the slanting light creates shadows, are the best times for distinguishing the tracks' outlines. Some indistinct, rounded prints look as though someone has pushed a washtub down into the mud, while many others clearly show the outline of a three-toed foot. Paleontologists have followed some of the trails for up to 20 steps; one set of multiple tracks is believed to have been made by giant saltwater crocodiles barely floating along in the water, propelling themselves along with their claws.

As you leave this fascinating site, take note of the grebes and ducks swimming out on **Clayton Lake**—and remember that many scientists believe today's birds are descendants of the fearsome creatures that walked the planet so many millions of years before our own species appeared. ■

Kiowa and Rita Blanca National Grasslands

Kiowa and Rita Blanca National Grasslands

■ 229,327 acres ■ Northeast New Mexico, near Mills and Clayton
■ Best seasons spring and summer ■ Camping, hiking, fishing, horseback riding, bird-watching, wildlife viewing ■ Contact the national grasslands, 714 Main St., Clayton, NM 88415; phone 505-374-9652.
svinet2.fs.fed.us/r2/nebraska/gpng/kiri.html

A VAST AREA OF GRASSLANDS once stretched across the midsection of North America, home to bison, pronghorn, prairie dogs, wolves, sparrows, and other wildlife suited to a prairie life. Plants ranged from shortgrass in the arid West to tallgrass in the Midwest, where more moisture was available. The grasses that covered the land seemed a modest sort of vegetation, but actually represented thousands of years of adaptation to a dry, windy environment, constantly grazed by enormous bison herds and regularly swept by fire. In their lushness, these grasslands tempted pioneers to plow them up and plant crops; in some places this produced rich agricultural lands, but in others it led to disaster. With severe droughts in the early 1900s, marginal areas suffered severe erosion. Much of the land simply dried up and blew away in the constant wind.

Like most of our national grasslands, the Kiowa and Rita Blanca were created after the Dust Bowl years of the 1930s, when the government bought abandoned farms and began restoring something like the original grass cover. Also like other grasslands, this preserve is a patchwork of public lands and private property, with cattle grazing on both.

What to See and Do

For visitors with an interest in natural history, the main activities here are driving the back roads to observe wildlife and, in a few places, walking across the rolling, open country to enjoy a taste of this Big Sky environment.

Whatever your pleasure, you should stop by the Kiowa/Rita Blanca ranger office in Clayton and buy a map that shows local roads and indicates which tracts are public. Also talk to a ranger about the best areas for wildlife viewing or hiking; management practices, such as grazing and prescribed burning, change the character of tracts from year to year.

Pronghorn (see sidebar p. 127) are common in this region. A few prairie dog colonies still exist, though disease causes the population of this species to rise and fall. Mule deer and kit fox also roam the grassland; while the latter is fairly common, to see one you need to drive back roads at night—and have some luck.

Birds are the most often-observed wildlife, ranging from the abundant horned lark, which flies up in small flocks from the roadside, to the golden eagle. The beautiful ferruginous hawk, a grassland specialist that has declined in many parts of its range, resides here year-round.

Two members of the shorebird family that prefer prairie over wetlands for nesting make their homes here. Long-billed curlew and threatened mountain plover breed locally and are most likely to be found in heavily grazed areas with shortgrass.

Human as well as natural history is part of the Kiowa and Rita Blanca National Grasslands. A segment of the famed **Santa Fe Trail** enters New Mexico north of Clayton, and today's hikers and horseback riders can travel along the actual ruts left by covered wagons in the mid-19th century as they traversed this important commercial route.

To walk the Santa Fe Trail, drive north from Clayton 12 miles on N. Mex. 406. Where the highway bends east, drive west 3 miles on a dirt road, then north 1 mile to an informational kiosk. Almost 3 miles of the trail are preserved here, marked in part with limestone posts. (These "Kansas fence posts" were often used in prairie areas where trees were scarce.)

This hike provides a glimpse of a time long vanished in the West, when virgin grassland stretched far beyond the horizon in all directions. As you follow the trail, listen for the songs of western meadowlark and lark sparrow. If the temperature isn't too hot or cold, you could come upon a bullsnake out searching for a rodent meal. Very large and often quite pugnacious, this species is nonvenomous, but you'll still want to give it a wide berth.

Walking the Santa Fe Trail makes a fine introduction to the grasslands, a landscape that was too long unappreciated. Early travelers simply wanted to get across it alive; settlers too often abused it; but you can enjoy it for the diverse and rewarding environment it truly is. ■

Pronghorn on the shortgrass prairie

Pronghorn, Not Antelope

Europeans who encountered a fleet, horned mammal on the New World prairie were reminded of the antelope of the Old World; the name antelope has been used for this species ever since.

Nowadays, though, people who want to be correct say pronghorn: This speedster isn't even related to the true antelope, but is instead an exclusively North American animal unlike any other.

Once, an estimated 30 million to 60 million pronghorn roamed grasslands from Canada well into Mexico. Overhunting, and possibly disease, reduced the species to no more than 30,000 by 1920. A ban on hunting allowed partial recovery, and today pronghorn are common in many parts of the West, though in nothing like their former numbers.

Out on the prairie there's nowhere to hide, so pronghorn developed two ways to escape from predators: They have enormous eyes and superb vision, the better to spot danger at long distance. Their windpipe, heart, and lungs are huge, which, combined with strong muscles and light bones, allows them to sprint at speeds up to 60 miles an hour and to run at 40 miles an hour for miles without stopping.

No predator can match such speed, so their only threat (before men with rifles) came from being taken by surprise; this they try to avoid by remaining in areas where shortgrass allows them to see any approaching menace.

While coyotes prey on pronghorn fawns, loss of habitat is the major factor affecting populations of the animal. Unlike deer, pronghorn normally refuse to jump fences, even low ones. Because they prefer to crawl underneath, fences that extend to the ground disrupt their nomadic existence. Thus, even a few strands of wire can prevent them from utilizing productive territory.

New Mexico Highlands and Rio Grande Valley

San Mateo Mountains receding to Gila National Forest

THE EARTH'S RESTLESS and fickle temperament is much in
evidence in southwestern and central New Mexico. Volcanoes that blew themselves to bits, a massive crack in the
Earth's crust, expansive lakes that dried up to powdery
sand, storms of fiery ash, huge blocks of rock that tilted
like broken-legged tables, barren alkali flats, rich veins of
mineral ores—all these have shaped the landscape of this
region. Although in many cases the old scars have been
prettified by grassland or forest or smoothed by erosion,

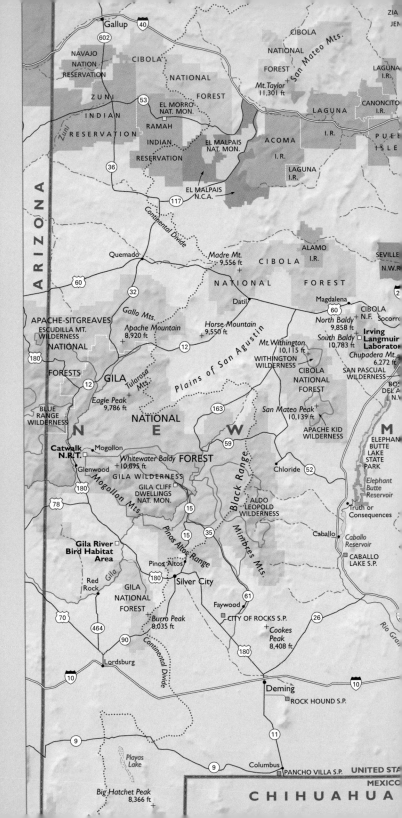

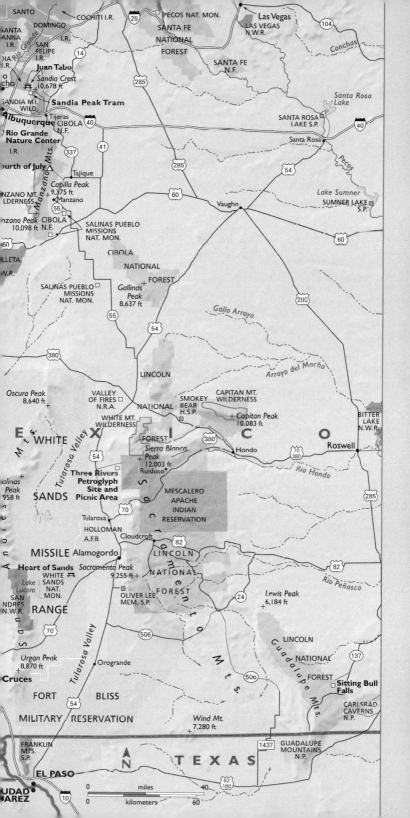

White Sands National Monument

signs of past mutability and violence remain.

Splitting the state north to south, the Rio Grande Rift reveals a narrow region along which the Earth's crust is literally pulling itself apart. Many fault lines underlie the rift zone and tectonic shifts have caused the rift floor to drop thousands of feet over the past 30 million years, though volcanic and erosional debris have substantially filled the resulting lowland.

Blocks of the crust were tipped and uplifted along the edges of the rift, creating mountain ranges such as the Sandias and the Sacramentos. Hot, upwelling magmas in and near the rift produced a volcanic landscape marked by features that include the volcanoes you see around Albuquerque and the Carrizozo lava flow northwest of the Sierra Blanca range.

Down the rift that bears its name flows the Rio Grande—like so many rivers much exploited and abused. Once a meandering, cottonwood-lined oasis for wildlife, it has been in recent decades dammed, contained by levees, and depleted along much of its length.

One of the region's most historic chapters was written in the Mogollon Mountains and the Black Range near Silver City. Here, a forestry official named Aldo Leopold led the push to create the world's first official wilderness area. Set aside within Gila National Forest in 1924, the Gila Wilderness has since been split; the eastern portion is now named for Leopold, who went on to become one of the founding figures of the American environmental movement.

Some of New Mexico's most rewarding hiking trails crisscross Gila National Forest, over volcanic peaks and through woodlands of ponderosa pine, Douglas-fir, spruce, fir, and aspen. Black bears, mountain lions, bighorn sheep, elk, mule and white-tailed deer, javelinas, and a host of smaller mammals find homes in the Gila, and the critically endangered Mexican gray wolf has been reintroduced near the Arizona border.

Near Alamagordo, the Tularosa Valley comprises a closed basin—that is, a "bowl" with no drainage to the outside—created by the pulling-apart action of the Rio Grande Rift. Once it was filled with a substantial lake; in these drier times, most water sinks into the ground or evaporates, with only small, ephemeral Lake Lucero as a legacy of its ancient ancestor.

The structure of the basin is one factor contributing to the development of the immense gypsum dunes at White Sands National Monument, one of the region's most striking sights. Here, geology isn't simply fascinating background for your visit—it's just plain fun to walk through this otherworldly landscape of dazzling white, wind-shaped sand.

Northward, mountains on the east side of the Rio Grande Rift—the Sacramentos, the Manzanos, the Sandias—all offer national forest wilderness areas to explore, as well as more accessible campgrounds, picnic areas, and short hikes. On many trails in the Sacramentos and the Manzanos, you'll probably be alone, or nearly so, practically any time of year; the Sandias, just a short drive (or tram ride) from the metropolis of Albuquerque, are far more frequented but no less enjoyable for the crowds sometimes found atop 10,678-foot Sandia Crest.

The Sandia Crest National Scenic Byway climbs the east side of the range, passing through varying life zones up to the coniferous forest covering the high peaks. By beginning your day in the cottonwood *bosque* at Albuquerque's Rio Grande Nature Center, you can easily visit an intriguing array of ecosystems—riparian, semidesert scrub, pinyon-juniper, pine, and spruce-fir—in just a few hours.

From the easy loop drive around Bosque del Apache National Wildlife Refuge to a backpacking trip in the Black Range, from the tracks of a beetle in White Sands' dunes to a glimpse of a black bear (in the forest that was home to Smokey himself), from a desert wildflower to a 100-foot Douglas-fir—the range of potential adventures is just what you'd expect from this large and diverse segment of wild New Mexico. ■

Storm from the Crest Trail, Sandia Mountain Wilderness

Gila National Forest

■ 3.3 million acres ■ Southwest New Mexico, around Silver City ■ Best seasons spring-fall. High-elevation roads and trails closed by snow in winter ■ Camping, hiking, fishing, mountain biking, bird-watching, wildlife viewing, pictographs ■ Camping fee ■ Contact the national forest, 3005 E. Camino del Bosque, Silver City, NM 88061; phone 505-388-8201. www.fs.fed.us/r3/gila

ENTICEMENTS TO VISIT Gila National Forest cover a wide range of interests and outdoor activities, from scenic drives to some of the most remote long-distance hiking trails in New Mexico. The Gila's more than three million acres encompass an equally broad range of habitats, from desert-scrub-grassland to riparian woods to spruce-fir forests on its peaks, topped by 10,895-foot Whitewater Baldy.

The mountains here were formed by volcanic activity in the Tertiary period, from 30 million to 5 million years ago, when gigantic volcanoes spewed forth their lava and ash and collapsed back into their own magma-emptied interiors. Erosion has worn away and disguised these ancient volcanoes, so that today's non-geologist traveler sees merely rugged, forested highlands dissected by river valleys. Intrusions of

Catwalk National Recreation Trail, Gila National Forest

igneous material in that violent time created rich mineral fields, spawn-
ing a boom-or-bust era of mining for silver, gold, and other metals.
Massive open-pit copper mines scar the terrain around Silver City, born
as a boomtown after silver was discovered there in 1870.

At the heart of the national forest lies Gila Cliff Dwellings National
Monument, preserving 700-year-old rock and adobe cliff houses. Just a
short walk away is the Gila Wilderness, the largest wilderness in New
Mexico and the world's first officially designated wilderness area. In the
northern part of the national forest, the Catwalk National Recreation
Trail, possibly the most unusual hiking trail in the state, combines history
and beauty in a short path up a picturesque canyon.

Mountain lions, black bears, bighorn sheep, elk, mule and white-tailed
deer, pronghorn, and javelinas find homes here, as do some notable birds
including Montezuma quail, northern goshawks, spotted owls, willow flycatchers, and red-faced warblers. The Gila River, one of the state's most
significant streams, provides crucial habitat for several rare fish species.

With more than 650 miles of hiking trails in its wilderness areas alone,
the Gila offers greater opportunity for exploration than most people could
ever begin to take advantage of. It deserves even more attention for its
wild mountains, its expansive forests, its wildlife, and its colorful past.

What to See and Do

The headquarters of Gila National Forest sits just north of US 180 on the east side of Silver City. Stop here for maps and information, then drive north on N. Mex. 15 through the town of Pinos Altos ("tall pines"), which boomed when gold was discovered in 1859.

Just beyond town, you enter the national forest as the highway heads up pretty Cherry Creek Canyon. As you travel the **Inner Loop–Gila Cliff Dwellings Scenic Byway,** the scenery only gets better. Once you cross the Continental Divide, you're officially in the West.

About 6 miles from Pinos Altos, after passing two campgrounds, watch for the **Signal Peak Trail** on the east side of the road. (If you come to Forest Road 154, you just missed it.) This steep, 1.5-mile walk ascends 1,800 feet through ponderosa pine and Douglas-fir to the summit of 9,001-foot **Signal Peak.** You'll find excellent views, both north across the national forest and south to the Chihuahuan Desert grassland to the south of Silver City.

You can also drive to the summit on Forest Road 154, which winds around to climb the east side of the peak (high clearance may be needed near the top).

Birders visit Signal Peak and vicinity to look for several southwestern specialty species including greater pewee, and Grace's, redfaced, and olive warblers. With luck you might spot a northern goshawk, often considered the fiercest of all American raptors; a female near her nest is a truly fearless and aggressive creature.

Abert's and red squirrels scamper through the conifers, and mule deer are seen most often early or late in the day.

Continue north on N. Mex. 15 as it winds through the **Pinos Altos Range,** topping a mesa where flocks of pinyon jays roam the scrubby pinyon-pine-juniper woods. The road continues down to an intersection at Sapillo Creek, where you head north toward **Gila Cliff Dwellings National Monument** (*Silver City, NM. 505-536-9461. www.nps.gov/gicl. Adm. fee*).

In 6 miles, be sure to stop at the **Senator Clinton P. Anderson Wilderness Overlook** for a panorama of the Gila River Valley and the Gila Wilderness stretching out to the north and west.

Just a mile past the little community of Gila Hot Springs, look for the **Heart Bar Wildlife Area** on the east side of the road; the riparian habitat along the West Fork Gila River and an adjacent small pond is home to bobcat, gray fox, wild turkey, and the strikingly handsome common black-hawk.

Not far beyond is the visitor center, where you'll find information on the national monument (just 2 more miles down the road) and on the **Gila Wilderness,** the 557,873-acre area surrounding it.

The popular 34-mile Middle Fork Trail begins by the visitor center and runs up the **Middle Fork Gila River.** Backpackers can make loop or one-way trips of several days; anyone can do a day hike, following the stream for any distance. Use caution when the water is high.

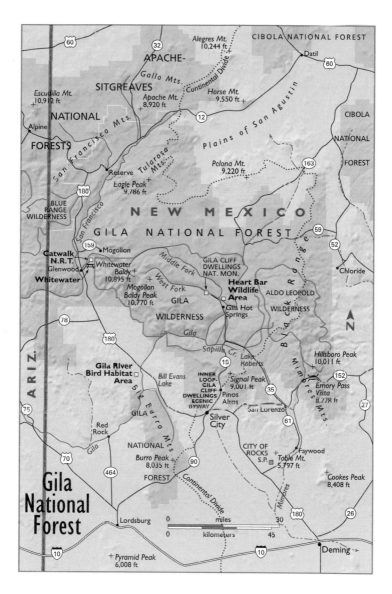

Gila Cliff Dwellings National Monument

Farther north along N. Mex. 15, watch for the short **Trail to the Past,** near the Scorpion Corral Campground, leading to Native American pictographs. At the road's end is the parking area for

Gila Cliff Dwellings National Monument. Here, a 1-mile, self-guiding loop trail passes seven shallow caves eroded in cliffs of Gila conglomerate—rock composed of volcanic debris cemented together by sedimentary material. Five of the caves contain Pueblo-style stone structures built by people of the Mogollon culture about 1270; they were occupied for only a short period before being abandoned.

At the far end of the parking lot is the trailhead for the popular hike up the **West Fork Gila River.** With a wilderness map, advance preparation, and advice from rangers, a variety of multiday backpacking trips can begin from here.

One favored route follows the **West Fork Trail** upstream 2 miles, takes **Big Bear Trail** across a mesa 7 miles to join the **Middle Fork Trail,** and follows it back to the visitor center for a loop of about 24 miles.

Alternatively, walking 3 miles straight up the West Fork Trail makes a beautiful and easy day hike, especially nice if you can arrange to be on the trail early in the morning. Beginning under high cliffs, the route passes through meadows to cross the rocky stream near beaver dams. Alligator junipers, pinyon pines, willows, and cottonwoods border the trail; spotted towhees sing from brushy areas and belted kingfishers rattle as they fly over the ponds. On a hillside, skeletons of ponderosa pines testify to a small fire; just beyond, the trail enters a narrower, steep-sided canyon.

Aldo Leopold Wilderness

When you leave this area and return to the highway intersection at Sapillo Creek, take N. Mex. 35 southeast. A stop at Lake Roberts can be productive for marsh birds, waterfowl, and other wildlife.

The road crosses the Continental Divide (back to the "East") and follows the Mimbres River to join N. Mex. 152. Turn west to return to Silver City. To drive up into the rugged Black Range, turn east. In 19 winding miles you reach **Emory Pass Vista,** with its panorama over the Rio Grande and Caballo Reservoir to the San Andres Mountains, 70 miles away. Emory Pass is one route into the 202,016-acre **Aldo Leopold Wilderness**.

The Leopold is more rugged and far less visited than the Gila Wilderness, and many of its access roads are long, rough, and difficult. Before planning a trip here, talk to a ranger at the Black Range District Office *(505-894-6677)* or the Wilderness Ranger District Office *(505-536-2250)*.

You can easily sample the Leopold wilderness, though, by hiking north from Emory Pass Vista on N. Mex. 152 to 10,011-foot Hillsboro Peak; the **Crest Trail** gains 1,820 feet in a bit less than 5 miles as it in part traces the wilderness boundary. This hike passes beneath ponderosa and southwestern white pines, Douglas-fir, and aspen on its way to a fire lookout tower in a meadow atop the peak, where you can see broad-tailed hummingbirds feeding on flowers in summer.

Back in Silver City, drive west and north on US 180 for 25 miles; turn south on a county road signed for Bill Evans Lake. After 4 miles, go straight where the paved road turns left to the lake, and continue 5 miles to the **Gila River Bird Habitat Area** at the Gila National Forest boundary.

Though this riverside spot may not be as spectacular looking as the peaks to the east, its riparian zone

Fall foliage along the Gila River, Gila National Forest

represents one of the most threatened environments in the Southwest. Free-flowing streams with their wooded riparian zones have been widely destroyed by land-clearing, over-grazing, dams, and other alterations; a number of species dependent on this habitat have declined with its loss.

By exploring the cottonwoods, sycamores, oaks, pinyon pines, and junipers along the wide channel of the Gila River here, you'll have a chance to see birds including common black-hawk, zone-tailed hawk, Montezuma quail, yellow-billed cuckoo, willow flycatcher, Lucy's warbler, and summer tanager. Watch also for mule deer and javelinas. Though you won't see them, threatened fish such as the loach minnow swim in the waters here.

Catwalk National Recreation Trail

Continue north on US 180, with the craggy Mogollon Mountains on the east, to Glenwood; turn east on the road to the Whitewater picnic area and the famed **Catwalk National Recreation Trail.**

Here a route pioneered by 19th-century miners leads up a stunning canyon, partially on a steel catwalk suspended from the walls bordering the narrow chasm. Volcanic cliffs loom high above the rocky bed of **Whitewater Creek,** which drops down the canyon in a series of small waterfalls. Arizona sycamore, Arizona walnut, Rio Grande cottonwood, Emory and Gambel oaks, and netleaf hackberry border the stream, and the haunting song of the canyon wren echoes between the cliffs.

This is a popular, often crowded walk, but don't pass it up for that reason; do it on a weekday if possible, or early in the morning.

The catwalk portion of the trail ends a little more than a mile up the canyon at a metal bridge; the **Whitewater Creek Trail** continues for some 16 miles, reaching the Gila Wilderness boundary about 2.5 miles from the picnic area.

Adjoining trails allow backpackers to explore far up into the Mogollon Mountains toward Grouse Mountain, Hummingbird Saddle, Whitewater Baldy, and Mogollon Baldy Peak.

To access the most popular trail into the Mogollons, drive less than 4 miles north of Glenwood on US 180, turn east onto N. Mex. 159, and drive 13 miles to **Mogollon.** First a mining boomtown, then a ghost town, this picturesque community is now experiencing a rebirth as a tourist destination; it's worth a visit even if you're not interested in the trails beyond.

Continue 8 more miles *(road is closed until late spring by snow)* to the parking area at Sandy Point, where the Crest Trail, marked to Mogollon Baldy Peak, heads south into the Gila Wilderness. At this elevation (9,100 feet, and quickly climbing to more than 10,000), the lush forest comprises Douglas-fir, southwestern white pine, Engelmann and blue spruce, white and corkbark (subalpine) fir, and aspen.

Hummingbird Saddle, 4.8 miles along, makes a fine day-hike destination. (Any hummingbirds you see will be broad-tailed in summer, plus rufous in fall.) Backpackers often continue 7 more miles to the top of 10,770-foot **Mogollon Baldy Peak** for its grand views. ■

Aldo Leopold and the Gila

Pioneer conservationist Aldo Leopold is known as the founder of the science of game management and, especially, as the author of *A Sand County Almanac*—a classic collection of nature essays that has inspired environmentalists since it was published in 1949, a year after its writer's death.

A Midwesterner, Leopold, after graduating from Yale Forest School in 1909, joined the Forest Service and began working in Arizona and New Mexico. As time passed, he saw wolves and grizzly bears disappear, saw how roads allowed access to lands formerly untouched, saw fewer and fewer places where nature existed on its own terms.

He came to believe that America required something that had never before been imagined—or needed: tracts of land where, by law, the modern world was kept out, and humans were temporary visitors.

In 1924, at the urging of Leopold and like-minded colleagues, the world's first officially designated wilderness was established around the headwaters of the Gila and Mimbres Rivers in the Mogollon Mountains and the Black Range.

The Gila Wilderness began as a 755,000-acre area; today, after boundary changes (and, alas, a bisecting road) it exists as two separate units: the Gila on the west and the Aldo Leopold on the east, totaling just over 760,000 acres.

America's map shows many wildernesses today—in large part because of the example created by Aldo Leopold. When you hike here, you're in a fit place to contemplate, as Leopold wrote, that the land is not a commodity but "a community to which we belong."

City of Rocks State Park

■ 680 acres ■ Southwest New Mexico, 28 miles northwest of Deming off
N. Mex. 61 ■ Best seasons early spring-early fall ■ Camping, hiking ■ Adm. fee
■ Contact the park, P.O. Box 50, Faywood, NM 88034; phone 505-536-2800

THE NAME ON THE MAP may be a
little puzzling, but it's certainly
worth the short trip from Deming
or Silver City to visit this park set
in the Chihuahuan Desert grassland of the **Mimbres River Valley.**
Only if you know the geologic history of the region will you be prepared for the scene at the end of
the entrance road—and even then
you're bound to be amazed by
what you find.

Parry agave, City of Rocks State Park

More than 30 million years ago,
a series of volcanic eruptions,
centered about 19 miles north of
today's park, covered the surrounding area with pumice, ash,
and lava. As the material settled,
heat "welded" it into rock called
tuff; as it cooled and compacted,
vertical cracks developed. With the
passage of millennia, erosion—by windblown dust, rain, plant roots, and
cycles of freezing and thawing—widened the cracks and shaped the
resulting rock columns into huge, smooth, oddly shaped forms. Some
house-size and standing up to 50 feet tall, these monoliths do indeed give
the impression of a "city" on the plain, or perhaps an outdoor display of
gigantic, free-form sculptures.

A 0.75-mile walking trail leads from the botanical garden through the
middle of the rocks to the North Suburb Area, and you can clamber
around and explore these spires and blocks to your heart's content (bring
plenty of film). Be sure to drive the short spur off the entrance road to
the slightly higher observation point. From here you have a wide-angle
perspective on the park, as well as views of nearby volcanic features. Just
a mile northeast, **Table Mountain** is a mass of soft-bedded rhyolite tuff;
14 miles southeast, 8,408-foot **Cookes Peak** formed when magma
intruded into sedimentary rock that has since largely eroded away.

Many other igneous formations surround the park, while copper-
mine tailings to the northwest testify to the region's abundant mineral
resources. Zinc, gold, lead, and copper have been mined nearby, along
with the metal for which Silver City was named. ■

Gypsum dunes, White Sands National Monument

White Sands National Monument

■ 144,420 acres ■ South-central New Mexico, 14 miles southwest of Alamogordo off US 70 ■ Best seasons spring and fall. The park, adjacent to White Sands Missile Range, occasionally closed for brief periods during military testing ■ Camping, hiking ■ Adm. fee ■ Contact the national monument, P.O. Box 1086, Holloman Air Force Base, NM 88330; phone 505-679-2599. www.nps.gov/whsa

THE DAZZLING SAND DUNES that cover 275 square miles of New Mexico's Tularosa Valley create one of the most striking sights in the Southwest, but they wouldn't exist if not for a particular series of geologic events. White Sands is one of the few places in the world, in fact, where the right conditions prevail to produce extensive dunes of the bright white mineral called gypsum.

More than 250 million years ago, repeated evaporation of a shallow sea laid down a layer of gypsum, a type of calcium sulfate, in the sedimentary rock that formed here. Much later, after the region had been uplifted into a dome, a section collapsed between fault lines, forming a graben, or basin—a small-scale part of the Rio Grande Rift that cuts across the state from north to south (see sidebar p.165). The sides of this uplifted dome stand as today's San Andres and Sacramento Mountains, to the west and east of what is now called the Tularosa Valley.

As these mountains erode, rain and snowmelt carry the water-soluble gypsum and other minerals into the basin. In most regions, a river would then transport the still dissolved gypsum to the sea—but the Tularosa Valley has no outlet; the minerals build up in ephemeral Lake Lucero, where evaporation leaves them as a powdery white crust of sodium chloride and gypsum crystals. Prevailing strong southwest winds then pick up the gypsum crystals, carrying them northeast where they accumulate as tall dunes. Winds continue to push the sand formations, moving them slowly but relentlessly northeastward at a rate of 30 feet a year.

Forty percent of this gypsum dune field, the world's largest, is protected within White Sands National Monument, where trails and a scenic road through the dunes allow you to experience this unique environment, and to see how plants and animals adapt to its harshness. Lake Lucero, the source of the white sands, is located 15 miles southwest of the main park road, and is accessible only on monthly ranger-led tours; ask at the visitor center about the schedule for this and other programs.

What to See and Do

At the **visitor center,** just off US 70, you can learn about White Sands geology and ecology before starting on the park's 8-mile (one way) **Dunes Drive.**

For the first couple of miles, you'll have dunes on the south and Chihuahuan Desert grassland on the north. Just as the road enters the dunes, stop and walk the 1-mile **Big Dune Nature Trail,** which loops out across the great waves of sand.

The trail booklet, available for a small fee, will help you get the most out of this easy hike; you can identify such typical plants as four-wing saltbush, soaptree yucca, rubber rabbitbrush, Mormon tea, and skunkbush sumac, and learn about their various adaptations to this habitat.

While 240 vascular plants grow in the **Tularosa Valley,** only about 60 can survive in the dune field—including, rather surprisingly, Rio Grande cottonwood, which somehow exists in a place that receives only 8 inches of rain a year and has very limited soil and nutrients.

As a dune approaches, some plants survive by growing taller, staying above the rising tide of sand. Notice the "pedestals" formed where roots hold together a column of soil after a dune crest has moved past a plant.

Note, too, the greater plant variety in the low interdunal areas; higher levels of nutrients and moisture here create a more fertile environment—though it will eventually be covered by moving dunes.

Farther west, the wheelchair-accessible **Interdune Boardwalk**

Ground Cuckoo

While at White Sands, you may see New Mexico's state bird: the greater roadrunner. Like the cartoon version, the real critter can trot along at a good pace—up to 20 miles an hour. Its thick legs and strong toes are well adapted to a terrestrial life, but the roadrunner can also fly.

A member of the cuckoo order (its scientific name, *Geococcyx,* means "ground cuckoo"), the roadrunner uses its long beak to nab lizards, snakes, insects, scorpions, centipedes, and small mammals.

Following pages: Hikers, White Sands National Monument

interpretive trail loops for 0.3 mile through an area demonstrating the importance of this habitat.

Animals live here, too, though most are shy or nocturnal, or both, and so rarely seen. If you're lucky enough to visit White Sands after a period with little wind, you'll find the ground absolutely covered with traces of desert dwellers. The treadlike pattern of a caterpillar, the hieroglyphics of a darkling beetle, the X's of a roadrunner, the paired dots of a pocket mouse—all mark the dunes, along with occasional tracks of larger creatures such as coyote, kit fox, or badger.

Though you probably won't see them, several animals here have evolved a lighter-than-normal coloration for better camouflage from predators. The Apache

A Fragile Crust

The dark, crusty material in White Sands's interdune areas is actually an essential part of life here. Called cryptobiotic soil, it comprises an interdependent community of living things that includes cyanobacteria and other algae, fungi, and lichens. In this nutrient-poor environment, the crust provides a hospitable place for plant life, fixing nitrogen from the air and building soil.

You can destroy cryptobiotic soil and break the chain of life simply by stepping on it. As you explore the dunes, always avoid walking across this fragile crust. Learn more about it on the park's Interdune Boardwalk.

pocket mouse, the earless lizard, and a few insects show this adaptation to their white-sand world.

As you drive, you may note that dunes exist in varying shapes. The first part of Dunes Drive passes through an area of parabolic dunes, where plants anchor the extremities of a formation while its middle is pushed by the wind, creating an inverted U-shape. Later, the road traverses barchan dunes, formed where winds fashion crescent shapes in areas with limited sand, and transverse dunes, created when barchan dunes join in long ridges. Nearer Lake Lucero (and not accessible by the drive) are dome dunes, low mounds of sand that are the first to form downwind from the gypsum deposits along the lakeshore.

After winding through the dunes, the drive makes a short loop at Heart of the Sands picnic area. Here the **Alkali Flats Trail** leads across the dunes to the now dry bed of **Lake Otero,** a body of water that filled most of the Tularosa Valley in the last ice age, just a few thousand years ago. Having long since evaporated, Otero left an extensive moonscape of mineral crust to the west of White Sands.

This walk follows posts across the otherwise featureless dunes for a 4.6-mile round-trip; make sure you have plenty of water and use caution if you plan to go the entire distance. Even hiking part way, you'll experience the dunes' vastness, and appreciate their variety.

As long as you park in a designated area, you're free to walk out across the sand anywhere in the national monument. ■

Oliver Lee Memorial State Park

■ 640 acres ■ South-central New Mexico, 12 miles south of Alamagordo off US 54 ■ Best seasons spring and fall; spring is best for birding ■ Camping, hiking, bird-watching, wildlife viewing ■ Adm. fee ■ Contact the park, 409 Dog Canyon Rd., Alamogordo, NM 88310; phone 505-437-8284. www.emnrd.state.nm.us/nmparks

SET AT THE MOUTH of spectacular **Dog Canyon,** a deep gash in the side of the Sacramento Mountains, this little gem of a park encompasses the junction of a perennial stream with the arid Chihuahuan Desert—a blend of habitats that hosts a diverse range of plants and animals. The water and lush growth of the canyon attracted both Native Americans and European settlers. Preserved here are rock walls and an irrigation system built by an immigrant French homesteader in the 1890s.

Claret cup cactus, Oliver Lee Memorial SP

Beginning at the visitor center, the **Dog Canyon Interpretive Trail and Boardwalk** (a half-mile loop) offers an easy look at the park's natural history. Rio Grande cottonwood, velvet ash, netleaf hackberry, desert willow, and Texas mulberry grow in the riparian zone, while on the drier slopes nearby, you'll see sotol, New Mexico agave, ocotillo, cane cholla, creosote bush, and various prickly pears and yuccas. Along the streambed grow cattail, horsetail, and, at seeps along the canyon wall, maidenhair fern, yellow columbine, and giant helleborine. White Apache plume and the sunflowerlike blooms of skeletonleaf goldeneye create color in summer, and in fall lanceleaf sumac turns red on the canyon walls.

Black-chinned hummingbird, ladder-backed woodpecker, violet-green swallow, pyrrhuloxia, canyon towhee, and Scott's oriole are among the park's breeding birds; along the trails you might spot crevice spiny lizards, Texas horned lizards, western diamondback and black-tailed rattlesnakes, gray foxes, or javelinas.

The **Dog Canyon National Recreation Trail** also begins at the visitor center, but requires more time (8 hours round-trip) and energy than the boardwalk trail. It climbs the canyon walls under towering cliffs of limestone and dolomite, gaining 3,100 feet in 5.5 miles to reach Forest Road 90B in **Lincoln National Forest** (see pp. 148-153). At the crest of this imposing escarpment, you'll have a fabulous view of **White Sands National Monument** (see pp. 142-46) in the Tularosa Valley far below. ■

Hikers in the White Mountain Wilderness, Lincoln National Forest

Lincoln National Forest: Northern Districts

■ 926,000 acres ■ South-central New Mexico, east of Alamogordo and north of Ruidoso ■ Best months April-Nov. High trails and roads often snow-covered in winter ■ Camping, hiking, mountain biking, bird-watching, petroglyphs ■ Camping fees ■ Contact the national forest, 1101 New York Ave., Alamogordo, NM 88310; phone 505-434-7200. www.fs.fed.us/r3/lincoln

BEAUTIFUL FORESTS, mountain meadows, wilderness areas, great views, and varied trails are a few of the highlights of Lincoln National Forest's two northern ranger districts, Sacramento and Smokey Bear, both easily accessible from Alamogordo and the bustling tourist destination of Ruidoso. A scenic byway, a world-renowned observatory, and a fascinating Native American petroglyph site add to the regional attractions.

As an interesting topographical distinction, a hiker who climbs to the summit of 11,580-foot Lookout Mountain and looks out (or rather, down) on the Tularosa Valley is taking in an elevation difference of more than 8,000 feet—the greatest sight-line elevational change in New Mexico. While this part of the national forest doesn't drop that low, it does encompass life zones from the Chihuahuan Desert to spruce-fir forest and alpine tundra on its high peaks.

The Lincoln's White Mountain Wilderness barely misses 12,003-foot Sierra Blanca peak, the highest mountain in southern New Mexico; snow that lingers on this summit long into summer gave it the name "white mountain." Lying within the Mescalero Apache Indian Reservation, Sierra Blanca is believed to be sacred by the tribe and is off-limits to hikers, except with permission from the tribal office (505-671-4494).

What to See and Do

Sacramento Ranger District

From US 54/70 just north of Alamogordo, drive east on US 82 toward the resort community of Cloudcroft, set at an elevation of 8,663 feet in the **Sacramento Mountains.** As you reach the final switchbacks before town (about 15 miles from US 54/70), watch for the **Osha Trail** parking lot.

This easy, 2.6-mile loop, with interpretive signs, makes a fine introduction to the area, passing through an attractive forest of ponderosa pine, Douglas-fir, quaking aspen, Gambel oak, and bigtooth maple, to list some of the more common trees. After a steep little climb from the parking lot, the trail stays fairly level; on the west side of the loop, you'll have a good view out over the Tularosa Valley to White Sands National Monument (see pp. 142-46)and the San Andres Mountains 60 miles to the west.

Continue toward Cloudcroft a short distance and watch for a turn south into the **Trestle Recreation Area** (Day-use only). Interconnected trails descend a slope for close looks at two trestles left from the Alamogordo and Sacramento Mountain Railroad. Nicknamed the Cloud-climbing Railroad, this

line was established in the late 19th century to bring timber from the mountains to Alamogordo and ceased operation more than a half century ago. The trails here are part of an extensive (in-progress) rails-to-trails conversion; one finished trail is a self-guided nature walk that identifies some of the local trees and shrubs.

There may be someone in the reproduced rail depot at the parking lot to provide information; if not, the Lincoln National Forest's Sacramento Ranger District Office (505-682-2551) is just ahead in Cloudcroft, near the intersection of US 82 and N. Mex. 130.

Drive south on N. Mex. 130 and in less than 2 miles, turn west on N. Mex. 6563. Known as the **Sunspot Scenic Byway,** this route certainly is scenic—especially at overlooks where you have views out over the white-sand dunes.

In 0.2 mile you'll reach the national forest's Slide Campground and the northernmost trailhead for the **Rim Trail.** As its name implies, this path follows the edge of the Sacramento escarpment south for 28 miles, often in forest but with views of the Tularosa Valley here and there.

Few people walk the entire distance; with a map, short hikes of varying distances are possible, since side trails and roads off N. Mex. 6563 intersect the trail many times along its length.

The scenic byway ends at the **National Solar Observatory** *(505-434-7000)* on 9,255-foot Sacramento Peak, where scientists conduct various research projects to learn more about the sun. A visitor center is open daily from May through October; tours are self-guided or guided *(Fri.-Sun.; fee)*.

Return north on N. Mex. 6563 about 10 miles from the observatory and turn east on Forest Road 164. In 3.7 miles you'll reach **Bluff Springs,** where there's a beautiful waterfall, and fine hiking and mountain biking on nearby trails, old logging roads, and the beds of abandoned railroad spurs. Wild turkeys are plentiful here amid the Douglas-fir, white pine, ponderosa pine, and aspen; the elusive spotted owl nests in this area, too.

Smokey Bear Ranger District

While the Sacramento Mountains east of Alamogordo are sedimentary rock—their massive escarpment created when the block of the Tularosa Valley dropped thousands of feet—the part of the range northwest of Ruidoso has a different origin. **Sierra Blanca Pcak,** the high point of the Sierra Blanca range of the Sacramento Mountains, consists of igneous material formed when an ancient volcano discharged lava and ash across the landscape.

To begin your exploration of the national forest's Smokey Bear Ranger District take N. Mex. 48

north from Ruidoso about 5.5 miles and turn west on N. Mex. 532. In less than a mile, turn north on Forest Road 117, which climbs steeply alongside Little Creek. The upper part of this road can be quite rough at times; check with the district office in Ruidoso (505-257-4095) about its condition before making the drive.

About 5 miles up the road, you'll reach the parking area for the **Crest Trail**; this path runs 21 miles across the high ridges of the Sierra Blanca range, ending near Nogal Peak on Forest Road 108 northwest of Bonito Lake.

Hiking the Crest Trail is the most scenic way to experience the 48,800-acre **White Mountain Wilderness** *(505-257-4095),* but it's a serious backpacking trip requiring a car shuttle. Walking even a part of the trail will take you through some of the habitats for which these mountains are known: splendid woods of Engelmann spruce, subalpine and white fir, Douglas-fir, and aspen, with grassy meadows interspersed.

Continue up Forest Road 117 a steep half mile to **Monjeau Lookout** for a great panoramic vista of the Sierra Blanca range and the valleys that crease its slopes. Then drive back down to N. Mex. 532 and turn west toward Ski Apache downhill ski area. This very winding road is one of the most scenic drives in the state; 9 miles into the drive, pull over at **Windy Point Vista** to enjoy the view.

Just before the ski area entrance, you'll find the parking lot for the **Scenic Trail** on the north. From the trailhead, this route climbs 0.6 mile to join the

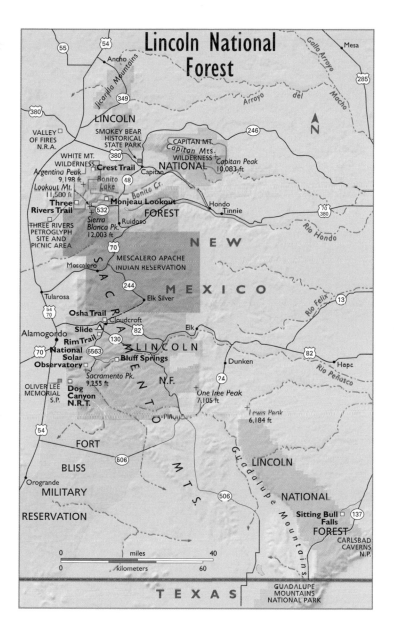

Crest Trail (here about 5 miles from the trailhead on Forest Road 117). Beautiful meadows and coniferous woods make this short trail worthwhile by itself, but it's also used as the route to the top of

11,580-foot **Lookout Mountain,** the highest point in Lincoln National Forest.

Follow the Scenic Trail to the Crest Trail and turn west; proceed for 2 miles and turn south on the

Smokey Bear

Smokey Bear, the Forest Service symbol of fire prevention, began life in 1944 as an illustrated poster showing a bear pouring water on a campfire. In 1950, after a fire ravaged the Capitan Mountains of Lincoln National Forest, firefighters found a badly burned black bear cub in a tree. Naming him Smokey, after the poster bear, officials eventually sent him to the National Zoo in Washington, D.C.

Smokey Bear (*not* Smokey "the" Bear) became so popular that in 1964 he was given his own zip code. He died in 1976 and was buried in Capitan at **Smokey Bear Historical State Park** (*102 Smokey Bear Rd. 505-354-2748*). A museum tells his story and that of fire-prevention education.

Lookout Mountain Trail for the climb to the summit. This route gains almost 1,700 feet in 3.4 miles, which at this altitude makes it a fairly strenuous walk— but fabulous views of Sierra Blanca and the Tularosa Valley wait at the top.

The most popular trails in the White Mountain Wilderness begin at the Argentina Canyon/Bonito trailhead. To reach it, drive north from Ruidoso about 9.5 miles on N. Mex. 48; at the sign to Bonito Lake, turn west on N. Mex. 37. In 1.3 miles, turn west onto Forest Road 107; the road curves around the lake and continues west, changing to dirt, then dead-ends at the trailhead. Several trails begin here and lead up to the Crest Trail (see opposite).

The **Three Rivers Trail**—the major trail into the White Mountain Wilderness from the steep west side of the Sierra Blanca range— begins 9 miles past the **Three Rivers Petroglyph Site and Picnic Area** (*505-525-4300. Adm. fee*), overseen by the Bureau of Land Management (*505-525-4300*).

To reach the petroglyph site, drive north of Alamogordo 30 miles on US 54 and turn east on well-marked Forest Road 579, which leads 14 miles to the base of the mountains. At this historic site, interpretive trails wind past literally thousands of examples of Native American rock art, pecked into the dark desert varnish on basalt boulders by the Jornada Mogollon, a people who lived here between 1000 and 1400.

Continue to the end of Forest Road 579, where the Three Rivers Trail begins; it enters the White Mountain Wilderness almost immediately, climbing steeply for 6 miles to meet the Crest Trail.

As the trail rises from 6,800 feet to 10,400 feet, it travels from Chihuahuan Desert scrub through pinyon-pine-juniper woodland and ponderosa pine to mixed coniferous forest and meadows at the top; there are great views along the last 1.5 miles.

Going up and back makes a strenuous day hike. If you use trails that connect with the Crest Trail on the east side of the wilderness, you can set up a variety of one-way backpacking trips; however, this requires a long vehicle shuttle.

Bonito Creek and Argentina Canyon Loop

The popular trails beginning beyond the turnoff to the South Fork campground offer beautiful forest, wildflower-spangled meadows, and fine vistas. Trailheads for the **Bonito Trail** and the **Argentina Canyon Trail** are just steps apart at the west side of the parking area where Forest Road 107 ends.

To make a wonderful, moderately strenuous hike of about 6.5 miles, begin on the Bonito Trail, heading up **Bonito Creek** through Douglas-fir, white fir, ponderosa pine, oak, and aspen. In the first miles, you pass the remains of two old mines on the creek's south side.

In 1.3 miles, where Bonito Creek and the Bonito Trail turn south, follow the **Little Bonito Trail** west up Little Bonito Creek. Sometimes fairly steep, the trail in 1.2 miles intersects with the **Cut Across Trail;** continue on the Little Bonito trail for the longer loop. In another 0.3 mile, the Little Bonito

Trail meets the Crest Trail, the 21-mile ridge route across much of the wilderness area. Turn north here, and soon you'll have excellent views as you reach the high point of the hike at 9,100 feet, below Argentina Peak.

After following the Crest Trail for 1.2 miles, turn east on the Argentina Canyon Trail at Argentina Spring. From here, it's a 2.5-mile descent through the canyon to the Argentina Canyon trailhead. You'll pass through extensive aspen groves and a deep chasm with tall Douglas-firs. This species grows taller than any other tree in the Southwest, and these are suitably impressive specimens.

For a shorter (about 5.2-mile) loop, after you've hiked 1.2 miles up the Little Bonito Trail, take the Cut Across Trail east. Rising to a ridge with good views down the Bonito Creek drainage, this shortcut reaches the Argentina Canyon Trail in about a mile; turn east to return 1.7 miles to the trailhead. ■

N. Mex. 532, Sacramento Ranger District, Lincoln National Forest

Bosque del Apache National Wildlife Refuge

■ 57,200 acres ■ Central New Mexico, 20 miles south of Socorro off N. Mex. I ■ Best months Nov.-March ■ Hiking, bird-watching, wildlife viewing ■ Adm. fee ■ Contact the refuge, P.O. Box 1246, Socorro, NM 87801; phone 505-835-1828. southwest.fws.gov/refuges/newmex/bosque.html

IT'S A FAMILIAR STORY: People driving down the highway spot a National Wildlife Refuge sign, pull in to drive the auto-tour route, and then stop at the refuge office demanding to know where all the animals are. They were expecting a zoo, rather than a place where wild animals live.

From fall through spring, Bosque del Apache is exactly what that kind of visitor believes all refuges to be like. It's certainly no zoo, but tens of thousands of big, spectacular birds throng roadside fields and wetlands here, creating one of the country's most exciting wildlife-viewing

Snow geese, Bosque del Apache National Wildlife Refuge

experiences. Whether it's the wild trumpeting of sandhill cranes or the vision of a huge flock of snow geese put to flight by a passing bald eagle, a wealth of memories will reward visitors to this refuge, just minutes off I-25. A 12-mile auto-tour loop, five trails, and several observation platforms make the refuge easily accessible to everyone.

Though Bosque del Apache covers nearly 90 square miles, the focal point of the refuge is the central 7,000 acres stretching along 9 miles of the Rio Grande. A *bosque* (Spanish for "woodland") of cottonwoods and willows borders the river, with adjacent man-made ponds supplementing the area's natural wetlands. The refuge lies in the western part of the central flyway and is a traditional migration route for geese, ducks, and sandhill cranes, which follow the Rio Grande as they move between their northern breeding grounds and southern wintering areas.

Once the river meandered freely across its flat floodplain, regularly overflowing its banks and cutting new channels to create oxbow lakes and ephemeral marshes rich in wildlife. With much of its flow now impounded by dams or diverted for agriculture, the Rio Grande needs help to provide habitat for the creatures that depend on it. Refuge management includes re-creating some of the river's natural meander channels, clearing invasive tamarisk (also called salt cedar, an alien shrub that displaces native vegetation), establishing new stands of cottonwoods, manipulating water levels in artificial wetlands, and planting crops for wildlife food.

Bosque del Apache was established in 1939, in part to provide a wintering ground for the then endangered "greater" sandhill crane—a race of a gray, long-legged species that nests from Siberia to Cuba. These handsome, 4-foot-tall birds mate for life, and often are seen in family groups of a pair of gray adults and one or two brownish young, though they also commonly rest or feed in flocks. Their loud *gar-oo-oo* call can be heard for a mile or more. Today, 13,000 or more of these cranes winter on the refuge, along with 30,000 geese (mostly snow geese) and more than 60,000 ducks. Up to 20 bald eagles take advantage of this concentration of birds, preying on sick or injured ducks and geese. While cranes and waterfowl are Bosque del Apache's most visible creatures, you'll find many more species here—of mammals, reptiles, and amphibians, as well as birds.

The majority of the refuge is arid Chihuahuan Desert, which, combined with the riverside bosque, wetlands, and farm fields, creates a mosaic of habitats that translates to a great diversity of wildlife. You might spot a Gambel's quail, a black-tailed jackrabbit, or a Texas horned lizard in the desert on one side of the road, and turn to see a neotropic cormorant or a muskrat in the marsh on the other side, while a northern harrier flies past a herd of mule deer in a nearby field.

Visits to Bosque del Apache are enhanced by one of the most extensive volunteer programs of any national wildlife refuge, with knowledge-

Birders on observation platform, Bosque del Apache NWR

able people leading tours, staffing the visitor center, and assisting visitors at observation areas. Most refuge visitation and programs occur from November through March, when large winter flocks of cranes and waterfowl are present. But even a summer visit can be exciting, when you can search for breeding birds including herons, egrets, bitterns, ten species of ducks, lesser nighthawk, the endangered southwestern willow flycatcher, Lucy's warbler, and lesser goldfinch. Of the more than 370 species that have been seen on the refuge, about 115 actually nest here if conditions are suitable. The presence of breeding waterbirds depends on the availability of water for rookery sites.

What to See and Do

Stop first at the refuge's visitor center on the west side of N. Mex. 1, 8 miles south of the little town of San Antonio. Plantings showcase typical vegetation of the Chihuahuan Desert, and feeders attract finches, sparrows, and other birds. Inside you'll find an extensive selection of nature books, as well as maps, wildlife checklists, and other information.

The refuge tour begins nearby, on the east side of N. Mex. 1. This 12-mile route is divided into two shorter sections: the Marsh Loop and the Farm Loop; unless you're pressed for time, you should make the entire circuit.

Marsh Loop

As you head out on the Marsh Loop, in fall through spring you immediately begin seeing some of the waterfowl for which Bosque del Apache is known, including Canada goose, mallard, northern pintail, northern shoveler, redhead, and others.

The most conspicuous birds, though, are the snow geese, flying, swimming, or walking in huge, cackling flocks. Like many other places, Bosque del Apache has seen significant increases in snow goose

Refuge Celebration

One of the most successful and popular of the many bird-watching festivals held across the country is the annual Festival of the Cranes, celebrated the third week of November at the Bosque del Apache National Wildlife Refuge and in the nearby city of Socorro. Refuge tours, guest speakers, children's programs, identification workshops, and art exhibits are among the attractions. As many as 10,000 people attend, enjoying wildlife and diverse events, from musical concerts to astronomy star parties. For information, call the Socorro Chamber of Commerce (505-835-0424).

numbers in recent years, as the population of this Arctic-breeding fowl has skyrocketed for reasons that are not clear.

About 14 percent of the white geese are Ross's goose, the snow's very similar but smaller relative. (Note the latter's proportionately smaller bill, the lack of the dark "grinning patch" between the upper and lower beaks, and the

Another Crane

Among the thousands of sandhill cranes that winter at Bosque del Apache NWR, you might spot a whooping crane, the sandhill's larger relative. Most members of this endangered species breed in Canada and winter on the Texas coast. Beginning in the 1970s, wildlife officials tried to start a separate population in Idaho, placing whooper eggs under sandhill foster parents. This program has been abandoned because the whoopers imprinted too strongly on the sandhills, resisting mating with other whoopers. Only a handful remain in the Idaho flock.

more angular profile between the forehead and bill.)

The 1.5-mile **Marsh Overlook Trail** lets you get off the loop road for closer inspection of wetlands bordered by cattails, bulrushes, and phragmites (common reed). Shorebirds can be abundant in spring and fall. Look for greater and lesser yellowlegs; spotted, western, and least sandpipers; long-billed dowitcher; Wilson's phalarope; and many other species. American avocet and black-necked stilt, both striking, long-legged birds, nest here.

On the back side of the refuge, the 2-mile (round-trip) **Rio Viejo Trail** follows an old channel of the Rio Grande with a bosque of young Rio Grande cottonwoods. Once, regular flooding dispersed cottonwood seeds along the riverside, renewing woodlands; today, refuge personnel divert water to

simulate natural flooding and restore this disappearing habitat.

Nearby, the 2-mile (round-trip) **River Trail** traces the Rio Grande under mature Rio Grande cottonwoods; in spring and summer this trail can be flooded and can have lots of mosquitoes.

Farm Loop

The road heads north past tamarisk, willows, and honey and screwbean mesquites to the **Farm Loop,** where the greatest numbers of wintering sandhill cranes are usually found.

Viewing is usually best in early morning or late evening, when the geese and cranes are leaving or returning from daily trips to feed in surrounding fields and cropland. The sight of skeins of calling birds settling in for the night creates the kind of thrilling scene for which the refuge is famed.

Two trails running west of N. Mex. 1 offer Chihuahuan Desert flora and fauna, as well as expansive views of the refuge and the Rio Grande Valley. The **Canyon Trail,** beginning south of the visitor center, makes a 2.5-mile loop through a fairly shady canyon, with a moderate elevation gain.

The **Chupadera Wilderness Trail,** much more strenuous, leads 5 miles (one way) to the top of 6,272-foot Chupadera Mountain, gaining 1,700 feet in elevation along a path with no shade and no water. Stamina, preparation, and six hours are required for this hike into the **Chupadera Wilderness.** Just a half mile along, though, is a vista point with a great view over the refuge—a good destination if you can't do the entire trek. ■

Water Canyon

■ 9,600 acres ■ Central New Mexico, 15 miles west of Socorro off US 60
■ Best months April-Nov. Road can be closed by snow at high elevations
■ Camping, hiking, bird-watching ■ Contact Magdalena Ranger District, Cibola National Forest, P.O. Box 45, Magdalena, NM 87825; phone 505-854-2281. www.fs.fed.us/r3/cibola

THIS BEAUTIFUL CANYON in the volcanic Magdalena Mountains west of Socorro offers easy access to varied habitats, excellent for bird-watching, hiking, or just enjoying some fine scenic views. A dirt road, rough but usually passable for cars, leads almost to the top of 10,783-foot **South Baldy** and a web of trails provides the chance to explore mixed deciduous and coniferous woods and mountain meadows in Cibola National Forest.

Turn south from US 60 onto Forest Road 235, the main canyon road, passing through grassland dotted with yucca and cholla. Look for prong-horn and black-tailed jackrabbits, and for raptors including golden eagles, Swainson's and red-tailed hawks, and American kestrels. As you enter the canyon and gain elevation, pinyon pine, junipers, and oaks border the road, and typical birds include black-chinned hummingbirds, ash-throated flycatchers, western scrub-jays, and black-throated gray warblers.

The paved portion of the road ends at a primitive campground 4.5 miles from US 60, under the tall bluff of **Water Canyon Mesa.** Narrowleaf cottonwoods, Arizona walnuts, Gambel oaks, and alligator junipers grow in this pretty creekside setting, home to acorn woodpeckers, plumbeous vireos, spotted towhees, and hepatic tanagers. A nice hike begins by taking Forest Road 39 to the west; drive a short distance to the trailhead for the **Copper Canyon Trail.** This route follows the canyon 4 miles to a ridgeline between South and North Baldy peaks, gaining almost 3,000 feet.

Forest Road 235 becomes dirt-surfaced and rough past the camp-ground; as it climbs, the surrounding woodland begins to include pon-derosa pine, white fir, Douglas-fir, Englemann spruce, and aspen. Wild turkeys, Abert's squirrels, and mule and white-tailed deer live here, along with rarely seen black bears and mountain lions. Some of the nesting birds of the upper canyon are southwestern specialties at the northern edge of their ranges, including elf owls, Hutton's vireos, bridled titmice, and olive and red-faced warblers.

About a half mile past the campground, the **Water Canyon Mesa Trail** leaves the road on the east; great views reward those who reach the top of this short but steep 3-mile loop hike.

The road ends near South Baldy's summit. Here you'll find the **Irving Langmuir Laboratory for Atmospheric Research** (505-835-5423. Open to visitors mid-June–mid-Aug.), dedicated to the study of thunderstorms, hail, and lightning. A popular day hike, the **North Baldy Trail** begins just beyond here, following ridgelines about 6 miles to 9,858-foot **North Baldy.** Lightning storms are frequent; take shelter when bad weather threatens. ■

Manzano Mountains

■ 100,000 acres ■ Central New Mexico, 30 miles southeast of Albuquerque via N. Mex. 337 and N. Mex. 55 ■ Best months April-Nov. Areas on east side of mountains usually closed by winter snow ■ Camping, hiking, bird-watching ■ Contact Mountainair Ranger District, Cibola National Forest, P.O. Box 69, Mountainair, NM 87036; phone 505-847-2990. www.fs.fed.us/r3/cibola

AT THE HEART OF THIS steep and rugged range southeast of Albuquerque lies Cibola National Forest's 36,970-acre **Manzano Mountain Wilderness,** crossed north to south by the 29-mile **Manzano Crest Trail.** Traversing open ridgelines in many places, the trail affords great views over the Rio Grande Valley to the west and the Estancia Basin to the east.

Several hiking routes lead up to the Crest Trail from the east, as do four from the west: the **Trigo Canyon, Salas, Comanche,** and **Osha Trails,** accessible from the John F. Kennedy Campground east of Belen. You can also drive up to the Capilla Peak Campground to reach the Crest Trail and enjoy its views without gaining elevation on foot.

The most popular destination within the Manzanos is the **Fourth of July Campground,** 7.5 miles west of Tajique on Forest Road 55. A brilliant display of fall color, rare in these parts, is provided by extensive stands of bigtooth and Rocky Mountain maples; quaking aspen and Gambel oak costar in the show, adding gold and yellow to the maples' scarlet and orange.

A variety of loop hikes are possible here. For one, follow the **Fourth of July Trail** up the canyon into the wilderness area to intersect the **Cerro Blanco Trail,** turning south on the latter to Forest Road 55; walk back along the road for a loop of about 5 miles. An attractive option is to turn north on the Cerro Blanco Trail for about a half mile to meet the Crest Trail, then return down the Cerro Blanco Trail to the road.

The trailhead for the **Albuquerque Trail** is located on Forest Road 55, about a half mile east of the turnoff to the Fourth of July Campground. This easy walk up a small creek leads to more stands of bigtooth maple, ending in about 2 miles at the border of the Pueblo Isleta Indian Reservation. You can loop back along the Fourth of July Trail or any of the other connecting paths.

The west side of the Manzanos comprises the steep edge of the Rio Grande Rift (see sidebar p. 165). The tilted block that forms the Manzanos is gentler on the east side, and forests are generally lusher. As you ascend, either by trail or on New Canyon Road (FR 245) to Capilla Peak, the woodland changes from pinyon pine and junipers to oaks, maples, and ponderosa pine; aspen, Douglas-fir, Engelmann spruce, and white and subalpine fir grow higher. Black bears and mule deer are fairly common in the mountains, and wild turkeys have been reintroduced. Nesting birds include mountain chickadees, hermit thrushes, and western tanagers. ■

Southward view of Manzano Mountains

Sandia Mountains

■ 60,000 acres ■ Central New Mexico, just northeast of Albuquerque off
N. Mex. 165 ■ Best months April-Oct. Trails are snow covered in winter;
road and tram access continues to ski area on Sandia Crest ■ Camping, hiking,
mountain biking, cross-country skiing, bird-watching ■ Parking fee at recreation
areas ■ Contact Sandia Ranger District, Cibola National Forest, 11776 Hwy. 337,
Tijeras, NM 87059; phone 505-281-3304. www.fs.fed.us/r3/cibola

IN 1540, A SPANISH EXPLORER visiting a Native American pueblo on the Rio
Grande wrote, "To the east there is a snow-covered mountain range, very
high and rough." His description of the Sandia Mountains, which rise
abruptly on the eastern edge of Albuquerque, is as accurate today as it
was in the 16th century. These highlands have long served as the city's
major playground; more than two million people travel to them every

Cane cholla cactus along the Pine Trail, Sandia Mountains

year, and their pinnacle, 10,678-foot Sandia Crest, is by far the most-visited mountain in New Mexico.

The Sandias form part of the east rim of the Rio Grande Rift, the great, down-dropped basin that splits New Mexico. The top of the Sandias is easily accessible by two means: One is a tramway that runs from the eastern edge of Albuquerque to the summit. The Sandia Peak Tram, the longest aerial tram in the United States, covers 2.7 miles as it ascends more than 4,000 feet. On the east, Cibola National Forest's Sandia Crest National Scenic Byway winds to the top, passing picnic areas and trailheads along the way. (The only two national forest campgrounds in the Sandias are reservation only group sites.)

Much of the western slope of the Sandias is protected within the 37,800-acre Sandia Mountain Wilderness, which sees a great deal of day-hiking because of its proximity to Albuquerque and its many convenient trailheads. The wilderness is bisected by the tramway and a

Engelmann's prickly pear bloom

downhill ski area; at the top of the tram you'll find a national forest visitor center and a restaurant. To the east of the wilderness lies the scenic byway. As a result, Sandia Mountain Wilderness is probably the state's least "wild" wilderness.

This is not to say that the Sandias lack natural-history interest. In fact, just the opposite is true. Because of their swift rise from desert to an elevation of more than 2 miles, from terrain that receives only about 10 inches of precipitation a year to heights that receive nearly three times that, the Sandias encompass a wide range of flora and fauna. You can hike or drive from scrubby desert grassland with cholla, pinyon pine, and juniper up through ponderosa pine and oak, into forests of Douglas-fir, subalpine (corkbark) fir, Engelmann spruce, and aspen.

What to See and Do

To drive to the top of Sandia Crest, leave I-40 east of Albuquerque at Tijeras, drive north 6 miles on N. Mex. 14, then turn west on N. Mex. 536—the **Sandia Crest National Scenic Byway.** After 2 miles, a side road on the left leads to the Sulphur Canyon and Cienega Canyon picnic areas, both of which offer a chance to explore ponderosa pine forest with other conifers and aspen intermixed. There is a short, wheelchair-accessible nature trail at 7,600-foot **Cienega Canyon,** or you can continue on the **Cienega Trail** from the picnic area, ascending for a little more than 2 miles to meet the **Crest Trail,** where you'll have great views into canyons on the Sandias' steep western slope.

About 3 more miles up the scenic byway is the parking area for the popular **Tree Springs Trail,** another way to reach the Crest Trail. Here at 8,300 feet, Douglas-fir has become the dominant tree; as you hike up 2 miles to the Crest Trail you may see birds such as red-naped sapsuckers, cordilleran fly-catchers, red-breasted and pygmy nuthatches, and MacGillivray's warblers. The much sought-after flammulated owl, a strictly noctur-nal bird only about the size of a bluebird, nests here—but it's not often found.

At the Crest Trail junction, it's only about another 1.6 miles north to the upper terminal of the aerial tramway. You can return to the Tree Springs Trail via ski trails and the **10-K Trail** to avoid in part retrac-ing your path to the parking lot.

Continuing up the highway, you reach the Capulin Spring picnic area and the adjacent Capulin Snow Play Area, popular with cross-country skiers and oth-ers who'd rather go down a snowy slope on an inner tube than on skis.

About a dozen switchbacks later, the road ends at **Sandia Crest.** Take time here to enjoy the view to the west, with Mount Taylor and the Jemez Mountains on the horizon and sprawling Albuquerque below.

Crest Trail

From here, you can hike part of the **Crest Trail,** a 29-mile route that traverses the wilderness from north to south. If you walk about 2 miles south along the trail, you'll reach the upper tram terminal and the national forest visitor center; most people, though, head north 2 miles, passing a cluster of elec-tronic towers and descending toward **North Sandia Peak**,

Rio Grande Rift

Though the low terrain that splits New Mexico in half north to south is often called the Rio Grande Val-ley, it wasn't carved by flowing water. It began to form long before there was a stream traversing the landscape. About 30 million years ago, the crust of the North Ameri-can tectonic plate began to split here. Over millions of years, the land between two roughly parallel fault systems sank—in some areas as much as 5 miles below the higher ground bordering it.

At first the nascent Rio Grande Rift comprised a line of closed basins, with no drainage from one to the other. Gradually, erosion carried material into the basins, partially filling them. Massive volca-noes, fed by magma rising through the faults, erupted alongside the rift, their ash and lava also raising its level. Eventually, it became flat enough that the Rio Grande could begin its journey from the Rocky Mountains to the Gulf of Mexico.

The Rio Grande Rift is quite narrow in Colorado, widening to about 30 miles near Albuquerque and to 80 miles or more in the southern part of the state.

The rift continues to widen today, even if usually imperceptibly. Occa-sional minor earthquakes show, though, that things remain in motion far below the placid river.

where you'll find more great views at various overlooks.

Here you're in woodland of Engelmann spruce and corkbark fir—the latter a southwestern sub-species of subalpine fir with especially thick, ridged bark.

Violet-green swallows and white-throated swifts zoom around cliff faces, achieving a graceful flight that the hang gliders who launch here can only dream of. In meadows, look for broad-tailed hummingbirds flitting among the flowers. Listen for them, too: The wings of the male broad-tailed produce a musical whistling trill, which makes them sound like mechanical toys as they buzz past.

On the west side of the Sandias, the most popular of the trails leading up the steep canyons is probably **La Luz,** a strenuous climb of nearly 8 miles that begins at Cibola National Forest's Juan Tabo picnic area in northeastern Albuquerque, reached by taking Forest Road 333 east from N. Mex. 556 (Tramway Road).

Gaining 3,600 feet along the way, La Luz Trail ends at the upper tramway terminal; many hikers ride the tram back down, taking a 2-mile connecting trail back to the Juan Tabo area from the lower tram terminal. Or, you can take the tram up and walk down the trail—easier on the lungs but harder on the knees.

Beginning nearby (continue north less than half a mile on a spur road at the entrance to the picnic area), the **Piedra Lisa Trail** heads north for 5 miles to another trailhead on Forest Road 445, south of N. Mex. 165. Many people, however, hike only the first 2 miles, gaining 1,000 feet to a granite ridgeline called the **Rincon.** You'll have excellent vistas along the route as you traverse pinyon-pine-juniper habitat. ◼

Rio Grande Nature Center

◼ 270 acres ◼ Central New Mexico, in Albuquerque at western end of Candelaria Rd. ◼ Best seasons fall-spring ◼ Hiking, bird-watching ◼ Adm. fee ◼ Contact the center, 2901 Candelaria Rd. N.W., Albuquerque, NM 87107; phone 505-344-7240

SEEN FROM AN AIRPLANE, or a high viewpoint like the nearby Sandia Mountains, the Rio Grande appears as a ribbon of green in the arid and urbanized landscape around Albuquerque. Set on the river northwest of the city center, the Rio Grande Nature Center provides an accessible means to explore the riparian cottonwood and willow forest—locally known by the Spanish term *bosque*—that serves as a refuge for an array of wildlife.

From the parking area, a short trail leads to the **visitor center,** where you'll find books, exhibits, and a viewing window overlooking a 3-acre cattail pond. A changing lineup of birds can be seen here throughout the year, including the colorful wood duck. Look also for pied-billed grebes, Canada geese, gadwalls, mallard, cinnamon teal, common moorhens, and American coots on the water, and in the edge vegetation for great blue herons, black-crowned night-herons, Virginia rail, and soras.

Take the trail west from the visitor center, crossing a drainage ditch and the Rio Grande levee, to reach the 0.8-mile **Bosque Loop Trail** and the 1-mile (one way) **River Walk;** both wind through the bosque to overlook the river. Coyotes, beavers, and raccoons are occasionally seen, though birds are always more conspicuous residents. The more common breeding species include black-chinned hummingbirds, northern flickers, western wood-pewees, white-breasted nuthatches, bewick's wrens, rufous-sided towhees, and black-headed grosbeaks. Along the river, look and listen for killdeer and belted kingfishers, both of which often loudly announce their presence before they're seen.

Although the bosque here can be vibrant with life in a lovely verdant setting, all is not well with this ecosystem. The river once flowed freely south from the Colorado mountains to the Gulf of Mexico, a linear oasis in a dry landscape. Floods regularly drove it out of its banks, spreading nutrients and seeds and regenerating its vegetated borders. Today, though, dams check floodwaters, irrigation ditches siphon away much of the remaining flow, and levees—like those adjacent to the nature center—contain the river's urge to meander.

Some of the huge Rio Grande cottonwoods here are a century old, but not nearly enough new growth is occurring to replace the regal, old trees. Instead, Russian olive and tamarisk, introduced species, are taking over extensive areas of riverbank. Levees have dried up places that once were seasonal marshy wetlands, destroying essential habitat. The river carries far less silt than it once did, and flows faster and deeper.

In the stretch between Cochiti Dam and Elephant Butte Dam, 7 of the 19 original native fish species have disappeared. The Rio Grande silvery minnow, once abundant, declined to near extinction in the late 1990s, the latest victim of a wounded river environment.

There are no quick solutions to the Rio Grande's situation, and there will be no recovery from some of its losses. Those who visit—walking trails, rafting the upper reaches, or visiting Bosque del Apache to the south—should value the habitat that remains, and encourage restoration efforts all along this grand river. ■

American coot

Arizona Highlands

Lost Dutchman State Park, Superstition Mountains

IN BETWEEN ARIZONA's Colorado Plateau, with its famous
national parks and monuments, and the Basin and Range
region of the south, with its cities and desert resorts, lies
a transition zone of rugged mountains dotted with some
of the state's finest natural areas. The area has been given
differing names—the Arizona Mountains, the Central
Highlands, the Rim Country—but no matter what it's
called, it's a rewarding destination for travelers in search
of either sight-seeing vacations or adventure travel.

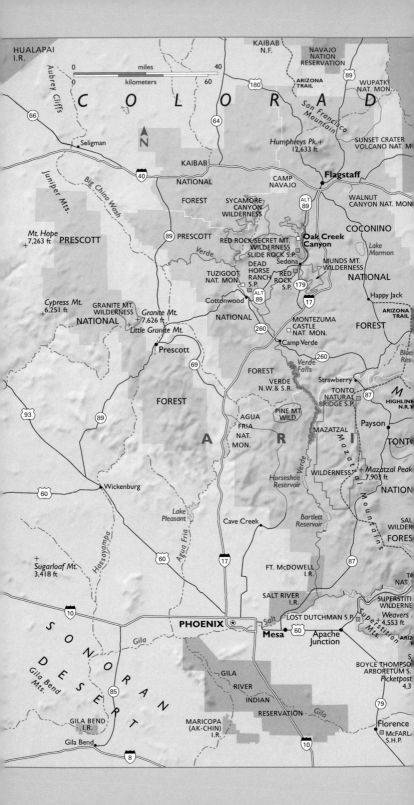

HOPI INDIAN RESERVATION

P L A T E A U

NAVAJO NATION RESERVATION

Window Rock

Little Colorado

HOMOLOVI RUINS S.P.

eor Crater

Winslow

Painted Desert Visitor Center

ZUNI I.R.

West Sunset Mt. 6,612 ft

East Sunset Mt. 6,840 ft

Holbrook

PETRIFIED FOREST NATIONAL PARK

Dry Lake

Little Colorado

ZUNI I.R.

Zuni

Snowflake

St. Johns

ACHE-SITGREAVES

Heber Overgaard

Mogollon Rim Visitor Center

NATIONAL   FORESTS

LYMAN LAKE S.P.

Lyman Lake

OLLON

Pinedale

260

Show Low

Springerville

SGATE DERNESS

O

N

A

Pinetop-Lakeside

POLE KNOLL REC. AREA

Mexican Hay Lake

ESCUDILLA MT. WILDERNESS

WHITE

R

I

M

WHITE MOUNTAIN SCENIC BYWAY

MT. BALDY WILDERNESS

Escudilla Mt. 10,912 ft

SIERRA ANCHA WILDERNESS

MOUNTAIN

White

Baldy Peak 11,403 ft

White Mts.

BIG LAKE REC. AREA

Alpine

APACHE

San

Black

APACHE

eodore osevelt ke

SALT RIVER CANYON WILDERNESS

SAN

CARLOS

RESERVATION

BEAR WALLOW WILDERNESS

Hannagan Meadow

BLUE VISTA

SITGREAVES

RAIL ENIC WAY

Globe

APACHE

RESERVATION

Rose Peak 8,786 ft

BLUE RANGE PRIMITIVE AREA

NATIONAL

San Carlos Reservoir

CORONADO TRAIL SCENIC BYWAY

Blue

FORESTS

San Francisco

Santa Teresa Mts.

Gila

Clifton

CORONADO N.F.

GILA BOX RIPARIAN N.C.A.

No national parks lure the hit-the-high-spots tourists to these central mountains; these visitors mostly see them through a car window on the way from Phoenix to Grand Canyon or Petrified Forest National Parks. Instead you'll find parts of several national forests, wilderness areas, and a few state parks, all lower profile than the big brochure-cover attractions elsewhere in the state. This is not to say that the trails here are deserted, only that a high percentage of visitors are Arizonans who know and appreciate this in-between land.

The exception to that last statement is the Sedona area, quite justly celebrated for the beauty of its red-rock country, and notorious, perhaps, for its New Age mysticism and "energy vortices." You'll encounter tourists aplenty here throughout the year, but don't let that stop you from visiting, driving through Oak Creek Canyon, and hiking some of the trails in the adjacent wilderness areas. While sites close to town can be crowded, many outlying trails provide a degree of solitude.

The most distinctive physical feature of the region, the Mogollon Rim stretches from northwest of the town of Sedona east to the White Mountains, an abrupt escarpment that unequivocally marks a portion of the southern edge of the Colorado Plateau. In places, jumbled, eroded rocks create a sloping transition from top to bottom, while in other spots sheer palisades of rock hundreds of feet high give the Rim a walled-fortress appearance. Around Payson, hiking trails trace the Rim along its top and base in an area of popular national forest campgrounds, recreation areas, and fishing lakes. Not far away in a narrow canyon below the Rim, Tonto Natural Bridge State Park preserves one of the state's most unusual rock formations.

Wilderness areas within this region encompass a conspicuously wide range of environments. Just east of Phoenix, the volcanic Superstition Mountains are largely covered by scrub vegetation consistent with their location at the edge of the Sonoran Desert. Saguaro, chollas, and other cactuses border the trails, along with agaves, shrubs, and trees such as jojobas, sumacs, acacias, and oaks. While not rising to high elevations, trails here offer plenty of challenges to hikers traversing these rough and rocky uplands. Legends of a lost gold mine still cling to the Superstitions, even after the failures of countless prospecting expeditions.

A short drive northward, the peaks of the Mazatzal Wilderness rise within sight of the Mogollon Rim, their forests of pinyon and ponderosa pines, junipers, and oaks representing a transition between the desert to the south and the spruce-fir woodland of the White Mountains to the east. Visited less often than some of the other areas, the Mazatzals allow hikers as much isolation as they want in wild terrain where mountain lions, black bears, and mule deer roam. The Verde River, part of which is included in the National Wild and Scenic Rivers System, borders the Mazatzals on the west; white-water rafting is popular on one segment of the river during spring runoff.

Volcanic activity built the White Mountains, near Springerville and Alpine in eastern Arizona. Massive eruptions about five million years ago

Autumn leaves, Oak Creek Canyon, Coconino National Forest

left lava and hardened ash piled in deep layers, burying a large segment of the Mogollon Rim. With elevations topping 11,000 feet, the White Mountains are cloaked in coniferous forest and intermingled aspen groves, home to a range of high-country wildlife. Such elusive birds as blue grouse, spotted owls, three-toed woodpeckers, and pine grosbeaks reside here, along with one of the state's densest elk populations. Broad tracts of grassland interspersed with the forest add to the ecological diversity. Trails that attract hikers in summer also make the White Mountains one of Arizona's most popular cross-country skiing destinations. Some of the wilderness discoveries here are accessible only to hikers or horseback riders, but the Coronado Trail Scenic Byway, the White Mountains Scenic Byway, and the Terry Flat loop road south of Escudilla Mountain offer superb scenery to all.

The Arizona Highlands may be geographically in-between, but there's nothing middle-of-the-road about their wild beauty. Whether you want to catch your supper in a mountain creek, raft a river, or leave civilization behind on a wilderness trail, you'll find contentment here. ◼

Storm clouds over upper Boynton Canyon

Sedona and Oak Creek Canyon

■ 240,000 acres ■ Central Arizona via Ariz. 89A between Flagstaff and Sedona
■ Best seasons fall through spring ■ Camping, hiking, bird-watching ■ Adm. fee
to state parks; parking fee at some recreation areas ■ Contact Sedona Ranger
District, Coconino National Forest, P.O. Box 300, Sedona, AZ 86339; phone
520-282-4119. www.fs.fed.us/r3/coconino

DEBATE CONTINUES OVER whether there's any sort of mystical energy ema-
nating from Sedona, but there's no doubt that the place is full up with
contradictions. In few sites do wilderness and civilization, ethereal splendor and raw commerce, quiet canyons and traffic-choked roads exist in
such intimate proximity.

The town of Sedona is one of the most popular and highly promoted
tourist destinations in Arizona, with two officially designated national
forest wilderness areas crowding its very borders, and another just a few
miles away. In Sedona you can literally cross the fence from a luxury
resort into a wilderness area (and a dazzling one, at that). Here, a goodly
number of people arrive in town and immediately acquire maps of
wilderness areas and a map of New Age energy vortices, which in two
cases actually coincide. Here, some of the state's most preservation-
worthy scenic areas exist hard by a town rapidly growing into a city, with
all the fast-food, subdivisional, mall-culture sprawl that implies.

What brought about this collision of ethoses? Pure beauty. Whatever
you think of Sedona's commercialism, its blend of money and mysticism,
you can't argue that it's located amid some of the most beautiful surroundings imaginable. For that, you can thank an accident of geology.

In the Sedona area, dozens of spectacular canyons have cut back into the edge of the Colorado Plateau, creating high-walled gorges exposing some of the same beautifully hued layers of sandstone, limestone, and shale seen on the walls of the Grand Canyon. Oak Creek Canyon is bisected by Ariz. 89A, one of the most famous scenic roads in America, which makes its grandeur accessible to all but also often leads to crowding at its picnic areas, trailheads, and at famed Slide Rock State Park. In the Sycamore Canyon Wilderness (see p. 183), by contrast, foot and horse trails provide the only access into the gorge's wild heart.

But the scenes that have made Sedona famous, that have adorned countless calendars and picture books and attracted vacationers and permanent residents, are red-rock buttes, towers, spires, cliffs, and multifarious other formations that arise from the rolling land at the canyons' mouths. Here, in the Permian period more than 300 million years ago, sand built up in a deposit hundreds of feet thick, some layers originating as a beach formation and some as great dune fields. Over the eons it was compressed into sandstone, tinted red by the presence of iron. Exposed by subsequent erosion, this relatively soft rock has been shaped by water and wind into fantastic forms, some of which are hinted at by names such as Cathedral Rock, Coffeepot Rock, Rabbit Ears, and Ship Rock.

Much of this red-rock scenery can be seen from roadsides, at places such as celebrated Red Rock Crossing, just southwest of Sedona. Several local companies offer off-road-vehicle tours of the region, most simply for great views, others specializing in subjects such as wildlife or Native American rock art.

For those who prefer to leave their vehicles behind, an extensive trail system within Coconino National Forest, which surrounds Sedona and includes the Red Rock/Secret Mountain Wilderness, provides close-up experiences of this gorgeous terrain. You'll find trails here suitable for all abilities, and in fact some of the most splendid scenery is accessible along some of the easiest trails. At this writing, Sedona and the Coconino National Forest are cooperating to build a system of trails that eventually will circle the town, making access even easier to the landscape that brought everyone here in the first place.

If you're one who's exasperated by crowds, who prefers to feel alone in a wilderness miles from another human, then you should stick to long-distance trails farthest from town, or perhaps visit

Horned Lizards

Throughout most of Arizona you may come across various types of horned lizards; a half-dozen species are present in the state. Often called "horned toads," these small, round-bodied animals are reptiles, not amphibians. Some possess the unusual ability to squirt blood from their eyes, an odd but apparently effective defensive tactic. Especially favoring ants as food, horned lizards can be found from dry deserts to mountain coniferous forests.

on a weekday in winter. (If you can arrange to be here right after one of the fairly infrequent snows, usually occurring from January through March, red-rock country truly can seem magical.) Otherwise, simply accept that any place this accessible and this beautiful is going to lure multitudes of visitors, and enjoy sharing the fun with your fellow hikers.

Summer is not the best time to visit Sedona, Oak Creek Canyon, and red-rock country. Not only are the vacation crowds present, but the canyons can be hot and, in some places, fairly shadeless. The direct over-head sun doesn't make for good photography, either, and you're going to want to take lots of pictures. In spring or fall you certainly won't find a deserted town, but hiking conditions will be more pleasant, and the longer period of slanting light at the beginning and end of day puts a golden burnish on the deep-red rocks.

What to See and Do

If you approach Sedona from Flagstaff on Ariz. 89A, your intro-duction to Oak Creek Canyon will be a dramatic one. You'll be traveling across a section of the Colorado Plateau covered in basalt from lava that erupted from the San Francisco Mountain area (see pp. 60-63 and 67), north of Flagstaff. This hard layer is one of the factors that have kept the edge of the Colorado Plateau from eroding into a slope—so when you arrive at the canyon, you arrive very, very suddenly.

At the **Oak Creek Vista** 12 miles south of Flagstaff, you can gaze down the drainage and admire the multicolored west wall of the canyon. You'll see the same sand-stone, shale, and limestone found in the upper walls of the Grand Canyon, created by deserts and seas dating back 300 million years. Like a layer cake of strawberry, toffee, and vanilla, the canyon side rises 1,000 feet above spring-fed **Oak Creek**. Note that the east wall is much lower than the west, in part because of slippage along a fault line that runs through the canyon.

If you have time to think of anything at all as you negotiate the hairpin turns leading down into the canyon, you will no doubt admire the ingenuity of the road's engineers. Eventually (not as quickly as you wish, perhaps), you'll arrive at the narrow, tree-shaded canyon floor, heading south toward Sedona. Some of the most popular natural attractions in the area are located along the next dozen miles of highway.

Hiking

Many hikes are possible as you drive along Ariz. 89A. Trails are on both sides of the road, most climb-ing fairly steeply out of the canyon back to the plateau above. The **Cookstove Trail** (beginning at the Pine Flat Campground) and **Hard-ing Springs Trail** (beginning at the Cave Springs Campground), for example, both ascend to the Col-orado Plateau on the east side of Oak Creek Canyon, offering great views in return for gaining about 800 feet in 0.7 mile. Going up Harding Springs and back down Cookstove makes a nice loop trip.

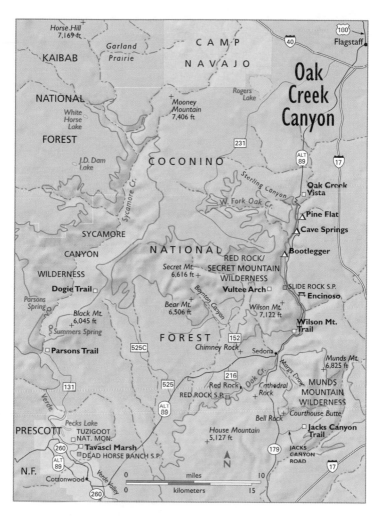

Oak
Creek
Canyon

The **A.B. Young Trail** begins at the Bootlegger Campground and climbs the west canyon wall, gaining about 1,500 feet in 2.4 miles to reach a lookout tower. There (if it's occupied and the occupants give you permission to go up) you'll have a superb panorama of the canyon and the Colorado Plateau, with San Francisco Mountain on the horizon to the north. (You'll have great views even if you don't go up the tower, too.) The trail passes from riparian woods along Oak Creek up into chaparral with manzanita and scrub oaks, reaching ponderosa pine woodland atop the canyon wall. Early settlers used this trail as a path along which to take their cattle to summer pasture on the higher, cooler plateau.

The **Wilson Mountain Trail** is a vigorous climb that you'll enjoy most if you leave early, take it slowly, and plan on spending pretty much all day going up and

Stepping carefully along the West Fork Oak Creek

back. It's 5.6 miles one way, with most of the 2,300-foot elevation gain coming quickly as you hike west from the creek. You don't have to get to the top to enjoy great vistas of the canyon, but if you do you'll want to spend time looking out across Sedona and the **Verde Valley** to the south and **Sterling Canyon** to the northwest. The trailhead is located just north of the Midgely Bridge, with an alternative (and shadier) start 3 miles farther north on Ariz. 89A near the Encinoso picnic area.

Guided Hike:
West Fork Oak Creek

The hike up the **West Fork** of Oak Creek is often called the "No. 1 hike in Arizona"—and the truth of that claim could be asserted whether you're talking about popularity or beauty. Easily accessible just off Ariz. 89A, and offering a wondrous red-rock landscape in return for an easy walk, West Fork attracts nearly every ambulatory soul who visits the area. To get the most out of this hike, and to share it with the fewest number of hikers, visit on a weekday and try to be at the trailhead at dawn.

Although there's very little elevation gain along the 3 miles of maintained trail here—hence the "easy" description—less mobile folks should note that you must cross the creek several times along the way, hopping over sometimes slick rocks. Shoes with a good tread, or hiking sandals, could be a good idea, though plenty of people do fine in sneakers.

To start the hike, drive north from Sedona about 10 miles on Ariz. 89A, and watch for the **Call of the Canyon day area** (Fee) on the west side of the highway. Park here and cross Oak Creek using the footbridge.

Before reaching the canyon of the West Fork, you'll walk downstream along Oak Creek a short distance, passing through an old apple orchard. The initial settler arrived in Oak Creek Canyon in 1876, and in the first decades of the 20th century, farming was a thriving enterprise along the stream; apples and other fruits were especially popular. Nowadays it's mostly wildlife that enjoys the bounty of the old orchards, although apples are still cultivated and harvested at Slide Rock State Park, downstream a few miles. You'll also pass the ruined buildings of a long-abandoned tourist resort, including an odd cave room in the cliffside.

After signing in at the Forest Service registration post, you'll head generally northwest along the West Fork, passing under walls of red and buff sandstone. The crystalline water of the creek is home to rainbow and brown trout; anglers sometimes try their luck along this stretch of stream, though Oak Creek itself is more popular.

Arizona sycamores, Arizona walnuts, ponderosa pines, alligator junipers, cottonwoods, bigtooth maples, box elders (also a kind of maple), and Douglas-firs are some of the trees you'll be walking beside and under along the path. The last named species is not a true fir. If you want to get technical about it, notice how the needles of the Douglas-fir have short petioles (or stems); true fir needles lack petioles. The cones of true firs stand upright on the branches, while Douglas-fir cones hang down. In favorable locations, these evergreens can grow larger than any other Arizona tree.

Where the creek makes a relatively sharp left bend, stop to admire the way erosion has sculpted intricate patterns in the sandstone of the wall opposite the trail. Imagine how long it would take flowing water to scoop even a quarter inch from the rock, and then multiply that...oh, as many times as you want. The Colorado Plateau began rising some 60 million years ago, so the forces that have carved its rim have had plenty of time to work.

Listen for the descending song of the canyon wren, echoing between the cliffs. Other nesting birds you might spot include white-throated swifts, western wood-pewees, violet-green swallows, common ravens, bridled titmice, and summer tanagers.

In places, at times, pools along the creek are deep enough for swimming, or at least for submersion. Lots of flat rocks beside the stream make great spots to sit down and eat a snack, or bask in the sun, or just enjoy the birdsong and sound of the wind.

The officially maintained trail ends at the 3-mile mark, and most people turn around here. Those willing to wade (or even swim) and/or push through thick chaparral on hillsides can continue their explorations upstream. Some folks hike all 14 miles to the top of the canyon and another trailhead on Forest Road 231, reached from Flagstaff. This requires backcountry skills and shouldn't be attempted when there's a chance of storms. In

Not Quite a Pig

Across much of southern and central Arizona, but especially in canyon bottoms with oaks, you may come across a small herd of javelinas, or collared peccaries. These mammals, which can stand about 2 feet high, are covered in coarse light and dark hairs that give them a grizzled appearance. Though they resemble pigs, javelinas are in a different, New World family.

Javelina

Thanks to a musk gland on their backs, which gives off a skunky scent, javelinas are often smelled before they're seen. Females usually give birth to two young, and these little piglets look quite appealing as they trot along with the rest of the herd, rooting for acorns, fruit, insects, lizards, and even snakes.

Where they have become accustomed to humans, javelinas are fairly tame. As with all wild animals, though, it's better to watch, and admire, from a distance.

some spots canyon walls narrow to deep, constricted passages, providing no escape for hikers should water begin to rise suddenly.

Red Rock/Secret Mountain Wilderness

You can reach trails into the **Red Rock/Secret Mountain Wilderness** by driving west from Sedona on Ariz. 89A and turning north on Dry Creek Road (Forest Road 152). The **Boynton Canyon Trail** is a favorite of many locals, though to enjoy it you must begin the hike by skirting a resort development in the mouth of the canyon—a disconcerting beginning for a wilderness experience. Ascending only 500 feet in 2.5 miles, this easy walk begins in dry pinyon-pine-juniper habitat before entering woods of oak, maple, and alligator juniper. Up the canyon, some of the walls towering above you are not red but a bright, almost unnatural orange.

Nearby trailheads for the **Fay Canyon, Long Canyon,** and **Secret Canyon Trails** each offer access to similar relaxed hikes of less than 10 miles, leading into beautiful red-rock canyons. The **Vultee Arch Trail,** beginning near the **Secret Mountain Trail,** is an easy walk up Sterling Canyon that leads in less than 2 miles to Vultee Arch, a small natural arch on a hillside. The **Brins Mesa Trail** can be accessed by two trailheads, one on Forest Road 152 and the other on the northern edge of Sedona (drive north from Ariz. 89A on Jordan Road); along this route you'll have close views of **Coffeepot Rock** (well named) and **Chimney Rock,** among other formations.

Munds Mountain Wilderness

Covering 18,150 acres just southeast of Sedona, **Munds Mountain Wilderness** provides more fine trails, with easy access from town. Five miles south on Ariz. 179, you'll find the trailhead for the easy 4-mile loop through scrub vegetation around Bell Rock and Courthouse Butte, two famous local formations. (Bell Rock lives up to its name, while it takes more imagination to see a columned courthouse in the butte.)

Continue a couple of miles south on Ariz. 179 and turn east on Jacks Canyon Road to reach the trailhead for the **Jacks Canyon Trail.** This moderately strenuous hike gains 1,100 feet in 5.7 miles to join the **Munds Mountain Trail,** from which it's a steep climb farther to the top of Munds Mountain. Here you'll find one of the best vistas of red-rock country anywhere in the area.

The easy **Margs Draw Trail** can be accessed from various trailheads, including one on Schnebly Hill Road east of Sedona and another reached by turning east on Sombart Lane from Ariz. 179 about one-third mile south of Schnebly Hill Road. You'll have good views of Crimson Cliffs and Munds Mountain on this route, which also provides access to the formation that local folks call Snoopy Rock. (From the right angle, the rock does indeed look like the famous cartoon dog, lying on his back atop his doghouse.)

No one can visit Sedona without driving to the spot southwest of town known as **Red Rock Crossing,** with its famous view of **Cathedral Rock,** the best known symbol of red-rock country. From Ariz. 89A west of Sedona, take Red Rock Loop Road south and follow signs to the picnic area at the crossing on Oak Creek, where photographers gather at sunset to capture the spires and cliffs in the last light of day. If you'd like to hike to the base of Cathedral Rock, you can drive south from town on Ariz. 179, turn west on Back of Beyond Road, and follow it to a parking lot on the south side of the road.

Area State Parks

Just north of the Encinoso picnic area, **Slide Rock State Park** *(Sedona. 520-282-3034. Adm. fee)* combines Oak Creek history with one of Arizona's most popular swimming holes—though that term doesn't quite do the place justice. The 43-acre park occupies the site of a pioneer homestead, where a settler who arrived in the canyon in 1907 built an irrigation system (still in use today) and established an apple orchard. On warm days,

happy crowds gather at **Slide Rock,** a natural water slide where Oak Creek sluices down slippery rock chutes for short but fun rides. Nearby, pools between a series of small waterfalls make great wading or swimming sites. If you intend on sliding Slide Rock, for the sake of safety and decorum wear some old sneakers or water sandals and sturdy shorts over your swimsuit. The park presents guided nature and history walks regularly, and in fall visitors can watch the apple harvest.

Located off Red Rock Loop Road, 286-acre **Red Rock State Park** *(Sedona. 520-282-6907. Adm. fee)* encompasses several miles of trails through riparian habitat along Oak Creek. Dedicated to environmental education, the park offers guided nature walks, among other programs. It would not be a bad idea to stop here first before exploring the Sedona area in order to get a fine first lesson in local flora and fauna. ■

At Slide Rock State Park

Sycamore Canyon Wilderness

■ 55,937 acres ■ Central Arizona, 20 miles west of Sedona off Ariz. 89A
■ Best seasons fall through spring ■ Camping, hiking ■ Contact Sedona
Ranger District, Coconino National Forest, P.O. Box 300, Sedona, AZ 86339;
phone 520-282-4119. www.fs.fed.us/r3/coconino

Sunlight on Sycamore Canyon

YOU'LL FIND SOLITUDE, red-rock terrain, and desert, forest, and riparian environments in Sycamore Canyon Wilderness, which essentially adjoins Red Rock/Secret Mountain Wilderness on the west. A number of trails enter this 20-mile-long canyon, some accessed by dirt road from Flagstaff and others from roads leading south of I-40, west of Flagstaff. Two trails in the southern part of the wilderness, the Dogie Trail and the Parsons Spring Trail, provide a good sampling of its landscape.

To reach the trailhead for the **Dogie Trail,** drive about 5 miles west from Sedona on Ariz. 89A and turn north on Forest Road 525; at a junction in less than 3 miles, go west on Forest Road 525C about 8 more miles to a parking area at Sycamore Pass; from here it's a short walk to the saddle where the trail starts. The view from this spot is worth a drive even if you don't intend to hike down to the canyon floor, 5.4 miles away. You'll pass through pinyon-pine-juniper woods, with an occasional smooth-bark Arizona cypress, a special tree of this region. At **Sycamore Creek** (dry most of the year here), the Dogie Trail intersects the **Taylor Cabin Trail,** where you can turn right up the drainage. With a good map, various loop and one-way shuttle hikes are possible. Bear in mind that the canyon can be very hot in summer, when hiking is usually inadvisable.

An easy, beautiful hike, the **Parsons Trail** is reached by a rather roundabout trip from Sedona. Take Ariz. 89A southwest about 20 miles to Cottonwood, then go west on Main Street to the turnoff to **Tuzigoot National Monument** (see p. 185). Just after crossing the Verde River, turn west on Forest Road 131 (Sycamore Canyon Road) and drive 11 miles to the trailhead. The hike leads 4 miles up a riparian zone along Sycamore Creek, perennial here thanks to the flow of Summers Spring and **Parsons Spring,** the latter the destination for this hike. You'll see plenty of the Arizona sycamores for which the creek was named as you walk under multicolored cliffs. ■

Cottonwood trees along the Verde River, Dead Horse Ranch State Park

Dead Horse Ranch State Park

■ 325 acres ■ Central Arizona, I mile north of Cottonwood off Ariz. 89A
■ Best seasons spring and fall ■ Camping, hiking, canoeing, fishing, mountain
biking, horseback riding, bird-watching ■ Adm. fee ■ Contact the park, 675
Dead Horse Ranch Rd., Cottonwood, AZ 86326; phone 520-634-5283.
www.pr.state.az.us

ECOLOGISTS ESTIMATE THAT 90 percent or more of Arizona's original riparian habitat—the lush streamside woodland of cottonwoods, willows, and
associated vegetation—has been lost to land-clearing, dams, overgrazing,
and lowering of the water table. Declining, too, have been populations of
animals dependent on this environment, including amphibians, beavers,
river otters, and birds such as willow flycatchers.

The Verde River, which runs southward through the center of Arizona, supports green corridors of riparian habitat in several stretches,
including Dead Horse Ranch State Park and the 461-acre riparian corridor known as the Verde River Greenway, a 6-mile segment of river near
Cottonwood. Just a short drive from Sedona, this often overlooked spot
makes a rewarding side trip.

What to See and Do

From Main Street in Cottonwood,
take North Tenth Street north and
cross the **Verde River** to reach the

state park; drive east and park at
the lagoon, a pond with marsh
vegetation circled by a walking

trail. There you could find a great blue heron standing on the bank, searching for fish and frogs.

Walk south a short distance to the **Greenway Trail** bordering the Verde River, where you can stroll through the corridor forest alongside the usually placid stream. This stand of large Fremont cottonwoods (which gave the nearby town its name) and Goodding willows is considered the finest along the length of the Verde. When water levels permit, it can be fun to put in a canoe for a quiet paddle along the Verde in the greenway area. Anglers often line the banks, casting for stocked trout.

You might come across mule deer, javelinas, or raccoons as you walk here, especially if you're out at dawn or dusk. More likely than mammals, though, are birds in a wide variety attracted to the riverside woods. Look here for nesting green herons, common blackhawks, yellow-billed cuckoos, black phoebes, and beautiful hooded orioles.

Miles of paths loop through the park, with even more trails extending into adjacent Coconino National Forest. The **Lime Kiln Trail** (2.1 miles one way) follows part of a 19th-century wagon road that ran from Sedona to Jerome; the remains of an old kiln used for converting limestone to lime can be seen along the way. Following this trail, the **Thumper Trail** and the **Raptor Hill Trail** make a loop of about 7 miles, popular with hikers and mountain bikers.

Tavasci Marsh

Just north of the state park, **Tavasci Marsh** ranks with the region's most productive wetland areas. Administered by the state game and fish department, this tract of cattails, bulrushes, and open water can be reached from a trailhead in the north part of the state park or from a parking area at nearby **Tuzigoot National Monument** *(4 miles N of Cottonwood off Ariz. 89A. 520-634-5564. www.nps.gov/tuzi. Adm fee).* The name Tuzigoot means "crooked water," referring to the meandering course of the Verde River and to Pecks Lake, an oxbow lake of the Verde. An observation deck at the marsh allows for scanning the water for birds, beavers, and otters.

The national monument itself is well worth a visit while you're in the area. This 42-acre site protects the remains of a hilltop pueblo occupied by the Sinagua Indians between 1000 and 1400, with more than a hundred rooms, including two- and three-story structures. ∎

A Rare Rose

In spring, look for the white or yellowish flowers of the endangered Arizona cliffrose on hillsides north of the Verde River. This Arizona shrub is known from only a handful of sites; the population around Dead Horse Ranch State Park is the healthiest still extant. An evergreen that grows 5 feet tall, the cliffrose has been harmed by grazing, poor reproduction, and off-road vehicles. Because of its presence, hikers in Dead Horse must stay on the trails.

Granite Mountain Trail

■ 9,700 acres ■ Central Arizona, 9 miles northwest of Prescott at end of Granite Basin Rd. ■ Best seasons spring and fall. Cliff-climbing face closed Feb.–mid-July for peregrine falcon breeding season ■ Hiking, rock-climbing, bird-watching ■ Parking fee ■ Contact Bradshaw Ranger District, Prescott National Forest, 2230 E. Hwy. 69, Prescott, AZ 86301; phone 520-445-7253. www.fs.fed.us/r3/prescott

THREE REASONS EXPLAIN WHY the Granite Mountain Wilderness is one of Arizona's most popular wilderness areas: It's located just a few miles outside the growing city of Prescott; it's easily accessible from the city on a paved road; and it offers superb scenery along a 4.1-mile trail that begins as more of an easy stroll than a hike.

From the Metate Trailhead at an elevation of 5,600 feet, the Granite Mountain Trail skirts tiny **Granite Basin Lake** as it passes through an attractive woodland of ponderosa and pinyon pines, Emory and Gambel oaks, and Utah and alligator junipers, with Fremont cottonwoods, velvet ashes, and willows in riparian areas. Soon the trail reaches the wilderness boundary, passing between **Little Granite Mountain** to the south and **Granite Mountain** to the north, though the latter's summit isn't visible from this angle. Granite Mountain's flanks are composed of huge rounded boulders of granite dating from Precambrian times, 1.7 billion years ago, creating a spectacularly beautiful landscape. Most people are content simply to admire the view, but rock climbers find Granite Mountain one of the state's most challenging venues for their demanding sport.

Peregrine falcons, those fast-flying lords of the air, nest on Granite Mountain's cliffs, and lucky hikers may spot one soaring high above or zooming toward earth in thrilling dives that can reach over 100 miles an hour. Birders are more likely to spot acorn or hairy woodpeckers, canyon wrens, pygmy nuthatches, spotted towhees, or bridled or juniper titmice. Collared lizards are common here, and both western diamondback and black-tailed rattlesnakes live among the rocks.

As the trail gradually climbs and nears **Blair Pass,** 1.3 miles along, you'll pass among chaparral thickets of turbinella oak (with thick, prickly leaves that resemble holly), manzanita (with urn-shaped flowers that show it's a member of the heath family), mountain mahogany, and Wright's silk tassel, with cholla and prickly pear interspersed.

At the pass, you've gained only 200 feet in elevation, and the easy part of the hike is finished; over the next 2.8 miles of switchbacks you'll ascend nearly 1,400 feet to reach a viewpoint at 7,185 feet on the south side of Granite Mountain. Most of the elevation is gained fairly quickly from Blair Pass, which allows you to catch your breath and enjoy the last half mile of the hike; the panorama at trail's end, overlooking Prescott toward the Bradshaw Mountains, is well worth the effort. ■

Two- and four-footed hikers in the Granite Mountain Wilderness

Mogollon Rim

A PORTION OF THE southern edge of the Colorado Plateau is marked with geologic certitude by the Mogollon (moge-ee-YONE) Rim, an escarpment that runs from central Arizona southeast to the White Mountains. Cut by ancient rivers and recent erosion, the Rim ranges from a few hundred feet high to around 2,000 feet in its central section, where cliffs rise above the Verde River and Tonto Creek watersheds.

The Mogollon Rim reaches its greatest glory in the Payson area. Here Ariz. 260, coming from Camp Verde, drops off the Colorado Plateau and then rises again on its way east to Heber. Trails, roads, and recreation areas offer countless ways to experience the landscape both below and above the rim in this vicinity.

For backpackers, the **Highline National Recreation Trail** runs for 51 miles below the rim, from a trailhead just east of Pine to another on Ariz. 260 about 25 miles east of Payson. For drivers, Forest Road 64 (Control Road) also runs from near Pine to Ariz. 260, paralleling the Highline trail on the south. The trail and the road pass through the area burned by the Dude Fire of July 1990, which raged across 24,000 acres of forest. This fire also destroyed the cabin of famed western author Zane Grey, who used the Mogollon Rim

Hikers on the edge of Mogollon Rim in Apache-Sitgreaves National Forests

Mogollon Rim

as a writing and hunting retreat in the 1920s.

Beginning at the trailhead near Pine, the 8-mile **Pine Canyon Trail** heads north up a beautiful canyon and climbs the rim to Ariz. 87; walking 2 miles to **Dripping Springs** is a fine day hike.

To visit **Hellsgate Wilderness,** drive 12 miles east of Payson on Ariz. 260, turn south on Forest Road 405A, and continue less than a mile to the trailhead. From here the route drops 1,500 feet in 6 miles into a canyon on Tonto Creek.

Ariz. 260 ascends the rim about 30 miles east of Payson; near the top you'll find the Forest Service's Mogollon Rim Visitor Center, open from May through September. Forest Road 300 travels west from here along the top of the Rim, with side roads and trails leading to some breathtaking vistas. The easy, scenic **Rim Lakes Vista Trail** begins on Forest Road 300 just off Ariz. 260 and runs along the edge of the rim for 3.5 miles.

Forest Road 300 parallels the rim all the way to Ariz. 87, north of Strawberry. So, too, does a segment of the 138-mile **General Crook Trail,** which stretches from Dewey (east of Prescott) to Pinedale (between Heber and Show Low). This route was blazed in 1872 by Gen. George Crook, who traveled the rim in a campaign to subdue Apache tribes. General Crook preferred to ride mules, which were more surefooted than horses; today you can walk or ride a mountain bike along his historic route.

For more information on the region, contact Black Mesa Ranger District, Apache-Sitgreaves National Forests *(2748 Hwy. 260, Overgaard, AZ 85933. 520-535-4481. www.fs.fed.us/r3/asnf),* Blue Ridge Ranger District, Coconino National Forest *(HC 31, Box 300, Happy Jack, AZ 86024; 520-477-2255. www.fs.fed.us/r3/coconino),* or Payson Ranger District, Tonto National Forest *(1009 E. Hwy. 260. Payson, AZ 85541; 520-474-7900. www.fs.fed.us/r3/tonto).* ∎

Verde Wild and Scenic River

■ 40 miles ■ Central Arizona, southeast of Camp Verde ■ Rafting season usually March-April ■ Fishing, rafting, kayaking, canoeing ■ Contact Verde Ranger District, Prescott National Forest, P.O. Box 670, Camp Verde, AZ 86322; phone 520-567-4121. www.fs.fed.us/r3/prescott, or Payson Ranger District, Tonto National Forest, 1009 E. Hwy. 260, Payson, AZ 85541; phone 520-474-7900; or Cave Creek Ranger District, Tonto National Forest, 40202 N. Cave Creek Rd., Scottsdale, AZ 85262; phone 480-595-3300. www.fs.fed.us/r3/tonto

FROM ITS BEGINNINGS as intermittent desert washes and creeks below the Colorado Plateau, the Verde River runs south for 180 miles to join the Salt River just east of Phoenix, draining a substantial part of central Arizona along the way. Its watershed encompasses several tributaries, including Sedona's famed Oak Creek, Wet Beaver Creek, East Clear Creek, and the East Verde River.

A 40-mile middle stretch of the Verde has been designated as the state's only official Wild and Scenic River. During the late winter and early spring period of rains and snowmelt, depending on water level, the Verde provides an exciting white-water adventure for river runners; a leisurely short float can also be made downstream from the historic town of Camp Verde.

The scenic section of the Verde begins at Prescott National Forest's **Beasley Flats picnic area,** about 8 miles south of Camp Verde, and continues 18 miles to the tiny settlement of Childs. Class II and III rapids offer challenges to rafters, and **Verde Falls** can rate even higher, depending on the river's flow; experience and caution are needed—especially since, in case of trouble, help could be a long time arriving in this isolated area. To run this section requires a long shuttle on a steep, winding dirt road. Commercial rafting companies offer trips on the Verde, and local firms can provide shuttle service. For information on rafting possibilities, contact the Camp Verde Chamber of Commerce *(385 S. Main St., Camp Verde, AZ 86322. 520-567-9294).*

For those who would like to sample the Verde without running the Beasley-to-Childs section, the 8-mile trip from Camp Verde to Beasley Flats makes a relaxing day trip past cottonwoods and willows. Most of the land along the river here is private, but a public-access site located at the confluence of Clear Creek offers a chance to stop for lunch.

Downstream from Childs, the Verde enters the **Mazatzal Wilderness** part (see pp. 192-93) of Tonto National Forest, and for 22 miles becomes an official wild river, but even above the wilderness the river rewards rafters with picturesque bluffs and canyons.

A number of factors affect the Verde's level and floatability throughout the year; contact the local ranger districts of the Tonto or Prescott National Forests for advice before planning a trip. The ranger offices can also provide a detailed guide to the river. ■

Tonto Natural Bridge State Park

■ 160 acres ■ Central Arizona, 13 miles northwest of Payson off Ariz. 87
■ Best seasons spring and fall ■ Hiking ■ Adm. fee ■ Contact the park,
P.O. Box 1245, Payson, AZ 85547; phone 520-476-4202. www.pr.state.az.us

SOME PEOPLE CONSIDER geology a
rather dull subject, but such is definitely not the case at Tonto Natural Bridge State Park. This small
park, set in a steep-sided valley
below the Mogollon Rim, protects
what is believed to be the largest
travertine bridge in the world.
Don't imagine a freestanding arch;
instead, you'll find a tunnel 400
feet long, 183 feet high, and up to
150 feet wide—a huge, open-
ended cave, so to speak.

Around 300 million years ago,
a sea covering this region left
behind organic material that
formed a layer of limestone, topping previously accumulated
igneous rock. Faulting and erosion
later shaped **Pine Creek Canyon;**

Robust hedgehog cactus

water seeping through the limestone of the canyon wall created springs
that deposited a thick "dam" of travertine (formed from the dissolved calcium carbonate of limestone) in the canyon bottom. As more millennia
passed, **Pine Creek** wore through the dam, and the result was a mam
moth natural bridge, complete with stalactites and "draperies" like those
inside typical underground caves.

A walking path loops across the broad top of the bridge, with side
trails leading to four ground-level viewpoints offering varied perspectives
of the bridge. The **Gowan Loop Trail,** about a half mile long, leads rather
steeply down to Pine Creek and an observation deck for a look inside.
Spring water runs to the south end of the bridge and then spills off the
edge, creating a picturesque misty shower falling to the rocky creek bed.

At the north end of the parking lots, you'll find the **Pine Creek trailhead;** a developed path leads to the creek bed, where you can make your
way downstream (using caution on the slippery rocks) to the bridge, past
large boulders of purple sandstone. Along Pine Creek, note two trees with
distinctive appearances. Alligator juniper has blackish bark broken into
rectangular blocks like the hide of the animal whose name it shares; the
bark of smooth-bark Arizona cypress peels off in thin layers, exposing
smooth, reddish inner bark. ■

Mazatzal Wilderness

■ 252,500 acres ■ Central Arizona, 40 miles northeast of Phoenix off Ariz. 87
■ Best seasons spring and fall ■ Camping, hiking, horseback riding, fishing, hunt-
ing, bird-watching ■ Contact Payson Ranger District (east side), Tonto National
Forest, 1009 E. Hwy. 260, Payson, AZ 85541; phone 520-474-7900; or Cave
Creek Ranger District (west side), Tonto National Forest, 40202 N. Cave Creek
Rd., Scottsdale, AZ 85262; phone 480-595-3300. www.fs.fed.us/r3/tonto

AT MORE THAN A quarter million acres, Mazatzal is the largest national
forest wilderness area in Arizona. Its rugged mountains, the highest
Mazatzal Peak at 7,903 feet, rise beside scenic Ariz. 87 between Mesa and
Payson, tempting adventurous hikers to explore their canyons and ridges.
This is in large part remote and solitary country, though, so anyone venturing out on long hikes or backpacking trips should be sure of his or her
abilities, experience, and preparation.

Erosion-resistant rock of volcanic origin gives the eastern flanks of the
Mazatzal Mountains their steep aspect. Scrubby woods of pinyon pine,
oak, and juniper cover the lower reaches, with ponderosa pine above and
some Douglas-fir at the highest elevations. Black bears and mountain
lions range through the Mazatzals, the latter feeding primarily on mule
deer. Vegetation on the lower western side of the Mazatzals has a more
arid aspect, with saguaro cactus, ocotillo, paloverde, and other typical
Sonoran Desert plants growing on the slopes beside the **Verde River** (see
p. 190), which flows through the wilderness area for 22 miles.

The Mazatzal Wilderness is among the oldest in the Southwest, having
been given that status in 1940, and expanded in size in the years since.
Around 240 miles of trails wind through the area, some well-maintained
and relatively popular, others difficult to follow and seldom used. The
Mazatzal Divide Trail, the 29-mile path that's the major north-south
route through the wilderness, comprises a segment of the **Arizona Trail,**
which runs 790 miles from the Mexican border to Utah (see sidebar p.
248). Contact the ranger districts for information on trail conditions.

The most used routes into the wilderness begin on the east side of the
Wilderness at the Barnhardt trailhead, easily reached by turning west
from Ariz. 87 onto Forest Road 419 near the community of Rye. The road
climbs through grassland to a parking lot 4.7 miles from the highway,
within sight of the sheer cliffs of the **Mogollon Rim,** 20 miles to the
north. The **Barnhardt Trail** heads west through fairly open woods of
Emory oak, manzanita, one-seed juniper, alligator juniper, and pinyon
pine, with agave and sotol intermixed. You might see three "cousin" bird
species here: western scrub-jay, Steller's jay, and Mexican jay. The last
named, an Arizona specialty that roams in flocks of a dozen or more and
habitually gives its *week* call, lives here near the extreme northern edge of
its range. Overhead, their more distant relative the common raven utters
its croaking call, while noisy acorn woodpeckers flit from tree to tree. The
Barnhardt Trail climbs 1,800 feet into ponderosa pine forest to reach the

Mazatzal Divide Trail after 6.2 miles; this makes a nice day-hiking destination. At times in spring and after summer rains, two waterfalls provide a scenic diversion along the fairly strenuous trail ascent. Also beginning at the Barnhardt trailhead, but heading north, the **Half Moon Trail** is another good day hike, gaining only 300 feet in elevation on its 3-mile route to meet the **Rock Creek Trail,** which is a steep route up to the Mazatzal Divide.

Sheep Bridge, a picturesque suspension footbridge across the Verde River, is a favorite trailhead on the west side of the Mazatzal Wilderness; a long drive on one of two dirt roads is necessary to reach it, though, and a call to the Cave Creek Ranger District to inquire about road conditions is advisable before a trip. One route begins in Carefree and follows Cave Creek Road north 35 miles to Forest Road 269, which runs east 12 miles to a dead end at the river. The other leaves I-17 at the Bloody Basin exit and follows Forest Road 269 for 39 miles southeast to the bridge.

One popular destination from here is **Willow Spring,** 8 miles to the east, reached on a trail that climbs from desert vegetation into cooler oak-juniper woods. The **Verde River Trail** heads north from Sheep Bridge, continuing 28 miles to the northern boundary of the wilderness area. This low-elevation route is too hot for summer hiking; though a backpacking trip covering its entire length requires a long shuttle, hiking out and back, a shorter distance can make a good day or overnight trip in cool weather, offering the chance to experience Arizona's only officially designated Wild and Scenic river. ■

Sheep Bridge, Mazatzal Wilderness

Superstition Wilderness

■ 160,200 acres ■ Central Arizona, east of Apache Junction off Ariz. 88 and US 60 ■ Best seasons spring and fall. Hiking is inadvisable in summer ■ Camping, car camping, hiking, horseback riding ■ Parking fee at trailheads ■ Contact Mesa Ranger District, Tonto National Forest, P.O. Box 5800, Mesa, AZ 85211; phone 480-610-3300. www.fs.fed.us/r3/tonto

THERE ARE PLENTY OF reasons why the mountains of Superstition Wilderness in **Tonto National Forest** are such a popular destination for backpackers, day-hikers, and horseback riders. First, of course, is their location, just a short drive from Mesa, Scottsdale, and other suburbs of Phoenix. (Keep this in mind if you're thinking about visiting on a nice weekend from fall through spring, when trailhead parking lots can seem a little too mall-like.)

Second, these volcanic mountains have just the sort of rugged outline that inspires the imagination and invites exploration: What's behind those eroded bluffs and hills? What's the view like from that pass?

Then there's the evocative name, and to go with it a legend of lost gold that won't go away no matter how many times historians and geologists have debunked it. Top this off with a famous and visually striking

Weavers Needle, Superstition Wilderness

physical landmark and you have the Superstition Mountains, home of one of Arizona's most-visited wilderness areas.

With an elevation range of less than a mile, most of the Superstitions lack the desert-to-conifer (or Mexico-to-Canada) diversity of the southern "sky island" ranges. Nonetheless, the 160,200-acre Superstition Wilderness can provide challenging and rewarding hikes of varying lengths and solitude for those who go beyond weekend walks on its most popular trails.

More than 15 million years ago, massive volcanoes arose here, disgorging lava and ash over a wide area. After discharging their magma, these tall volcanoes eventually collapsed into their own empty interiors. Several of the resultant calderas overlap in the Superstitions, forming a jumble of volcano walls, lava flows, magma domes, and ash welded by its own heat into rock. All this has since been eroded into the steep cliffs, canyons, and craggy rock formations that characterize the range.

The best known site within the mountains, **Weavers Needle** raises its distinctively sloped point in the west-central Superstitions. Named for Paulino Weaver, a 19th-century trapper and miner, this eroded, sheer-sided spire has long been a regional landmark. It can be glimpsed from US 60, south of the range, but stands out dramatically from Ariz. 88 on the north, the federally designated **Apache Trail Scenic Byway.** This

"Jumping" Cholla

It surprises many people to learn that the angular, skeletonesque chollas are true cactuses. They're related to prickly pear, common over much of the United States. Some of the most familiar desert plants, chollas range from low mats to treelike forms 10 feet high.

Chain-fruit cholla and teddy bear cholla have terminal joints loosely connected to the rest of the plant. With their barbed spines, they easily attach themselves to passing animals (or hikers)—hence the folk name jumping cholla. This hitchhiking is means of propagation, since the separated joints root easily in favorable soil.

78-mile route winds east from Apache Junction through a stark desert landscape of rock, cactus, and narrow canyons. (Large recreational vehicles and trailers are not recommended on this sometimes tortuous road.)

A few ruins of Native American cliff dwellings still exist within the wilderness, and are of course fully protected by law. In the late 19th century, gold and other minerals were discovered nearby (the smaller Gold-field Mountains rise just to the west), but no mines were developed in the Superstitions. That didn't stop a legend from growing about a fabulous gold mine discovered by a German immigrant named Jacob Walz, who died in 1891, supposedly without revealing its location. In succeeding years, prospectors scoured the Super-stitions in search of the Lost Dutch-man Mine, guided by alleged clues left by Walz, or secret maps bought in the back rooms of saloons.

No one has ever found gold in the Superstition Mountains (except for the sunset glow of teddy bear cholla spines or the blooms of golden-flowered agave), and geologists say none is likely to be found. Historians have proven wrong some of the stories about Walz—yet the legend will probably live as long as people dream of instant wealth. The miner's name lives on at Lost Dutchman State Park (opposite), set on the western edge of the Superstitions.

The most popular portal into the Superstitions is the Peralta trail-head, accessed by taking a dirt road north from US 60, 8.5 miles east of Apache Junction. Three major routes branch out from the trailhead, including the very well used **Peralta Trail** up to **Fremont Saddle**—the most popular hike in the mountains. Many people hear that they can get a great view of Weavers Needle by walking a little over 2 miles, and often set out on this trail in midday, without water, with inappropriate footwear. As you return from the saddle (having, of course, hit the trail early in good shoes with plenty of water) you'll meet exhausted people asking, "How much farther is it?" and you'll reply, "Not too far, and it's worth it." This path ascends more than 1,300 feet in those 2 miles, and while it's not a difficult hike it's not just a relaxing stroll, either.

The Peralta Trail climbs a canyon through saguaro cactuses, acacias, paloverdes, jojobas, and scrub oaks, beneath palisades of rock eroded into weird and wonderful shapes. At the 3,760-foot **Fremont Saddle,** Weavers Needle rises to the north, shaped a little like a thumb tip. From other angles it has a more bifurcated aspect.

Hikers prepared for a strenuous 12-mile day hike, or for an overnight trip, can make a loop around Weavers Needle by continuing north on the Peralta Trail to the **Dutchman's Trail,** curving east to the **Terrapin Trail,** and then heading south to join the **Bluff Spring Trail** back to the trailhead. Sections of this route, especially the Terrapin Trail, can be hard to follow, so take an adequate map and know your own skills before setting out. You can also leave the Peralta trailhead on the Bluff Spring Trail and continue north on the Terrapin Trail to **Terrapin Pass** for a great view of Weavers Needle: a one-way route of 4.4 miles that's more difficult, but far less used, than the hike to Fremont Saddle.

The **First Water trailhead,** another popular entryway into the western Superstitions, is reached by driving northeast 3.5 miles from Apache Junction on Ariz. 88 and turning right onto a dirt road that winds 3 miles to a parking lot. Many different trails offer possibilities for loop trips, and those who arrange a shuttle can make one-way hikes to the Peralta trailhead or the **Canyon Lake trailhead,** 12.5 miles farther along Ariz. 88.

One popular day hike from First Water leads 3 miles to **Black Mesa,** a lava-capped ridge with a great perspective of Weavers Needle to the southeast. To make a loop, rather than an out-and-back hike, continue on the **Black Mesa Trail** to its intersection with the Dutchman's Trail, whence return to the First Water Trailhead for a route of about 9 miles.

Just south of the turn from Ariz. 88 to the First Water Trailhead is the entrance to 320-acre **Lost Dutchman State Park** (*5 miles NE of Apache Junction off Ariz. 88. 480-982-4485. www.pr.state.az.us. Adm. fee).* This site makes a good base for RVers or car campers. There's a short nature walk at the entrance that introduces a variety of desert plants, and trails branch out from the park into the wilderness area. The **Siphon Draw Trail** leads 1.6 miles up to the Basin (gaining 1,000 feet of elevation), with tremendous views along the way of Phoenix to the west.

While some trails in these mountains are well used and some routes are fairly short, don't underestimate the potential difficulties of travel here. This is true desert country, and water may not be available even at marked creeks and springs. Temperatures rise quickly in summer to well over 100°F. In the monsoon season (July through September), lightning can be a danger in exposed places and normally dry washes and canyons become fast-flowing rivers with frightening speed. Even if you're an experienced hiker elsewhere in the country, know the dangers of travel in this arid terrain before you set out.

If you're unsure of your desert wilderness skills but still want to see the Superstition backcountry, consider a horseback trip. Local outfitters can arrange pack trips with a guide, food, and camping gear, so all you need is the proper clothing. Contact the Tonto National Forest office in Mesa for names of outfitters. ∎

Following pages: Brittlebush below the cliffs of the Superstition Mountains

Boyce Thompson Arboretum State Park

■ 323 acres ■ South-central Arizona, 3 miles west of Superior on US 60 ■ Year round ■ Hiking, bird-watching, plant study ■ Adm. fee ■ Contact the park, 37615 U.S. Hwy. 60, Superior, AZ 85273; phone 520-689-2811. arboretum.ag.arizona.edu

Cactus garden, Boyce Thompson Arboretum State Park

SET AMONG RUGGED hills of volcanic ash and lava, this combination state park and research facility is well worth a day trip from Phoenix. Visitors with a serious interest in desert botany can spend happy hours wandering the trails, studying flora from around the world; arid-country residents can pick up information on gardening with plants that require little water; nature lovers can get a good introduction to species of the Sonoran Desert; and even those with little interest in reading plant labels will enjoy a beautiful and relaxing stroll around the arboretum trails.

The arboretum was founded in the 1920s with the goal of increasing public appreciation of the value of plants. Now jointly managed by the University of Arizona, Arizona State Parks, and the arboretum's private nonprofit corporation, the garden has become one of the leading desert research institutions in the country.

After stopping at the visitor center, take the trail through displays of drought- and heat-tolerant landscaping plants down toward **Silver King Wash,** where the path divides to make a loop totaling 1.5 miles. The trail circles around **Magma Ridge** beneath **Picketpost Mountain,** a lava-capped peak of tuff, or volcanic ash compressed into rock. Side trails lead to displays of Sonoran and Chihuahuan Desert plants and through gardens with dazzling arrays of cactuses, from compact species smaller than your hand to columnar species such as saguaro and barrel cactus. Everyone enjoys the bizarre, towering boojum tree—not a cactus but a relative of the common ocotillo—which appears to have forgotten that its roots should grow into the ground, not up in the air.

On the far side of Magma Ridge, the trail passes alongside **Queen Creek,** through an area with riparian trees such as Fremont cottonwoods, Arizona ashes, Arizona walnuts, and willows. An herb garden, a eucalyptus forest, and a legume garden (which includes common Arizona trees such as acacia and paloverde) are a few of the other attractions.

With its varied plantings, the arboretum attracts an excellent variety of wildlife, from birds to butterflies to lizards. Look for hummingbirds around blooming plants and for waterbirds at **Ayer Lake.** ■

White Mountains

■ 2.1 million acres ■ Eastern Arizona, south and west of Springerville ■ Best months April-Oct. Many recreation areas closed by snow in winter, when roads can be hazardous ■ Camping, hiking, fishing, mountain biking, cross-country skiing, bird-watching, wildlife viewing, ■ Contact Apache-Sitgreaves National Forests, P.O. Box 640, Springerville, AZ 85938; phone 520-333-4301. www.fs.fed.us/r3/asnf

GENERALLY SPEAKING, the White Mountains remain little known to out-of-staters, and that's just fine with most Arizonans. Let the tourists head for the Grand Canyon and the Painted Desert: The campgrounds, trails and streams of these highlands on the New Mexico border see enough traffic as it is. In fact, if a poll were taken asking outdoorsy Arizonans to pick their favorite getaway spot, the White Mountains just might win.

What's the attraction here? Better, maybe, to ask what isn't here. You can find dense coniferous forests, broad meadows, beautiful creeks, varied wilderness areas, excellent trails, scenic byways, mountain biking, winter sports, some of the state's best fishing, and abundant wildlife. Wildflower lovers and bird-watchers enjoy the diversity of the White Mountains, and even butterfly-watchers consider this area a hot spot for the number of resident species they can see in summer and fall.

Looking at a physical map, you might imagine the White Mountains to be part of the Mogollon Rim (see sidebar pp. 188-189), the escarpment that marks the southern edge of the Colorado Plateau. In fact, these mountains are the result of tremendous volcanic eruptions in the Tertiary period, more than five million years ago. Huge stratovolcanoes poured out thick lava and spewed ash over a vast area; the tallest of them is today's Mount Baldy, with its highest point, Baldy Peak, at 11,403 feet. The resulting mass of igneous material completely buries a substantial segment of the Mogollon Rim. Later, the mountains were shaped by glaciers, which cut U-shaped valleys in their higher reaches. In many years the White Mountains are among the snowiest places in Arizona, and high-elevation trails can remained covered through May or longer.

Mountain lions, black bears, pronghorn, mule and white-tailed deer, beavers, porcupines, and Abert's and red squirrels are just a few of the mammals found in the White Mountains, which also have some of the highest populations of elk to be found in the Southwest. But in recent years the most notable four-legged resident has been the Mexican race of the gray wolf, reintroduced here in the late 1990s amid much controversy (see sidebar pp. 204-205). Birders visit this area to search for species such as peregrine falcon, wild turkey, blue grouse, spotted owl, three-toed woodpecker, gray catbird, golden-crowned kinglet, and pine grosbeak.

Most of the White Mountains region lies within the jointly administered Apache-Sitgreaves National Forests, which have district offices in Springerville, Alpine, Clifton, Overgaard, and Pinetop-Lakeside. Bordering the national forests on the west is the reservation of the White Mountain Apache, who require permits for outdoor activities on their land. These are available at stores along US 60 and Ariz. 260 *(contact White Mountain Apache Tribe Game and Fish Department. 520-338-4385).*

Bear in mind that weekends and holidays can see campgrounds filled, lakes crowded with anglers, and wilderness trails lacking in solitude. When planning a trip, consider visiting in the fall when the aspen leaves are turning gold and fewer people are in the woods.

What to See and Do

Ariz. 260 and US 191 provide the major access to the White Mountains, meeting at the adjoining towns of Springerville and Eagar. The latter road is an attraction in its own right, officially designated the **Coronado Trail Scenic Byway.** Beginning at the national forest boundary near Clifton on the south at an elevation of about 6,400 feet, the road tops 9,000 feet on its 123-mile route north to Eagar. Great views are common along the way, most notably from the watchtower at **Rose Peak** (8,786 feet) and from the **Blue Vista** (9,184 feet), both with far-reaching panoramas

across mountains and lowlands.

In the vicinity of Blue Vista are several trailheads providing access eastward into the **Blue Range Primitive Area**, a 173,762-acre tract of rugged backcountry, bisected by the **Blue River,** where Mexican gray wolves have been reintroduced. ("Primitive area" was a federal term for a wilderness before the modern designation was created; in part because of today's political climate, the Blue Range has never been classified as a true wilderness, though it is managed as such.) Mountain lions, black bears, and elk roam here, and so do hunters and serious

Morning clouds over the Blue Range Primitive Area

backpackers; trails in the Blue Range are sometimes less well marked than elsewhere in the national forest, and map-reading skills are useful.

Forest Road 281, south of US 180, leads into the heart of the Blue Range, with side trails providing opportunities for short hikes. The **Blue River Valley** is at lower elevation than other parts of the White Mountains, and its trails are usually clear when many others are snow covered. Native American petroglyphs have been found in several spots; some are visible at the **Blue Crossing Campground,** on Forest Road 281 just north of the primitive area boundary.

Hannagan Meadow, a short distance north of Blue Vista, can swarm with butterflies in summer, including such beautiful species as Ferris's copper (a White Mountains endemic), Weidemeyer's admiral, hoary comma, California tortoiseshell, California sister, and Mormon metalmark. In winter, this area becomes a popular spot for cross-country skiing, with groomed trails attractive to skiers of all levels. Farther north, west of the town of Alpine, **Williams Valley** also offers fine cross-country skiing, and, like Hannagan Meadow, is great for mountain biking in the warmer months.

Northeast of Alpine you'll find one of the most beautiful spots in the White Mountains, great for mountain bikers, hikers, and as a scenic drive. Take Forest Road 56 east from US 191 to reach **Terry Flat,** where a 9-mile loop circles a broad meadow. (This unpaved road is bumpy at times, but is usually passable for cars; it's also a nice bike loop.) A 1951 fire in this area burned 23,000 acres, and the aspens that have grown up since

Mexican Gray Wolves

WOLVES evoke strong and divergent emotions in humans. Some people look into their expressive eyes and see the very essence of wildness, less an animal than a mystical symbol of freedom. They buy wolf T-shirts, put wolf posters on their walls, and even listen to recordings of wolf calls.

Other people have a seemingly visceral hatred of wolves, looking on them as vicious killers, and on their presence as a threat to humans and domestic animals. Their reaction, on hearing of a wolf in the vicinity, might be to reach for a gun.

Ecologists can afford neither sentimentality nor prejudice when they study our environment. They're likely to look on the wolf as an intelligent animal with an intricate social system that functions as a vital part of certain healthy ecosystems. They see areas in the American West where burgeoning elk populations are overgrazing and damaging their habitat, and they note the absence of a top predator that once preyed on them. They acknowledge that wolves do kill sheep, cattle, and other livestock, but see such attacks as a natural response to human invasion of territory that was once the wolf's, not as evidence of bloodthirstiness.

Unrelenting persecution by shooting, trapping, and poisoning caused the extirpation of the Mexican gray wolf (a subspecies of the gray wolf found in many parts of the Northern Hemisphere) in the Southwest by the mid-20th century. A few wolves

Mexican gray wolf

occasionally wandered across the border from Mexico, but even there the wolf was believed to have disappeared by 1980. For many years the only Mexican gray wolves known to exist lived in zoos and wildlife sanctuaries.

That changed in 1998, when the first wolves were reintroduced into the wild in the Blue Range of eastern Arizona, in what is known as the Blue Range Wolf Recovery Area in Apache-Sitgreaves National Forests. Wolves used in the program come from genetically pure sources in the United States and Mexico and are raised under conditions carefully designed to encourage wild behavior and minimize contact with humans. Wolves being considered for release live in natural settings in their normal social groups and are fed mainly road-killed native prey such as deer and elk.

The major site for captive wolf management is Sevilleta National Wildlife Refuge in New Mexico, a site closed to the public. Mexican gray wolves can be viewed, however, at several regional zoos including Albuquerque Biological Park, Living Desert Zoo and Gardens State Park at Carlsbad, New Mexico (see p. 115), the Arizona-Sonoran Desert Museum at Tucson (see pp. 256-57), and the Phoenix Zoo.

The release of 13 animals in two packs was part of a strategy to have a "viable, self-sustaining population of at least 100 Mexican wolves" in the species' historic range by 2005, according to the U.S. Fish and Wildlife Service's recovery plan. One hundred wolves don't seem like much of a threat to ranching and commerce in the American Southwest, but livestock growers (and politicians influenced by ranching money) reacted with virulence to the wolf recovery plan. Public hearings often turned into emotional battlefields, with wolf supporters and opponents angrily facing off before wildlife officials legally charged under the Endangered Species Act with ensuring the wolf's survival. Counties in New Mexico passed laws forbidding the release of wolves, knowing that federal rule superseded local regulations. Livestock growers and local governments have filed suit against the U.S. Fish and Wildlife Service to stop the wolf program, while a coalition of wildlife and conservation groups has intervened on behalf of the wolves to support reintroductions.

Despite the controversy, wolf restoration has continued. More wolves were released in 1999, and in 2000 two packs from Arizona were translocated to Gila National Forest (see pp. 134-140) in New Mexico. The program has had ups and downs: A few wolves have been shot (arrests have been made in one case), a couple have been killed by mountain lions, and one was killed by a car. As ranchers feared, wolves have killed livestock in both Arizona and New Mexico; in confirmed instances of wolf predation, owners have been repaid with funds from a private environmental group. U.S. Fish and Wildlife officials still face mostly hostile crowds at hearings whenever the issue is debated.

There are plenty of people, though, who dream of a time when the howl of the wolf will be heard again in the American Southwest. They believe the nearly 4.4 million acres of the Blue Range Wolf Recovery Area ought to be able to sustain several packs of Mexican gray wolves living freely and naturally in the wild. They think that a species that has appropriated so much of the world ought to find a way to share part of it with an animal that was here for thousands of years.

provide a truly spectacular sight in fall, when their leaves turn gold.

Just north of Terry Flat rises 10,912-foot **Escudilla Mountain,** the third highest peak in Arizona and the heart of the 5,200-acre **Escudilla Mountain Wilderness.** An easy trail to the top of this extinct volcano rises 1,300 feet in 3.3 miles, beginning in an aspen grove and continuing up into coniferous forest. Along the trail you'll pass through meadows dotted with wildflowers including sego lilies, Indian paintbrushes, cinquefoils, Rocky Mountain irises, yellow columbines, and many others.

White Mountains Scenic Byway

Some of the White Mountains' most popular areas lie south of Ariz. 260, part of the **White Mountains Scenic Byway.** The byway is a 123-mile route that loops through forests of ponderosa and southwestern white pine, Douglas-fir, blue and Engelmann spruce, subalpine and white fir, and aspen, with grassland interspersed. About 6 miles west of Eagar, look for the turnoff to the **South Fork Campground,** one of the best local birding areas. The campground takes its name from the South Fork Little Colorado River—the same river, in fact, that enters the Grand Canyon 200 miles to the northwest. American dippers can often be seen along the stream, where an "eastern" species, gray catbird, nests in riparian vegetation. At the end of the road, the **South Fork Trail** leads 7 miles up a canyon to **Mexican Hay Lake.** Peregrine falcons and spotted owls both breed in this area, and the beautiful trail makes a great hike

Forested land along the Little Colorado River, Apache-Sitgreaves National Forests

even for nonbirders, passing through a woodland of ponderosa pines, alligator junipers, Arizona sycamores, oaks, and aspens. If you can arrange a shuttle, walking from Mexican Hay Lake on Ariz. 261 down to the lower trailhead makes the 1,500-foot elevation change (from 9,000 to 7,500 feet) easier on the lungs.

About 8 miles farther west along Ariz. 260, the **Pole Knoll Recreation Area** comprises a series of loop trails best known for cross-country skiing, but also offering good hiking and mountain-biking possibilities. Just a few miles farther west you'll find the trailhead for the **Railroad Grade Trail,** a 21-mile path that follows an abandoned logging railroad route south to the Big Lake Recreation Area (intervening trailheads make shorter hikes possible).

Mount Baldy Wilderness

Probably the most popular hikes in the White Mountains are the two trails leading into **Mount Baldy Wilderness.** The **West Baldy Trail** is reached by turning south from Ariz. 260 onto Ariz. 273 and driving 9 miles to the spot known as Sheep's Crossing; continue another 3 miles to the start of the **East Baldy Trail.** Both hikes follow lovely little creeks (the west fork and east fork of the Little Colorado River, respectively) for part of their 7 miles up to join at a spot 200 feet below the rocky summit of **Baldy Peak.** (The summit lies within the White Mountain Apache Reservation and is considered sacred by that tribe; do not continue higher than the wilderness boundary, no matter how

tempting it is to reach the mountaintop.) By hiking up one trail and down the other and then taking a trail connecting the two you can make a loop of about 18 miles, gaining and losing about 1,900 feet of elevation.

Look for beavers as you walk along the streams, where trout await those who've packed in a fishing pole. Ponderosa pines, Engelmann and blue spruces, subalpine (corkbark form) and white firs, and aspens alternate with open meadows full of wildflowers. High-country birds such as blue grouse, three-toed woodpecker, gray jay, Clark's nutcracker, and pine grosbeak might be found here, though none are common and a sighting of even one should be considered lucky. More likely are species such as Steller's jay, gray-headed junco, western tanager, pygmy nuthatch, and brown creeper. Elk are often seen along the trails, and in fall the bugling of males adds to the experience of hiking in the wilderness.

Continue south on Ariz. 273 to the very popular **Big Lake Recreation Area,** where you'll find campsites and hiking and mountain-bike trails. **Big Lake** is one of many small lakes in the area that attract anglers hoping to catch trout and Arctic grayling.

North of Big Lake stretches a tract of about 10,000 acres of grassland, with only scattered patches of forest growing mostly on north-facing slopes. Although the reason for this mostly treeless expanse is still debated, some scientists believe the soil has had insufficient time to develop since the most recent volcanic activity. ■

Sky Islands and the Arizona Desert

Dune evening primrose and sand verbena,
Sonoran Desert in Cabeza Prieta National Wildlife Refuge

WHAT ON EARTH are "sky islands," and how did they come to rise amid southern Arizona's desert country? To answer that question, you need to look back in time eight million years and more, when geologic forces shaped this part of the state.

Here, as throughout much of the country west of the Rockies, stresses deep underground pulled apart the Earth's crust along fault lines, causing great blocks to drop thousands of feet; adjoining blocks tilted, raising

one edge skyward. During this slow process, the tops of the uplifted mountains were constantly being eroded into the adjacent sunken valleys, filling them with rocks and gravel and creating broad, flat plains. The result was a series of isolated mountain ranges surrounded by lowlands—high, forested islands in a sea of scrub and arid grassland.

Not all of southern Arizona's mountains were built this way; some rose earlier through upwelling of magma from far below the surface, and others were the result of massive volcanoes. But these, too, formed disjunct ranges that today comprise similar sky islands of high-elevation flora and fauna.

Southwestern and south-central Arizona lie within the Sonoran Desert, typified by the distinctive multiarmed saguaro cactus, whose beautiful white bloom is the state flower. Two of the finest showcases for the Sonoran Desert are Saguaro National Park, near Tucson, and Organ Pipe Cactus National Monument, south of Ajo. Both offer driving routes and hiking trails that let you experience the beauty of this exceptional environment. While the Mojave and Great Basin deserts receive most of

their rain in winter, the Sonoran has two rainy seasons: Summer "monsoon" rains bring a virtual second spring to the desert, allowing a great and surprising diversity of life to exist and even flourish in this often barren-looking landscape.

"Diversity," indeed, might be the one-word motto of southern Arizona. The proximity of 9,000-foot mountains wooded with ponderosa pines, Douglas-firs, and spruces to deserts dotted with creosote bush and cactus makes it possible to experience a great range of habitats within a very short distance. It's feasible—and very enjoyable—to hike along a desert wash in the cool dawn, and by the time midday heat arrives to be walking through shady high-elevation coniferous forest. The Chiricahuas, the Pinaleños, the Huachucas, the Santa Ritas, the Santa Catalinas—all offer this kind of desert-to-peak experience, in some cases only by hiking, and in others along a road, making the array of life zones accessible to all. The Sky Island Scenic Byway just outside Tucson is the most often traveled route to the high country, offering spectacular vistas as it winds 27 miles up Mount Lemmon.

Mexican poppies at Organ Pipe Cactus National Monument

Riparian (streamside) zones serve as linear oases in this arid land; they're among the most ecologically valuable, and most endangered, habitats in the Southwest. A high percentage of all species found in the region depend to some degree on riparian areas, which too often have been destroyed or degraded by dams, grazing, lowering of the water table, and assorted other factors. Several parks and natural areas protect remnant riparian tracts, including the San Pedro Riparian National Conservation Area (a site whose tremendous conservation value is far out of proportion to its prominence), Aravaipa Canyon, and the Nature Conservancy's Patagonia-Sonoita Creek and Hassayampa River Preserves. No nature-oriented trip to southern Arizona is complete without seeing one or more of these streamside areas, which provide invaluable refuges for fish, amphibians, reptiles, birds, and mammals extirpated from parts of their original ranges.

On the western edge of Arizona, the Colorado River has suffered as greatly as any stream in America from dams, levees, irrigation schemes, and other human-instigated factors. Once a swath of lush greenery in the hottest and driest part of the Sonoran Desert, it flows now as a tamed vestige of its former vigorous self, having lost a number of native species and been invaded by alien replacements. By visiting four national wildlife

Kofa National Wildlife Refuge

refuges strung along its lower reaches, and by using your imagination more than a little, you can figuratively reconstruct the old Colorado and thereby understand the importance of present protection and restoration efforts. All the refuges offer fine wildlife viewing, especially of wetland and riparian-habitat birds.

The list of southern Arizona's natural riches also includes grasslands that are home to pronghorn and several characteristic bird species. The Empire-Cienega Resource Conservation Area, southeast of Tucson, and Buenos Aires National Wildlife Refuge, west of Nogales, both provide an opportunity to explore this environment, where broad expanses of grasses glow golden tan much of the year but turn green with the arrival of summer monsoons.

Not all the region's attractions lie on the surface. Since its opening in 1999, Kartchner Caverns State Park, south of Benson, has been one of Arizona's most popular destinations, filled with spectacular formations in a multitude of colors.

So much, then, for the stereotypical idea that southern Arizona means desert. As fascinating and varied as that environment is, there's far more to the region than Sonoran plants and animals—enough to fill any naturalist's calendar for a vacation, a year, or a lifetime. ■

Chiricahua Mountains

■ 284,051 acres ■ Southeast Arizona, 35 miles southeast of Willcox
■ Best months April-Oct. ■ Camping, hiking, bird-watching, wildlife viewing
■ Adm. fee for national monument, user fee for national forest ■ High-elevation roads and recreation areas may be closed in winter ■ Contact Douglas Ranger District, Coronado National Forest, 3081 N. Leslie Canyon Rd., Douglas, AZ 85607, phone 520-364-3468; or Chiricahua National Monument, HCR 2, Box 6500, Willcox, AZ 85643, phone 520-824-3560. www.nps.gov/chir (national monument)

MANY THOUSANDS OF WORDS have been written about southern Arizona's "sky islands," but nothing can define that term like a long-distance view of the Chiricahuas. Seen from the flat Sulphur Springs or San Simon Valleys, these peaks soar more than a mile into the air, rising abruptly from the surrounding desert like jagged oceanic islands. Instantly you understand how these highlands can be home to plants and animals living in isolation, miles from others of their kind.

Cochise and Geronimo, leaders of the Chiricahua Apache, used the canyons of the Chiricahuas, and of the Dragoon Mountains to the west, as bases from which to attack the U.S. military forces who were trying to move the Apache onto reservations in the 1880s. As you explore this land, you'll see how hard it must have been to pursue the great warriors in the rugged terrain they knew well.

The human turmoils of the late 19th century were devastating to the Apache, but they pale next to the geological events of 27 million years ago, when volcanic eruptions formed the great bulk of the Chiricahuas' rocks. Something like the explosion of Mount St. Helens, only a thousand times more powerful, these eruptions spewed unimaginable amounts of ash and magma onto the surface. As the igneous material cooled, it formed the rhyolite of the Chiricahuas. Over time, erosion has created picturesque cliffs, pillars, and other formations throughout the area, making this one of southern Arizona's most scenic spots.

The most spectacular of these rock sculptures can be seen at Chiricahua National Monument, on the west side of the range. A scenic drive and 20 miles of hiking trails lead you through this striking landscape, including the geological fantasyland known as Heart of Rocks.

The great bulk of the Chiricahua Mountains lies within a division of Coronado National Forest, which provides campgrounds, picnic areas, hiking trails, and a dirt, but well-maintained, road that goes up and over the range, offering grand views along the way. The highest summits can be found within the Chiricahua Wilderness, an 87,000-acre area crisscrossed by trails and topped by Chiricahua Peak, rising to 9,759 feet. In 1994, an intense blaze called the Rattlesnake Fire burned nearly 28,000 acres here, blackening expanses of forest, causing extensive erosion, and

San Simon Valley, Chiricahua National Monument

ruining trails. While much mature woodland was destroyed, hikers in the high Chiricahuas can now witness the natural process of recovery, with wildflowers, shrubs, and young trees growing vigorously where a dense coniferous forest once stood.

A visitor to the Chiricahuas can easily sample an array of habitat types, from riparian woodland up through the oak-juniper zone and into coniferous forest with Douglas-fir, Engelmann spruce, and aspen. Both Apache and Chihuahua pine, two species with very limited ranges in the United States, grow commonly here.

Mountain lions and black bears roam the Chiricahuas, though they're seen here as seldom as elsewhere; the former often preys on white-tailed deer (of the small Coues variety), while the latter eats anything from berries and nuts to small mammals. Coatimundis travel in troops of a dozen or more at a time, and it's great fun to come across a band of these raccoonlike mammals climbing through the trees, bearing more than a little resemblance to monkeys. Look in pine-oak woods for the Chiricahua fox squirrel, a reddish species that's a specialty of these mountains. At the small end of the size spectrum, keep an eye out for the Chiricahua white, a butterfly whose U.S. range includes only southeastern Arizona and a small part of New Mexico. A resident of the pine forest, this butterfly species is strongly sexually dimorphic: Males are white and black, females orange and black.

The Chiricahuas are a celebrated destination among bird-watchers; in fact, from the little town of Portal on up to Rustler Park, you're bound to come across groups of binocular-toters, scanning the trees for some of the unusual species found here. Perhaps the most famed bird in these mountains is the elegant trogon, a gorgeous red-and-green creature that's one of the most highly prized finds in the region. Less showy but just as special is the Mexican chickadee, a mite of a bird that barely crosses the

Return of El Tigre?

Top predator throughout much of Mexico and Central and South America, the jaguar once also ranged through much of the Southwest, preying on deer, javelinas, coatimundis, rabbits, wild turkeys, and just about anything else it could catch. Essentially extirpated from the United States in the mid-20th century for killing livestock and for the black-market trade in its beautiful fur, the jaguar was seen afterward only as an extremely rare stray along the Mexican border.

In 1996, though, photographs confirmed two jaguar sightings in Arizona: one in the Peloncillo Mountains along the New Mexico border, and another in the Baboquivari Mountains west of the Chiricahuas. Because the big cat was thought not to occur in the U.S., it wasn't covered under the Endangered Species Act—an oversight corrected the next year. Now, many wildlife enthusiasts in the Southwest hope el tigre will appear again in our country's fauna and spread through Arizona's sky islands.

Mexican border into the high Chiricahuas. The list of other noteworthy birds is long and includes zone-tailed hawks, flammulated owls, magnificent and blue-throated hummingbirds (the latter the largest hummers in the United States), Strickland's woodpeckers, sulphur-bellied flycatchers, olive and red-faced warblers, and painted redstarts.

For beauty, geological interest, and wildlife, the Chiricahuas deserve their place among Arizona's most inviting natural areas. There's no better place to begin exploring the state's magnificent sky islands than here.

What to See and Do

Chiricahua National Monument

You'll understand the attraction of Chiricahua National Monument before you reach the entrance station. There's much to see along the 8-mile **Bonita Canyon Drive** up to 6,870-foot Massai Point, but you'll also want to get out and walk some of the park's trails. The hike to the top of **Sugarloaf Mountain** gains an easy 500 feet of elevation in 0.9 mile and the reward is a great panorama, including a view of famed Cochise Head, a profile crest 4 miles to the northeast.

It's a fairly difficult hike of about 3 miles one way to get to the **Heart of Rocks** area, where a 1-mile trail loops past such formations as **Pinnacle Balanced Rock, Punch and Judy,** and **Duck on a Rock.** Here you'll certainly see why the Apache called this area the Land of Standing-Up Rocks. There's great scenery, too, along the **Echo Canyon Trail,** a popular 3.5-mile loop that incorporates the **Hailstone Trail,** where you'll see volcanic hailstones. These unique objects formed as balls of mud in the swirl of erupting gas and ash.

From the national monument, drive south and then east on Pinery Canyon Road to reach the upper Chiricahuas. Take it slow and enjoy the views as you climb a half-mile in elevation in the 14 miles to **Onion Saddle.** (This winding dirt road is not suitable for large RVs or trailers.) At the saddle, turn south to reach the campground and picnic area at **Rustler Park,** 8,500 feet high.

Chiricahua Wilderness

Here, among pines, Douglas-firs, and aspens, trails head south into the **Chiricahua Wilderness,** administered by the Coronado National Forest. Many options for hikes and backpacking trips are available here, including a 4-mile walk to **Centella Point,** with great views into Cave Creek Canyon. Simply hiking a couple of miles toward Long Park will get you into areas that show signs of the big 1994 Rattlesnake Fire. Look for Mexican chickadees and red-faced warblers in the trees around Rustler Park.

The views are even better as you head down the slope on the east side of the Chiricahuas; take care on the narrow road as it passes from the high coniferous forest through pinyon-oak-juniper habitat to the lush woodland along **Cave Creek.** Just past the Sunny

Following pages: Echo Canyon Trail, Chiricahua National Monument

Flat Campground, turn south to reach the **South Fork Picnic Area,** one of the most famous bird-watching sites in America. Listen here for the hoarse *co-ah* call of the elegant trogon, especially where Arizona sycamores grow.

From South Fork, the 1.6-mile walk up a beautiful creek to **Maple Camp** offers great riparian habitat and excellent birding. As you walk through a forest of pine, Arizona walnut, velvet ash, silverleaf and Emory oak, Arizona cypress, and bigtooth maple, listen for the "squeeze-toy" call of sulphur-bellied flycatchers and watch for lovely painted redstarts.

Many other trails lead into the Chiricahua Wilderness. Some of the most popular begin near Rucker Lake Campground (*from US 191 4 miles N of Elfrida, go E on Rucker Canyon Rd. for 27 miles, then take FR 74 and 74E).* Strenu-ous hikes lead to the top of **Chir-icahua Peak;** for an easy day hike through superb scenery, follow the **Rucker Canyon Trail** upstream for 2.5 miles before returning. ■

Hikers in grottoes, Chiricahua National Monument

Muleshoe Ranch Cooperative Management Area

■ 49,120 acres ■ Southeast Arizona, 30 miles northwest of Willcox off Airport Rd. ■ Best months Sept.-May ■ Camping, hiking, horseback riding, bird-watching, wildlife viewing ■ Dirt access road can be muddy after rain; call ahead for conditions ■ Contact the management area, R.R. 1, Box 1542, Willcox, AZ 85643; phone 520-586-7072

VARIED REWARDS AWAIT WITHIN this tract of desert and mountains, set in the transition zone between the Sonoran and Chihuahuan Deserts. Day visitors can explore canyons where deciduous trees and shrubs line streamsides, while backpackers and horseback riders can range through semidesert grasslands or up into the rugged Galiuro Mountains, wild home of bighorn sheep, black bears, mountain lions, and golden eagles.

The "cooperative" in Muleshoe Ranch's name indicates an unusual agreement among the Nature Conservancy, the Bureau of Land Management, and the Forest Service, which share supervision. The most valuable treasures under their joint custody here are seven streams, five of them perennial, that create oases of riparian habitat in arid surroundings of desert grassland and scrub. Native fish are threatened everywhere in Arizona, but species such as speckled dace and Gila chub find sanctuary in Muleshoe's creeks.

On arrival, check in at the Nature Conservancy visitor center, where you can pick up a trail map and learn of recent wildlife sightings. An adjacent 0.75-mile nature trail makes a good introduction to Muleshoe; you might spot white-tailed or mule deer, and birding can be excellent in the woodland of velvet mesquite, netleaf hackberry, and Arizona walnut.

From the visitor center, walk or drive (four-wheel drive needed) a mile north along Jackson Cabin Road to **Bass Canyon,** a beautiful area with abundant wildlife. By walking down Bass Canyon and then back up **Hot Springs Wash** to the visitor center you can make a loop hike of about 3 miles. Zone-tailed hawks, common black-hawks, and gray hawks nest in the vicinity, along with other species including ladder-backed woodpeckers, black phoebes, bridled titmice, black-tailed gnatcatchers, and pyrrhuloxias, to name only a few. You might also see (or smell) javelinas or hognose skunks or come across a lumbering desert tortoise.

Rental cabins near the visitor center make it easy to explore Muleshoe at dawn, when wildlife is most active; as a bonus, lodgers can enjoy a dip in the ranch's natural hot springs. Those who prefer a wilder experience can head north to the BLM's **Redfield Canyon Wilderness** (*Safford Field Office, Bureau of Land Management, 711 14th Ave., Safford, AZ 85546. 520-348-4400*) or Coronado National Forest's **Galiuro Wilderness** (*Safford Ranger District, P.O. Box 709, Safford, AZ 85548. 520-428-4150*), where miles of trails offer solitude for those prepared for rugged travel. ■

Pinaleño Mountains rising above Roper Lake State Park

Pinaleño Mountains

■ 198,000 acres ■ Southeast Arizona, southwest of Safford off US 191
■ Best months June-Aug. ■ Camping, hiking, fishing, mountain biking, bird-watching, wildlife viewing ■ Camping fee ■ High-elevation recreation areas and visitor center closed in winter ■ Contact Safford Ranger District, Coronado National Forest, P.O. Box 709, Safford, AZ 85548; phone 520-428-4150

THE PINALEÑO MOUNTAINS rise 8,000 feet above the cotton fields along the Gila River to their north, topping out at 10,720-foot Mount Graham—the highest peak in southern Arizona. Located in the center of a triangle formed by the better known White, Chiricahua, and Santa Catalina Mountains, the massive Pinaleños are too often overlooked by travelers in the region, despite their rewarding natural features.

As you might imagine from the great elevational range they span, the Pinaleños compose an equally great diversity of flora and fauna. In the desert foothills around their base, typical vegetation includes velvet mesquites, ocotillos, sotols, Schott's yuccas, chollas, prickly pear cactuses, and creosotebushes. Above, a scrubby woodland of oaks, junipers, and manzanitas takes over, succeeded by silverleaf oaks and ponderosa pines (both the typical three-needled form and the five-needled variety called Arizona pine) and, at high elevations, Douglas-firs, Engelmann spruces, white and corkbark firs, and aspens.

All these life zones are easily accessible by way of the 37-mile **Swift Trail,** a driving route that leads from US 191 south of Safford up into the heart of the mountains, terminating above 9,000 feet and providing spectacular views along the way. Picnic sites and campgrounds dot the road from bottom to top, and an extensive trail system allows back-country exploration on foot, by mountain bike, or on horseback.

The Forest Service's Columbine Visitor Information Center, located 29 miles up the constantly winding Swift Trail at 9,600 feet, is usually open from Memorial Day to Labor Day; it's closed by winter weather the rest of the year, as are the last 11 miles of the road, which changes to dirt at mile 26. Maps and information are available here, and two fine day-hiking trails begin at the corrals across the road.

The **Ash Creek Trail** follows a stream 8.2 miles downhill, ending at a trailhead with an elevation of 4,200 feet. If you can arrange a shuttle, walking the whole route will take you through the range of Pinaleño life zones; you might, however, want to hike only the first 2.5 miles to **Ash Creek Falls,** a good out-and-back destination.

Wildflowers can be abundant along this trail, including Richardson's geranium, crimson and common (yellow) monkeyflowers, red cinquefoil, Franciscan bluebells, and many others. The endangered (but recovering) Apache trout, a small fish with a green back and yellowish sides, has been stocked in Ash Creek, where it sometimes hybridizes with introduced rainbow trout. (**Riggs Flat Lake,** near the end of Swift Trail, offers good trout fishing from spring through fall.) With luck, you might see a spotted owl or a northern goshawk along the trail; the Pinaleños host both of these superb raptors, though the fierce bird-eating goshawk is seen more often than the secretive owl.

From the corrals you can also climb **Webb Peak,** 1 mile away, offering great views of the Pinaleños and their surrounding valleys. To make a 3.2-mile loop, head east from the lookout on Webb Peak to join the Ash Creek Trail, and then walk back south to the corrals.

The Pinaleños host one of Arizona's densest populations of black bears, and wherever you hike you may see signs of their presence. Watch for places where bears have torn away the thick outer bark of corkbark firs (a form of subalpine fir) to feed on the inner bark. Look also for the small Coues variety of white-tailed deer, and for Abert's squirrel, with its big ears and bushy gray-and-white tail; not native to these mountains, it was introduced in the 1940s.

The most famous rodent in the Pinaleños is the Mount Graham red squirrel, an endemic subspecies of the red squirrel that's found throughout much of North America. As you explore, you may come across the squirrel's middens of Douglas-fir and Engelmann spruce cones. Highly endangered, with a total population of only about 500 individuals, this small squirrel was at the eye of a hurricane of controversy in the 1980s, when astronomers proposed building several observatories atop its mountain home to take advantage of the high elevation and clear sky. The debate that ensued was cut short when Congress bypassed endangered-species laws and ordered that three observatories be constructed.

A refuge of 1,750 acres has been set aside atop Mount Graham for the Mount Graham red squirrel; at this writing no entry is allowed, though that situation could change. ∎

Aravaipa Canyon Wilderness

■ 19,410 acres ■ Southeast Arizona, 23 miles southeast of Winkelman off Ariz. 77 ■ Best seasons spring and fall ■ Camping, hiking, wildlife viewing ■ Adm. fee; permit required ■ Contact Safford District, Bureau of Land Management, 711 14th Ave., Safford, AZ 85546; phone 520-348-4400

SOME WILD PLACES, generous in character, give their beauty freely. The Grand Canyon, for instance, offers drive-up marvels to all comers. Aravaipa Canyon Wilderness exacts a price from those who would enjoy its extraordinary environment. Not a financial one (the entry fee is nominal), but simply a bit of planning. The reward is a vibrant riparian zone along **Aravaipa Creek,** dramatic cliffs, and excellent wildlife viewing.

The wilderness that protects 10 miles of this perennial stream is administered by the Bureau of Land Management. Although the wilderness totals 19,410 acres, in practice hikers spend most of their time along the creek; to help preserve this fragile strip, a restriction of 50 visitors a day has been imposed, with trips limited to a maximum of three days (two nights). The required permits can be requested from the BLM Safford District office up to 13 weeks in advance. Call early, because the visitor quota is often filled quickly for weekends, especially in the best seasons of spring and fall.

Once you have your permit, there's still the matter of trip logistics. The canyon can be entered from either the west or east; the west can be reached over 12 miles of paved and dirt road that's passable for passenger cars, but to get to the east side you must drive about 45 miles on dirt roads, with high-clearance vehicles needed for the last 10 miles (call for road conditions before you visit). Even if your party has two vehicles, to set up a one-way hike through the canyon requires a very long shuttle (about 4.5 hours one way), so most people simply enter at one end, explore for as long as they have time, and return the way they came in. Those who go to all this trouble will see gorgeous cliffs of volcanic rock, beautiful specimens of Arizona sycamore and Arizona walnut, and common black-hawks, yellow-billed cuckoos, Bell's vireos and other birds. You also have an excellent chance of spotting desert bighorn sheep, which often appear on cliff tops above hikers.

There's no formal trail in Aravaipa Canyon. Hikers simply follow the creek, with the lay of the land forcing multiple crossings (which will entail wading through water ankle deep or higher—use extreme caution, and be alert for flash floods). Exploring some of the nine side canyons can be fun (and can lead to pretty pools and small waterfalls), but don't try rock-scrambling beyond your abilities.

Even with a limit on visitation, people can cause serious harm to such a confined and fragile ecosystem. Practice the lowest impact camping possible. Do everything you can to assure that generations to come will be able to enjoy one of the true natural treasures of the Southwest. ■

Hedgehog cactus in bloom, Aravaipa Canyon Wilderness

Cottonwoods on the San Pedro River, San Pedro Riparian National Conservation Area

San Pedro Riparian
National Conservation Area

■ 58,000 acres ■ Southeast Arizona, 7 miles east of Sierra Vista off Ariz. 90
■ Best seasons spring and fall ■ Hiking, fishing, mountain biking, bird-watching,
wildlife viewing ■ Contact Bureau of Land Management, 1763 Paseo San Luis,
Sierra Vista, AZ 85635; phone 520-458-3559

THE CARS SPEED ALONG Ariz. 90 between Sierra Vista and Bisbee, and the
drivers, if their minds aren't elsewhere, may notice that they cross a
bridge over a creek lined with tall cottonwoods. Only a few realize that
they've had a brief encounter with one of the most important natural
areas in the Southwest—a place that's been compared with the Grand
Canyon in its environmental significance.

This is the **San Pedro River,** which arises in the Sierra Los Ajos range
in Mexico and flows 140 miles north to its confluence with the Gila River
near Hayden, Arizona. While it lacks the immediate visual impact of a
mountain peak or a swath of unbroken forest, the San Pedro impresses
the biologists who've studied it as much as any natural feature on the

regional map. Beginning at the Mexican border, 40 miles of the river's riparian corridor have been protected as the San Pedro Riparian National Conservation Area, administered by the Bureau of Land Management. The designation recognizes the diversity of life that depends on the San Pedro, either as a permanent home or a temporary sanctuary.

Birds are always the first group of animals mentioned in connection with the San Pedro, and with good reason. Nearly 400 species have been seen along the river, and although some are onetime rarities, more than 100 resident species nest here, and perhaps 150 more use the river area regularly in migration or as a wintering ground. This vital site was the first in North America to be named a Globally Important Bird Area. The San Pedro's special breeding species include the gray hawk (the largest nesting population in the United States) and the tiny green kingfisher, the object of many a birding quest here. Common breeding birds include black-chinned hummingbirds, yellow-billed cuckoos, Lucy's warblers, yellow warblers, yellow-breasted chats, and summer tanagers.

Notable reptiles of the area include Mojave rattlesnake, Gila monster, Sonoran box turtle, Mexican garter snake, and desert grassland whiptail. Throughout the year, but especially in late summer, the San Pedro hosts an outstanding array of butterflies; common species include pipevine swallowtails, checkered whites, cloudless sulphurs, American snouts, and variegated fritillaries.

What to See and Do

The first step in exploring the San Pedro area is a stop at **San Pedro House** (*Ariz. 90, 7 miles E of Sierra Vista*), where a volunteer group operates a visitor center and gift shop. Trail maps, field guides, and expert advice will make your visit more enjoyable, and the trails that begin here lead to some of the most interesting areas along the river. Fremont cottonwoods, Goodding willows, Arizona walnuts, netleaf hackberries, and Arizona ashes grow along the river, where gray hawks make their nests.

The San Pedro area lies in the transition zone between the Chihuahuan Desert to the east and the Sonoran Desert to the west, and its vegetation shows characteristics of both regions. Beside the riparian strip, you'll find a savanna-like environment of mesquite and sacaton grass dominating some areas. On the higher ground away from the river grow creosotebush, tarbush, acacias, and other desert scrub plants.

By walking east from San Pedro House to the river, following it upstream, and then returning by way of **Garden Wash** and the Old San Rafael del Valle Road, you'll make a loop of a little over 2 miles and see a typical range of habitats. Trails at San Pedro are still being developed, so ask at the visitor center about current hiking possibilities. Eventually, a trail will border the river for 30 miles, allowing visitors to experience even more of the verdant ribbon of life that is the San Pedro. ■

Kubla Khan formation, Kartchner Caverns State Park

Kartchner Caverns State Park

- 550 acres ■ Southeast Arizona near Benson, 9 miles south of I-10 on Ariz. 90
- Year round ■ Camping, hiking, guided tours ■ Adm. fee; reservations recommended ■ Contact the park, P.O. Box 1849, Benson, AZ 85602; phone 520-586-4100 (information), 520-586-2283 (tour reservations)

BY THE TIME KARTCHNER CAVERNS STATE PARK opened in 1999, excitement about this underground wonder had built to almost rock-concert proportions. Calls to the reservation number jammed local phone lines and tours were booked weeks in advance. The beautiful formations contained within the cave would themselves have merited such attention, but the story behind its opening added even more to its renown.

In 1974, two spelunkers exploring the Whetstone Mountains made a discovery that all cave hunters dream of: a pristine cave never before seen by humans, full of gorgeous, colorful speleothems (the technical term for cave formations). Fearing damage to the fragile cave ecosystem, whether from deliberate vandalism or carelessness, they kept their find a secret for four years before telling the landowning Kartchner family. What followed were years of hush-hush meetings with conservation agencies and state officials before the site was added to the Arizona state park system in 1988 and word of the caverns' existence reached the public.

Preparing for visitor access meant elaborate planning and meticulous construction aimed at preserving this "living" cave, where formations—many of amazing delicacy—continue to grow. Airlocks, for instance, were installed on doors to prevent evaporation, since exposure to the extremely dry surface air could quickly have robbed the humid cave of its life-supporting moisture.

During construction, workers found a number of fossils, the most impressive of which were the bones of a giant Shasta ground sloth estimated to have lived 80,000 years ago. (A model of the 7-foot-long sloth is on display in the visitor center.) Paleontologists also identified the bones of an ancient horse and a bear, along with rabbits and packrats.

It was a quarter century from the cave's discovery to its opening as a park, but visitors are sure to find the wait worthwhile. Impressive displays in the **visitor center** offer an introduction to cave formation and ecology —preparation for the awe-inspiring journey into the earth.

Tours enter "rooms" sculpted by water flowing through crevices in the limestone of the Whetstone Mountains. When the water table dropped around 200,000 years ago, leaving the cave dry, moisture began seeping in from above, dissolving the limestone and redepositing it as speleothems such as stalagmites, stalactites, flowstones, draperies, and the striped formations known as cave bacon. Kartchner is especially rich in soda straws: thin, delicate shapes that hang from the ceiling. The cave contains the longest soda straw seen in any U.S. cavern, an incredible 21 feet 2 inches. (It isn't on the tour, but visitors can see a model in the visitor center.)

The centerpiece of the cave is a 58-foot-tall column called **Kubla Khan.** Arizona's tallest cave column, it ascends in layer after rounded layer—a giant's multiscoop ice-cream cone, perhaps. Kartchner holds the first known examples of formations called "turnip" shields, as well as several other unique or rare formations and mineral occurrences.

The tour passes through two large rooms, **Rotunda** and **Throne,** on its quarter-mile route. Eventually the trip will be expanded to include the Big Room, larger than the other two chambers combined.

Not everything in the caverns is inanimate. More than a thousand cave myotis bats inhabit the **Big Room** in summer, the females giving birth to pups and nursing them until they can leave the cave on their own. Bat guano provides nutrients for invertebrates such as mites, isopods, spiders, and crickets, all adapted to live in this dark ecosystem. Visitors are unlikely to see any of the cave critters, though, with the exception of occasional bats leaving the cave at dusk or returning at dawn.

The trail is fully wheelchair accessible, with only short steep sections, so nearly everyone can experience the grandeur of one of the most significant North American cave discoveries of the 20th century—a natural spectacle that's a secret no longer. ■

Birding in Southeast Arizona

THERE'S NO MORE enthusiastic group of nature lovers than birders, whose zeal to add new species to a life list (a record of all the different types of birds seen) spurs them on to spend vacations traveling around the country and, in many cases, around the world. To many of them, southeast Arizona ranks as the No. 1 birding destination in the United States, rivaled only by the lower Rio Grande Valley of Texas. Well over 400 kinds of birds have been spotted in the region south and east of Phoenix; of that number, several dozen either occur nowhere else in the country or are found more easily here than elsewhere.

Two factors primarily explain this avian richness. First is the great environmental diversity of southeast Arizona. A birder can easily walk a desert wash at dawn, move on to a riparian woodland in late morning, spend the afternoon in an oak savanna, and finish the day in a forest of pine, fir, and Douglas-fir—essentially traveling the equivalent of Arizona to Canada from sunrise to sundown.

Second is the region's proximity to Mexico. Many birds range only slightly across the U.S.-Mexican border, either as regular breeders or as strays. There's no ecological significance to this fact—political boundaries are, after all, only lines on a map—but birders who want to check off these species in the United States must come to this part of Arizona.

The list of local specialties includes some that are fairly common and easily seen, such as Harris's hawks, Gambel's quails, blue-throated hummingbirds, magnificent hummingbirds, Mexican jays, bridled titmice, curve-billed thrashers, painted redstarts, and yellow-eyed juncos.

A little searching, or luck, is usually required for others, including zone-tailed hawks, Montezuma quails, whiskered screech-owls, violet-crowned hummingbirds, Strickland's woodpeckers, northern beardless-tyrannulets, buff-breasted flycatchers, sulphur-bellied flycatchers, Mexican chickadees, olive warblers, and rufous-winged sparrows. And every birder hopes for a sighting of one of the regional rarities, such as ruddy ground-doves, buff-collared nightjars, plain-capped starthroats, eared

Elf owl in saguaro

Cactus wren

trogons, black-capped gnatcatchers, blue mockingbirds, flame-colored tanagers, or yellow grosbeaks.

Some of the sites covered in this guide rank among the most famous birding locations in North America. Every experienced birder has heard of (and probably visited) **Cave Creek Canyon** (see pp. 174-82) in the Chiricahua Mountains, the Nature Conservancy's **Ramsey Canyon Preserve** (see pp. 232-34) in the Huachucas, the **Patagonia-Sonoita Creek Preserve** (see pp. 239-40) near Patagonia, and **Madera Canyon** (see pp. 242-43) in the Santa Rita Mountains, to name only a few hot spots.

The regional birding itinerary also includes some smaller places that probably only birders would think of visiting. One of the smallest is the **rest area on Ariz. 82** just southwest of Patagonia, often called the "most famous rest area in America." (Famous among birders, anyway.) A flycatcher-like bird called rose-throated becard, rare in the United States, nests along the creek across from the parking area, and hundreds of birders have had their first sighting of the species here. The becard builds a bulky, football-size nest that hangs from the tip of a branch, usually near water. (If you look for this bird, don't cross the fence onto the private property beyond.) The rest area also hosts uncommon birds such as gray hawks and thick-billed kingbirds.

Most travelers don't put sewer ponds high on their list of must-see destinations; birders often do, though, for the waterfowl and shorebirds these artificial wetlands can attract. On Ariz. 90, some 3 miles east of Ariz. 92, the **Sierra Vista wastewater ponds** offer a viewing platform overlooking marsh vegetation where ducks and swallows often congregate. Beautiful yellow-headed blackbirds winter here in large flocks, and marsh wrens are also present in winter.

Birders in the Kartchner Caverns area drive another mile south and turn west into Coronado National Forest's **French Joe Canyon**, a rugged area in the Whetstone Mountains. (A high-clearance vehicle is needed for the primitive entrance road.) Here the rufous-capped warbler, an extremely rare bird in the U.S., has been seen in recent years; the even rarer Aztec thrush has been found as well, and the elusive Montezuma quail is sometimes spotted in the grassland mouth of the canyon.

Curve-billed thrasher

Acorn woodpecker

Huachuca Mountains

■ 75,000 acres ■ Southeast Arizona, west of Sierra Vista off Ariz. 92
■ Best months Jan.-April ■ Camping, hiking, bird-watching, wildlife viewing
■ User fee for Coronado National Forest ■ Contact Ramsey Canyon Preserve, 27 Ramsey Canyon Rd., Hereford, AZ 85615, phone 520-378-2785; Coronado National Forest, 5990 S. Hwy. 92, Sierra Vista, AZ 85615, phone 520-378-0311, or Coronado National Memorial, 4101 E. Montezuma Canyon Rd., Hereford, AZ 85615, phone 520-366-5515. www.fs.fed.us/r3/coronado

NOT AS FAMOUS AS THE CHIRICAHUA MOUNTAINS to the east, not nearly as popular as the Santa Catalinas to the north, the Huachucas must settle for encompassing some of the most beautiful canyons in southern Arizona, not to mention being home to one of America's most famous nature preserves.

Part of the reason the Huachucas (wah-CHOO-cahs) aren't as well known as some other ranges may be that much of their extent lies within the U.S. Army's Fort Huachuca military post. In fact, the Army allows visitors to enter freely, and Garden Canyon in the southern part of the post makes a wonderful destination. This is especially true for bird- and butterfly-watchers, but it also applies to anyone who wants to experience a lovely, lush mountain woodland.

As is true in other Arizona mountains, a visitor to the Huachucas can survey several different habitats. From semidesert mesquite grassland, you can climb through oak-juniper and pine-oak forests, and then hike even higher among ponderosa pines, Douglas-firs, and aspens. Beside creeks, Arizona sycamores provide the preferred nesting sites for the brilliant, long-tailed elegant trogons, while below them coatimundis amble along in curious troops.

What to See and Do

Most people enter the Huachucas at developed areas on the east side of the mountains; access points on the west side are reached via longer approaches on less maintained roads and trails.

Ramsey Canyon Preserve

The true treasure of the mountains is the Nature Conservancy's **Ramsey Canyon Preserve,** a spot so exceptional in its biological diversity that in 1965 it was named America's first National Natural Landmark. To visit the preserve, take Ariz. 92 south from Sierra Vista for 6 miles and turn west on Ramsey Canyon Road. Be aware that the preserve has parking for only 21 cars, and when the parking lot is full other visitors are temporarily turned away. There's no parking along the road, and reservations are not taken.

As delightfully attractive as it is environmentally significant, Ram-

Lower Ramsey Canyon, Huachuca Mountains

sey Canyon makes a trip to the Huachucas worthwhile all by itself. In 1993 a leopard frog that had been living in Ramsey Canyon was recognized as a species new to science. Appropriately named the Ramsey Canyon leopard frog, it was found to have the unusual characteristic of singing underwater (hence its scientific name *Rana subaquavocalis*). Known to reside only in Ramsey and several nearby sites, this fist-size amphibian has been the focus of intense conservation efforts since its discovery.

For many people the greatest joy here comes from simply watching the hummingbirds swarming at preserve feeders and flowers. Fourteen species of hummers have been reported here, including such rarities as white-eared and berylline hummingbirds.

Stop by the visitor center to chat with the knowledgeable staff and peruse the books and other available nature-related materials. If the hummingbird feeders are busy, it may be some time before you can bear to tear yourself away from these feathered gems. Eventually, though, you'll want to walk the trail up the canyon along spring-fed **Ramsey Creek** to further explore a sampling of the preserve's 380 acres.

Fremont cottonwoods, Arizona sycamores, bigtooth maples, and alligator junipers provide shade as you admire wildflowers and enjoy bird songs. Listen for the call of the sulphur-bellied flycatcher, the loud *week* of Mexican jay, and the liquid warbling of the beautiful painted redstart. You might spot a ridge-nosed rattlesnake in warm weather, but the common black-tailed rattlesnake is seen more frequently. More likely than either is a sighting of a mountain spiny lizard, with its pointy-scaled back, or an alligator lizard.

Coronado National Forest

From the trail up Ramsey Canyon, you can continue up the **Hamburg Trail** past Apache and Chihuahua pines, Douglas-firs, and Arizona madrones into **Coronado National Forest** and the 20,000-acre **Miller Peak Wilderness,** which is part of the national forest. After a mile, the trail reaches an overlook of Ramsey canyon, and 1.2 miles farther you'll arrive at **Hamburg Meadow.** With a trail map, all sorts of loop hikes are possible, but remember that you must be back to the preserve before the 5 p.m. closing time.

Continuing south on Ariz. 92 from Ramsey Canyon Road, you'll reach the turns to two other access points into the wilderness: **Carr Canyon** (1 mile south) and **Miller Canyon** (2 miles farther). The former road climbs all the way to the Ramsey Vista Campground at 7,200 feet, offering tremendous views along the way. (Be aware that this road is winding and steep, with sheer drops to the side.) The Miller Canyon road isn't so tortuous, but it ends at a trailhead at 5,750 feet; if you're intending to hike to any of the high peaks you'll have more climbing to do on foot.

Coronado National Memorial

Coronado National Memorial, which abuts the Mexican border, offers a few hiking trails in and around **Montezuma Canyon,** including a 0.75-mile climb to **Coronado Cave,** a 600-foot-long opening in the limestone of the Huachucas. You must obtain a free permit at the visitor center to enter the cave, and carrying at least one flashlight per person is required.

Many hikers use the memorial as the starting point to climb 9,466-foot **Miller Peak,** the highest point in the Huachucas. From a parking lot at **Montezuma Pass Overlook,** 3 miles west of the visitor center, the national forest's **Crest Trail** heads north 4.8 miles to a half-mile spur that leads to Miller Peak's summit. This fairly strenuous hike climbs 2,900 feet, with a great view waiting for you at the end. This, by the way, is the southern portion of the **Arizona Trail,** a 790-mile nonmotorized route that will eventually lead from the Mexican border to Utah (see sidebar p. 248).

Garden Canyon

Back in Sierra Vista, Fry Boulevard leads west to the main gate of **Fort Huachuca.** (At this writing a permit is not required to enter the post, but that could change.) Watch for signs for the road to **Garden Canyon,** reached by driving across the grassland for several miles and up into a beautiful mountain woodland. About 10 miles from the gate, less than a mile after the pavement ends, look for **Scheelite Canyon** on your left. A steep trail leads up under towering cliffs, through woods of oak, ponderosa pine, and Douglas-fir. Hundreds of birders come here each year to look for the rare Mexican spotted owl; Scheelite Canyon usually hosts a breeding pair.

The road deteriorates beyond Scheelite Canyon, but when it gets too rough for your vehicle, you can walk up to the pine woodland at **Sawmill Canyon;** if you haven't yet seen an elegant trogon, you could find the bird here. ■

Empire-Cienega Resource Conservation Area

■ 49,000 acres ■ Southeast Arizona, northeast of Sonoita off Ariz. 83 ■ Best seasons spring through fall ■ Camping, horseback riding, bird-watching, wildlife viewing ■ Dirt roads can be muddy after rain, rough and rutted anytime ■ Contact Bureau of Land Management, 12661 E. Broadway, Tucson, AZ 85748; phone 520-722-4289

THERE ARE PLACES IN THIS sprawling expanse of open country where travelers can get an inkling of what southern Arizona must have looked like when Spanish explorers and missionaries arrived in the 16th century. With the rugged Whetstone Mountains to the east, rising over rolling

Riders, Empire-Cienega Resource Conservation Area

grassland where pronghorn roam, the vistas in this resource conservation area take in a landscape of outstanding natural beauty.

The naturalness of the surroundings diminishes where roads and grazing cattle intrude, but it's the ranching heritage of this tract that kept it intact and prevented most development. The Empire Ranch once encompassed more than 600,000 acres; a part was sold and renamed Cienega Ranch, and in 1988 the Bureau of Land Management acquired ranchland to create today's resource conservation area. This is a multiple-use zone, not a park, so visitors are likely to come across working cowboys or hunters. As you explore, be sure to leave gates as you find them, whether open or closed.

The RCA is located in the Cienega Basin, with the Santa Rita Mountains to the west, the Empire Mountains to the north, and the Whetstones to the east. These ranges were formed by block faulting between 15 million and 8 million years ago. The uplands once rose much higher above the intervening basins, but over time erosion has carried much of the peaks' mass down into the valleys, which filled with debris. Today, the Empire-Cienega area sits on several thousand feet of gravel.

Bisecting the area, Cienega Creek, one of the few perennial streams in the region, creates a riparian oasis in the grassland and provides valuable wildlife habitat with its bordering cottonwoods, willows, and oaks. Aside from pronghorn (reintroduced here after being locally extirpated), Empire-Cienega is home to badgers, coatimundis, javelinas, ringtails, Gila monsters, and four species of rattlesnakes.

Living in or around the creek are three native fish— the endangered Gila topminnow, the rare Gila chub, and the longfin dace—as well as leopard frogs and canyon tree frogs. The presence of these wetland-dependent species in a generally arid climate (15 inches of precipitation a year) indicates the significance of Cienega Creek, which flows above ground northward 10 miles before its waters vanish into the earth.

What to See and Do

It has no formal trails, but the Empire-Cienega area can be explored by driving its roads and taking short walks into the grassland and along washes. The main roads can be treacherous after rain, and most of the secondary roads require high-clearance and/or four-wheel drive.

As you enter the area from Ariz. 83 about 8 miles north of Sonoita, follow dirt Empire-Cienega Ranch Road (signed as EC-900) east to an information kiosk, where you should study the posted map. (Taking notes wouldn't be a bad idea.) Continuing on this road will take you through grassland studded with mesquite and yucca to an old adobe ranch house and an area of oaks and tall cottonwoods.

Take Empire-Cienega Ranch Road (signed EC-901) northeast for about 6 miles to reach the streamside habitats of **Cienega Creek.** Those proficient with map and compass can make up their own walking routes, since hiking is allowed anywhere in the area. Local outfitters offer horseback tours, and this can be a fine way to experience Empire-Cienega; check with the Chamber of Commerce in Sonoita (520-455-5498) or Patagonia (520-394-0060).

Birders visit the area to see grassland species, including the beautiful Montezuma quail; though this species isn't rare in southern Arizona, its secretive habits can make it hard to find (as many a birder has discovered after fruitless searching). Cassin's and Botteri's sparrows are among the birds that wait for the summer monsoon rains to breed here.

Whether you're hiking, riding, or just driving, Empire-Cienega makes a fascinating destination— especially as a contrast to, say, the forested high country of the Santa Rita Mountains (see pp. 241-43). A visit here may not be quite as straightforward as a trip to a more developed natural area, but the rewards can be abundant. ■

Patagonia-Sonoita Creek Preserve

■ 850 acres ■ Southeast Arizona, near Patagonia off Ariz. 82 ■ Best months April-May and Aug.-Sept. Closed Mon.-Tues. ■ Guided walks, bird-watching, wildlife viewing ■ Contact the preserve, 150 Blue Haven Rd., Patagonia, AZ 85624; phone 520-394-2400

MOST ASSUREDLY RANKED AMONG THE top birding sites in the country, the Nature Conservancy's Patagonia-Sonoita Creek Preserve protects a beautiful stretch of one of the finest riparian habitats remaining in southeastern Arizona. A stop here is mandatory for any bird-watcher visiting the region, but even nonbirders should treat themselves to a stroll along tree-shaded **Sonoita Creek** to enjoy an outstanding example of an environment that once was common along southwestern streams.

From Ariz. 82 in Patagonia, a town founded in 1898 as a ranching and mining center, take Fourth Avenue northwest four blocks and turn left on Pennsylvania Avenue; cross Sonoita Creek and continue on Blue Haven Road about 1 mile to the preserve visitor center. Pick up a trail map here and ask about any recent wildlife sightings. There's a short, self-guided nature trail at the visitor center, with longer trails branching out toward the north. A worthwhile option for first-time visitors is to take a guided walk, offered every Saturday morning at 9 a.m., to get acquainted with preserve flora, fauna, and trails.

The **Creek Trail** winds along Sonoita Creek, past imposing specimens of Fremont cottonwood, some over 100 feet tall and thought to be 130 years old. Botanists consider this assemblage of venerable cottonwoods to be among the best in the state. Other common trees in the riparian woodland include velvet ash, velvet mesquite, canyon hackberry, Arizona walnut, and willow. Interspersed grassy clearings add to the diversity of the preserve and to the list of species it hosts.

In spring and summer, listen for the high whistles of the gray hawk, which it may emit as it soars just above the treetops or while sitting in a tall cottonwood. This handsome species, a preserve specialty, regularly nests along Sonoita Creek. Other notable breeding birds here include yellow-billed cuckoos, broad-billed hummingbirds, gilded flickers, Bell's vireos, Lucy's warblers, yellow-breasted chats, summer tanagers, lazuli buntings, and Abert's towhees. The preserve is known for hosting a variety of members of the flycatcher family, from the common black phoebe to the thick-billed kingbird, the latter found in the U.S. only in southern Arizona. The preserve's smallest flycatcher also boasts one of the longest, and oddest, names: northern beardless-tyrannulet, a small, plain, grayish species that lacks the stiff facial bristles that other flycatchers possess.

With luck you might spot a green kingfisher whirring by just above Sonoita Creek. Much smaller than the belted kingfisher, this scarce southwestern species isn't always present here. Its occurrence depends on water levels in the creek, which in turn depend on rainfall, most of which comes during the monsoon season from July through September.

Monsoon rains also mark the season of a less welcome species at the preserve: the chigger. This tiny mite larva burrows into the skin, causing intense irritation and itching in most people. The usual precautions, such as wearing long pants, tucking pants legs into socks, and applying repellent, will help make a summer visit more pleasant.

The Creek Trail intersects the **Railroad Trail** near the north end of the preserve; the latter path follows the old track bed of the New Mexico & Arizona Railroad, laid in 1882, and leads directly back south to the visitor center. On any of the preserve trails, watch for signs of white-tailed deer, badgers, gray foxes, coyotes, javelinas, and raccoons. You might also spot Arizona gray squirrels scampering through the trees or a desert cottontail "frozen" beside the trail, hoping you won't notice it.

The clear waters of Sonoita Creek are home to four species of native Arizona fish, including the endangered Gila topminnow. Four may not sound like many, but it's a significant number these days, after environmental abuse has degraded so much riparian habitat in the state. Research and water monitoring help assure that this stream will continue to be as secure for its wild residents as it is attractive to human visitors. ∎

Arizona Hummers

Arizona boasts the greatest variety of hummingbirds of any state. More than 15 species of these feathered gems have been spotted here. While some are very rare, a determined searcher could conceivably find a dozen types on a late-summer birding trip. To see that many, you must visit a range of habitats: Black-chinned hummingbirds, for instance, prefer desert lowlands, while broad-tailed and magnificent hummers are most common in mountains.

Arizona sycamores, Madera Canyon, Santa Rita Mountains

Santa Rita Mountains

■ 138,240 acres ■ Southeast Arizona, 35 miles south of Tucson off I-19
■ Best seasons spring-fall ■ Camping, hiking, guided walks, bird-watching,
wildlife viewing ■ User fees for national forest ■ Contact Nogales Ranger District, Coronado National Forest, 303 Old Tucson Rd., Nogales, AZ 85621;
phone 520-281-2296. www.fs.fed.us/r3/coronado

A BEAUTIFUL AND VERY ACCESSIBLE mountain canyon, a high peak with
spectacular views over much of southern Arizona, and some of the best
bird-watching in the country—these are the main ingredients that make
the Santa Ritas such a popular destination for outdoor enthusiasts. But
they're not the only items in this metaphorical natural stew. Add the
tangy smell of a desert grassland after a summer storm, the color of
columbines along a stream, the texture of alligator juniper bark, the
sound of wind in the pines...and this recipe could be a long one, indeed.

Like many of southeast Arizona's other sky island ranges, the Santa Ritas' elevation above the surrounding desert is the product of block faulting. In places on their western flanks, you can see "dikes" where magma flowed into thin cracks in surrounding rock, to be exposed by later erosion. The landmark called Elephant Head is one such intrusive element.

Just a short drive from Tucson, the Santa Ritas—and especially their main entry point, Madera Canyon, a Coronado National Forest recreation area—can be a little too popular on weekends in spring and fall. Keep in mind the two main rules for seekers of solitude: Visit on a weekday if possible, and arrive as early as you can.

What to See and Do

From I-19 at the small town of Continental, follow signs to **Madera Canyon,** taking White House Canyon Road (Forest Road 62) southeast across the desert scrub. In 7 miles, a well-marked turn indicates a right bend onto Forest Road 70 toward the canyon, about 5 miles ahead. (Continuing straight on unpaved Forest Road 62 will take you in less than a mile to a right turn to the Florida Canyon trailhead, another route into the mountains.)

Even if you want to explore Madera Canyon, don't rush across the intervening desert scrub and grassland without noticing its own special attractions. You're crossing a huge alluvial fan of eroded material, carried down from the Santa Ritas over countless millennia, now cut in several places by washes. At the third small bridge along Forest Road 70, you'll probably note a few cars parked alongside the road. These belong to bird-watchers, walking **Florida Wash** to look for phainopeplas, crissal thrashers, pyrrhuloxias, rufous-winged sparrows, varied buntings, and other desert species. Even if you're not a birder, walking a wash at dawn can be fun, as you enjoy the sights and sounds of the desert coming to life and possibly come across lizards, snakes, or Gambel's quail. As Forest Road 70 climbs, you enter grassy areas where Cassin's and Botteri's sparrows, both local specialties, sing after summer rains.

Madera Canyon

As you enter Madera Canyon you'll pass several parking lots and picnic areas. From any, you can access a nature trail (on the south side of the road) that parallels **Madera Creek** from the Proctor Road intersection to the parking lot at the end of the main road, gaining around 1,000 feet in elevation in a little over 2 miles. Walking a portion of this trail lets you experience the pine-oak woodland of the lower canyon before you head into its higher reaches. At the Bog Springs Campground, trails climb the canyon's east slope to several springs that make good day-hiking destinations.

Partway up Madera Canyon you'll pass **Santa Rita Lodge** (520-625-8746), a very popular base for visiting birders, butterfly enthusiasts, and other natural-history types. The hummingbird feeders here are nationally famous for the varied species they attract. Ask about guided walks and other nature programs offered seasonally. Elf owls, the smallest owls in North America, nest in old woodpecker holes in telephone poles around the lodge, and each night birders gather at dusk to watch these tiny creatures emerge.

Mount Wrightson Wilderness

The road up Madera Canyon ends at a picnic area and trailhead parking lots at an elevation of 5,400 feet; from the uppermost lot, trails climb canyons toward the Santa Rita highlands. Many hikers head for the summit of **Mount Wrightson,** the highest point in the Santa Ritas at 9,453 feet. The peak stands at the approximate center of the 25,260-acre **Mount Wrightson Wilderness,** a part of Coronado National Forest reached most often from Madera Canyon but also accessible from trailheads on its northern and southern borders. You can make loop or (with a shuttle) take one-way backpacking trips here, or simply day-hike up a trail and turn around whenever you feel like it.

If you're headed for the summit of Mount Wrightson you can choose from two popular routes that begin at the trailhead parking lots: The **Old Baldy Trail** covers 5.4 very steep miles; the **Super Trail** takes 8.1 miles to reach the top, but ascends more gradually on a better maintained path. The two trails merge briefly near Josephine Saddle at 7,080 feet, making varied loops possible.

Along the lower Super Trail, you'll pass through lush riparian woods of Arizona sycamores, alligator junipers (named for their rough bark), madrones, Arizona walnuts, and several oaks including silverleaf and Emory. Here in these lovely surroundings you might spot an elegant trogon, a medium-size red-and-green bird that's one of the showcase species of the Arizona borderland. Here, too, you might come upon a black-tailed rattlesnake, a common snake of lower and middle elevations. Not aggressive as rattlers go, this species is very handsome, patterned in black on yellowish tan; if you see one, admire it from a distance and leave it in peace.

As you climb, pines gradually compose more of the forest, which eventually includes Douglas-firs and aspens before reaching the final 0.9-mile spur to Mount Wrightson's rocky crest. The view from the top extends far into Mexico and takes in several of southern Arizona's sky island ranges. ∎

The Cat That's Not

Found throughout Arizona, the ringtail inhabits rocky cliffs and wooded canyons, where it sleeps all day and prowls all night for rodents, frogs, and other small creatures. Often called the ringtail cat, in fact it's more closely related to raccoons. With its big eyes and bushy tail, the ringtail has a lemurlike appearance—on the rare occasions it is seen. Although it is Arizona's official state mammal, it's a lucky resident, or visitor, who catches a glimpse of one.

Santa Catalina Mountains

■ 265,142 acres ■ Southern Arizona, on the northeast outskirts of Tucson
■ Best seasons summer (high country) and winter (desert) ■ Camping, hiking,
fishing, mountain biking, horseback riding, downhill skiing, bird-watching
■ Adm. and user fees ■ Snow closes high-elevation recreation areas in winter
■ Contact Santa Catalina Ranger District, Coronado National Forest, 5700 N.
Sabino Canyon Rd., Tucson, AZ 85750; phone 520-749-8700

AT ONCE IMPOSING AND INVITING, the Santa Catalina Mountains command
the horizon northeast of Tucson, their picturesque granite spires promising great scenery, and even greater vistas, for those who reach their high
country. From trailheads at the base, some with elevations of less than
3,000 feet, hiking trails climb all the way up Mount Lemmon, its conifer-
clad summit rising to 9,157 feet.

In real life, of course, relatively few people have the ambition and ability to gain well over a mile in elevation by shank's mare. As a notable
alternative, the Sky Island Scenic Byway ascends along 27 winding miles
to within a short stroll of Mount Lemmon's crest. Thanks to the road,
and to its proximity to the city of Tucson, Mount Lemmon is by far
the most-visited high point of southern Arizona's sky island ranges.

Climbing Mount Lemmon, Santa Catalina Mountains

Coronado National Forest provides abundant recreational opportunities in the Santa Catalinas, from roadside scenic lookouts and picnic areas to campgrounds and trails. In the southwestern part of the range, miles of hiking paths cross the 57,000-acre Pusch Ridge Wilderness, named for the prominent geological feature that dominates the view of the mountains from many angles.

The great range of elevation spanned by the scenic byway as it climbs these mountains means you can walk a desert path amid saguaros and ocotillos and in less than two hours be in a forest of white firs, Douglas-firs, and aspens. The highlands of the Santa Catalinas average about 20 degrees cooler than the Sonoran Desert below, which makes them a great midday retreat after an early morning hike in Saguaro National Park (see pp. 250-55) or a visit to the Arizona-Sonora Desert Museum (see pp. 256-57). Birders love this varied topography, for it means they can see typical desert birds such as cactus wrens and Gambel's quails and mountain species such as Steller's jays in an easy day trip.

With their easy access and range of recreational opportunities, the Santa Catalinas make an excellent introduction to the ecological diversity for which southeast Arizona is celebrated. Within a short time and a comparably short distance, you can experience the natural equivalent of a journey from Mexico to Canada—without leaving Tucson's backyard.

What to See and Do

Catalina State Park

An exploration of the Santa Catalina Mountains might begin with a visit to **Catalina State Park** off Ariz. 77 on the west side of the range *(520-628-5798. www.pr.state.az.us/parkhtml/ catalina.html; adm. fee).* Set in the desert along a wash called **Cañada del Oro,** this 5,511-acre park offers short loop trails and trailheads for long hikes up into the mountains. You'll also have a chance to visit the ruins of a village of the Hohokam, an agri-culture-oriented Native American people whose culture mysteriously disappeared in the 15th century and who are believed to be the ancestors of today's Tohono O'odham Indians.

The 2.3-mile **Canyon Loop** makes a nice early morning desert walk through mesquite scrub. For a longer and more challenging hike, begin the Canyon Loop on the **Romero Canyon Trail** and continue on the latter trail up along slopes covered in saguaro; in 1.1 miles you'll reach the boundary of the **Pusch Ridge Wilderness** and soon cross a divide into **Romero Canyon.** Here you can continue up an increasingly steep trail that, for backpackers, connects with other routes that lead to the top of **Mount Lemmon.** Catalina State Park is also home to an equestrian center for visitors who bring their own mounts.

Sabino Canyon

To visit beautiful **Sabino Canyon,** take Sabino Canyon Road north from Tanque Verde Road in north-eastern Tucson. The Forest Service operates a visitor center here with a bookstore; a private shuttle service *(520-749-2861. Fee)* runs a tram 3.8 miles up the canyon, with a spur into adjacent **Bear Canyon.** The tram eliminates private vehicles from the canyon, but this is still a very popular and often crowded area; try to arrive early and avoid weekends. (Hikers can enter the canyons at any time, without having to wait for the visitor center to open or the tram to begin operating.)

The tram ride offers narration on the canyon's natural and human history. By taking it to the top of its route, you can gain ele-

---

Hikers and Bighorns

Many hikes are possible in the Santa Catalinas, but be aware that certain areas may be closed part of the year to protect a critically threatened population of bighorn sheep. Numbers of bighorns in the Santa Catalinas have seriously declined in recent years, in part because of degradation of habitat and in part, it's believed, because of encroachment into their territory by hikers, who may not even be aware that their presence disturbs the sheep. Dogs are especially frightening to bighorns, probably invoking an ancestral memory of wolves; sheep will abandon an area simply because of the scent of a dog.

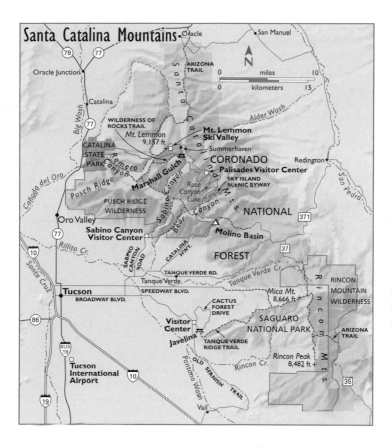

Santa Catalina Mountains

vation and save your energy for hiking up into the higher parts of the canyon. One fine loop ascends Sabino Canyon to a trail junction, heads east on the **East Fork Trail,** and then descends through Bear Canyon. This fairly strenuous 13.4-mile itinerary offers much of what makes the area so attractive: towering cliffs, waterfalls, seasonal swimming holes, and a riparian zone of cottonwoods, Arizona sycamores, alligator junipers, Arizona walnuts, and other trees.

Many hiking routes are possible here, and not all have to be difficult. Taking the shuttle to its terminus and then simply walking

down the paved road is an easy and appealing way to experience the pleasures of Sabino Canyon. Ask at the visitor center about guided bird walks and other natural history programs that might be offered.

Sky Island Scenic Byway

The Catalina Highway, which becomes **Sky Island Scenic Byway** *(Toll),* angles northeast from Tanque Verde Road 2.5 miles east of Sabino Canyon Road. Beginning along slopes dotted with majestic saguaro cactus, this sensationally scenic drive climbs steadily more than 6,000 feet to the summit of Mount Lemmon.

At **Molino Basin,** elevation 4,370 feet, you're entering a zone that receives between 15 and 20 inches of precipitation a year, compared with as little as 10 in the desert below. Growing here are pinyon pines, alligator junipers, and various oaks in a savannalike grassland, with manzanita in chapparal thickets. About 6 miles farther along, stop at one of the picnic areas in Bear Canyon to enjoy a woodland of Arizona cypresses, Arizona sycamores, and ponderosa and Chihuahua pines. Look for the little cliff chipmunk here, easily recognized by the stripes on its face.

Three miles beyond the picnic area, the fantastic rock formations at **Windy Point** (Milepost 14) will entice you to stop and enjoy the view of Tucson down below. The rock formations that make the Santa Catalinas so picturesque are formed of granite and gneiss, the latter metamorphosed by heat and pressure during periods of volcanic activity. Rain and occasional ice have sculpted the exposed granite here into cracked and creased cliffs and spires much favored by rock-climbers. The black-and-white birds you see zooming by on stiff, fast-beating wings are white-throated swifts, which nest in rock crevices. With luck, you might spot a peregrine falcon, which also breeds here.

Though it's only 7 acres, **Rose Canyon Lake** at Mile 17 is very popular for its rainbow trout fishing in spring and fall. A trail circles the lake, offering bird-watchers the chance to see species such as greater pewees, mountain chickadees, pygmy nuthatches, Grace's warblers, and hepatic tanagers—a far different set from the birds flitting through the desert scrub in lower Sabino Canyon. Here you're in the ponderosa pine forest, dominated by the most widespread

Arizona Trail

The Mount Lemmon Trail in the Santa Catalinas is part of the Arizona Trail, one of America's newest long-distance hiking routes. Winding from Coronado National Memorial, on the Mexican border, to the Utah state line north of the Grand Canyon, the trail covers 790 miles, the great majority of it on federal land. (Seventy percent of the trail crosses Forest Service land.)

In most places, such as in the Santa Ritas and in the Mazatzal Wilderness north of Phoenix, the Arizona Trail follows already designated trails; new segments are being built in other areas to link existing routes. The trail is open to nonmotorized use, such as hiking, horseback riding, and cross-country skiing. Mountain bikes are allowed on the trail except in official wilderness areas. (Alternative bike routes are being sought for these segments.)

The Arizona Trail has become a reality thanks to cooperation among government agencies and private landowners and to the work of volunteers from the Arizona Trail Association (602-252-4794. www.aztrail.org).

West face, Santa Catalina Mountains

pine in the West, growing from Canada well down into Mexico.

About 2.5 miles past the Rose Canyon Lake turnoff, stop at the **Palisades Visitor Center;** if you don't yet have maps of the area, buy them here to learn about hiking possibilities from trailheads along the byway. Soon after the visitor center, you enter the mixed conifer forest, where Douglas-firs and white pines appear among the ponderosa pines.

Five miles beyond the visitor center, in the town of Summerhaven, a spur road leads south to the Marshall Gulch picnic area. Trails here lead into **Pusch Ridge**

Wilderness, through an aspen forest and on to **Wilderness of Rocks,** a popular destination with stunning granite formations.

Back on the main road, continue past the ski area the last couple of winding miles to the top of Mount Lemmon. You won't find any vistas from the parking lot at the summit, but trails lead to various nearby lookout points and into Pusch Ridge Wilderness. Backpackers who arrange to be picked up at Catalina State Park or Sabino Canyon can hike down the mountain from here, experiencing all its life zones and getting fabulous views along the way. ■

Hiker with piece of dried saguaro cactus, Desert Nature Trail, Saguaro National Park

Saguaro National Park

■ 91,444 acres ■ Southern Arizona: Rincon Mountain District just east of Tucson on Old Spanish Trail and Tucson Mountain District just west on Kinney Rd. ■ Best seasons spring through fall ■ Backcountry camping, hiking, biking, horseback riding, bird-watching, wildlife viewing ■ Adm. fee ■ Contact the park, 3693 S. Old Spanish Trail, Tucson, AZ 85730; phone 520-733-5153 (Rincon Mountain District), 520-733-5158 (Tucson Mountain District); www.nps.gov/sagu; or Pima County Parks and Recreation Dept., 1204 W. Silverlake Rd., Tucson, AZ 85713; phone 520-740-2690

WHAT BETTER PLACE could there be to learn about the saguaro cactus, the monarch of the Sonoran Desert, than at the national park named for it? And it would take a dull soul, indeed, not to be fascinated by, and curious about, this magnificent plant after seeing the extensive stands of cactus within Saguaro National Park.

The park consists of two districts, one on the east side of Tucson, bordering the Rincon Mountains and Coronado National Forest, and the other west of the city in the Tucson Mountains. The Tucson Mountain District abuts Tucson Mountain Park, a Pima County park that preserves additional saguaro forest and offers more opportunities for hiking, biking, and horseback riding.

Though the saguaro may be the centerpiece of the national park, a whole range of flora and fauna awaits visitors here. From sparse desert flats with creosotebush and cholla to washes lined with mesquite and paloverde trees to *bajadas* (alluvial slopes around hills and mountains)

covered by saguaros, the terrain rises in the Rincon Mountain District to desert grassland and the peaks of the Rincons, with woodlands of ponderosa pines and Douglas-firs. An extensive system of trails provides access throughout the park, encompassing short, easy nature walks and strenuous backpacking routes all the way to the high point of the Rincons, 8,666-foot Mica Mountain. In addition, each district features a scenic loop drive.

It's wise to keep the seasons in mind when planning a visit to the desert. After wet winters, the spring wildflower display can be breathtaking: The brilliant gold of Mexican poppy is often the first-noticed bloom, while penstemons, lupines, desert marigolds, brittlebushes, and globe mallows contribute their colors. Many trees, shrubs, and cactuses also bloom, including creosotebushes, paloverdes, ocotillos, chollas, and hedgehog cactuses; desert birds are singing and nesting. Early summer may be a hot time to visit, but that's when the saguaro blooms. July brings the summer monsoon rains (see p. 258), ushering in a second spring of wildlife activity and flowering. In winter, plants and wildlife are less engaging, but moderate temperatures mean that hiking in the lowlands is comfortable all day.

What to See and Do

Rincon Mountain District

At the visitor center just inside the entrance to the park's **Rincon Mountain District,** you'll find books, maps, and exhibits and audiovisual programs on Sonoran Desert ecology. Outside, signs identify some of the more common plants you'll see as you explore the park. In spring, you'll soon become accustomed to the chugging call of the cactus wren and the sharp *whit-wheet* of the curve-billed thrasher, common around the entrance area.

The park's **Cactus Forest Drive** winds through rolling desert and across several washes as it makes an 8-mile loop from the visitor center. At the very least, you'll want to stop at the short, flat **Desert Ecology Trail;** here you'll learn some of the ways plants and animals adapt to the scarcity of water in the desert. The trail, appropriately enough, runs alongside a wash that sits dry as powder most of the year. This area receives only about 11 inches of rain a year; the top of Mica Mountain, which you can see peeking over the flank of Tanque Verde Ridge to the east, gets as much as 21 inches.

A map available at the visitor center shows the maze of trails north of the loop drive, also accessible from Speedway Boulevard and other streets on the park's edge. Loop hikes of practically any length allow exploration of the desert, but always be sure you have enough water before you leave a trailhead. For those with the proper knowledge and provisions, strenuous backpacking trails lead eastward from the visitor center into the wilderness area in the eastern section of the park, reaching the forest on Mica Mountain and 8,482-foot **Rincon Peak,** 7 miles

Following pages: Saguaros against a stormy sky, Saguaro National Park

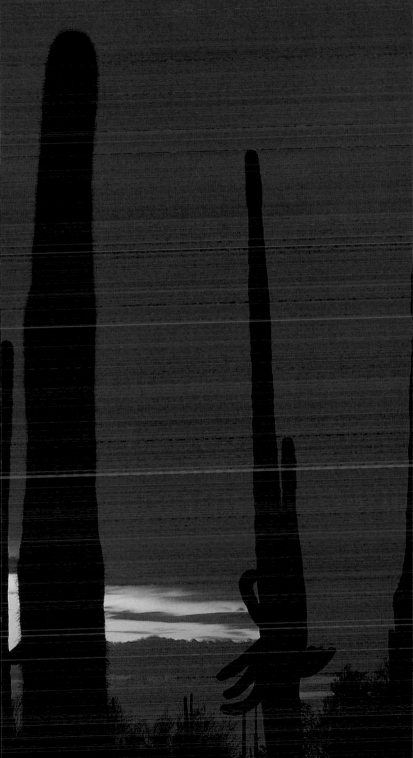

(as the raven flies) to the south.

If you don't have time for an all-day or overnight hiking trip, consider walking a part of the **Tanque Verde Ridge Trail,** which heads south and then east from the Javelina picnic area along Cactus Forest Drive. In return for 3 miles or so of fairly vigorous uphill hiking, you'll experience cactus desert, the grassland above, and a bit of oak-juniper forest on the ridge. You'll have good views of Rincon Peak to the east and Tucson down below to the west. In the grassland zone, note the plant with a tall flower stalk and a basal rosette of thick leaves rising about a foot high; one look at the sharp-tipped leaves and you'll know why Schott's agave is commonly known as shindagger. Sotol, also found here, has much longer and thinner leaves, which were used by Native Americans to weave mats and other household objects.

Tucson Mountain District

The desert plants and animals you'll find in the park's **Tucson Mountain District** are much the same as in the eastern unit, but the landscape looks very different. Here, huge cliffs of granite and rhyolite form the **Tucson Mountains,** topped by 4,687-foot **Wasson Peak**—far lower than the Rincons' summits. In the western part of the district, the striking **Red Hills** are composed of mudstone from an ancient lake bed and given their color by iron oxide.

Begin at the Red Hills Visitor Center, where the very short, wheelchair-accessible **Cactus Garden Walk** introduces desert plants; a mile north on Kinney Road, the

The Mighty Saguaro

Standing up to 50 feet tall and weighing eight tons or more, the saguaro seems to dominate the Sonoran Desert environment; with its tough skin and abundant spines, it exudes strength and vigor.

What we see in a full-grown saguaro, in fact, represents victory over long odds. The huge cactus begins as a seed the size of a pinhead, which must avoid being eaten by hungry animals. Next, it has to find a favorable germination site; young saguaros do best in the shelter of a "nurse" plant such as a paloverde or creosotebush. The tiny seedling then has to escape rodents, javelina hooves, and the boots of careless hikers; it may take

25 years to reach 2 feet in height.

After 50 years, the saguaro may overtop a person standing beside it, and as it continues to grow it exhibits marvelous adaptations to its arid surroundings. Its roots can spread 50 feet in all directions, the better to soak up water quickly. Woody ribs support its weight, but their flexibility, along with the cactus's pleated skin, allows tremendous expansion in volume. A saguaro may take in 200 gallons of water during one rainstorm.

During a life that may span 200 years, a saguaro can produce 40 million seeds. If only one survives to become an adult, the plant will have replaced itself by the time it dies—and that's all nature asks.

Visitors dwarfed by saguaro cactuses, Saguaro National Park

Desert Discovery Nature Trail, a half-mile loop, explores Sonoran Desert ecology in more depth. For a marvelous view of the **Avra Valley** to the west, take the 1.5-mile round-trip **Valley View Overlook Trail,** which you'll find on the park's 9-mile **Bajada Loop Drive.** This scenic route passes through some of the finest stands of saguaro found anywhere, with the giant cactus growing in amazing profusion on the hillsides.

A number of trails lead into the backcountry in the park and in adjacent **Tucson Mountain Park,** *(520 740-2690),* and with a map, numerous loop trips can be planned. The **Sendero Esperanza Trail** is the least strenuous route to Wasson Peak, leading 4 miles to the summit and offering great long-distance views along the way.

Many of the raptors you see from roads and trails will be red-tailed hawks, common across North America, but keep an eye out for Harris's hawk, a southwestern specialty feathered in chestnut, dark brown, and white. As usual, take care in rocky areas, which are home to western diamondback, tiger, and black-tailed rattlesnakes.

Few people are going to try to get close to one of the last mentioned reptiles, but the desert tortoise is another story. If you happen across one of these appealingly homely creatures, resist the urge to approach it or pick it up. Tortoises store water in their bodies to survive periods of drought, but often void their internal reserve when handled. An innocent attempt to examine a tortoise could endanger its life. ■

Arizona-Sonora Desert Museum

■ 21 acres ■ Just west of Tucson, adjacent to Saguaro National Park, Tucson Mountain District ■ Best months Nov.-April ■ Walking, wildlife viewing ■ Adm. fee ■ Contact the museum, 2021 N. Kinney Rd., Tucson, AZ 85743; phone 520-883-2702. www.desertmuseum.org

NO ONE INTERESTED IN NATURE who visits southern Arizona should miss the Arizona-Sonora Desert Museum. You may be eager to get to a park or wildlife refuge or to hit the trails in a national forest, but you'll be better prepared to enjoy what you do and you'll get more out of your travels if you take time to see this renowned Tucson attraction first.

The Arizona-Sonora Desert Museum is not a place you can stroll through in an hour; plan on spending three hours, or even more, for a leisurely visit. In summer, consider arriving when the museum opens at 7:30 a.m.; wildlife is more active, and you'll be finished before the hottest part of the day. Remember that the museum averages 87 days a years when the temperature tops 100°F.

As soon as you enter the gate, you'll realize that the name "museum" hardly fits the scene before you. Part zoo, part botanical garden, and part mini-nature preserve, the museum spreads over 21 acres, with 2 miles of walking paths. This private, nonprofit operation continues the vision of its founders, who in 1952 had a "brand-new idea" for a way to interpret their southwestern environment as a living, outdoor educational center, a desert in miniature.

The museum focuses on the Sonoran Desert, which stretches from Baja California and Sonora in Mexico to central Arizona and southern California. The most diverse of the four North American deserts, the Sonoran has milder winters and more summer rain than the others, conditions that support more than 2,000 types of plants. Among them are such distinctive species as saguaro and organ pipe cactuses, both found in Arizona, and the bizarre boojum tree of Sonora and Baja, Mexico.

Winding paths through the desert connect a series of exhibits, from naturalistic open-air displays with mountain lions, black bears, and ocelots to close-up views of tarantulas, scorpions, and other invertebrates. Among the most popular exhibits is the walk-in hummingbird aviary, where seven species of these glittering feathered jewels zoom past visitors, sometimes perching practically within touching distance. (You should resist the urge, of course.) When you leave the display, some of the same species will be hovering around feeders outside.

The **"Life Underground"** exhibit features nocturnal creatures you'd ordinarily have little chance to spot in the wild, including Merriam's kangaroo rats, lyre snakes, banded geckos, and kit foxes. The museum also hosts a number of Arizona's most endangered fish: This almost certainly will be your only chance to admire species such as Gila topminnows, Sonora chubs, desert pupfish, and razorback suckers. The museum may be the only opportunity you *want* to have to get close to a western diamondback or Mojave rattlesnake.

If you ever thought a cactus was a cactus, with perhaps only giant saguaro and prickly pear distinctive, you'll learn better at the museum's **Cactus Garden,** where dozens of species grow alongside other Sonoran Desert plants. You'll see how the paloverde tree uses its green trunk and branches for photosynthesis, and how the spiny and usually dead-looking ocotillo has adapted to grow leaves immediately after rain and shed them quickly when drought returns. The **Desert Garden** shows how native plants can be used for decorative landscaping; at certain times of year the flowering plants here teem with butterflies. For the curious traveler, a visit here brings great rewards in a better understanding of this unique and fascinating Southwestern ecosystem. ■

Desert cottontail

Desert hairy scorpion

Monsoon Season

For a newcomer to southern Arizona, the first summer thunderstorm can be an eerie experience. A brilliant July afternoon turns ominously black, lightning flashes, and the rain pours down in sheets so astonishingly dense you can hardly see. And then, in a matter of half an hour, it's over: The sky is blue again, the sun shines, and the storm might almost have been a dream.

Storm, Navajo Indian Reservation, Arizona

Rain in the desert? In summer? Most definitely so. These summer rains, locally called monsoons, set the Sonoran Desert apart from two other North American deserts —the Mojave, and the Great Basin—where rain occurs mostly in winter. Having two rainy seasons gives the Sonoran more diversity of flora and fauna and supports the growth of the tall shrubs, trees, and tree-like cactuses such as saguaros and organ pipes that give this region its distinctive appearance. These same summer rains, fed by moist air moving up from the Gulf of Mexico, fall on the semi-desert grasslands to the east of the Sonoran Desert, turning dry, golden grasses lush and green.

Many plants and animals have adapted their annual life cycles to this second springtime, which usually lasts from July through September. Wildflowers and some cactuses burst into bloom, providing nectar for butterflies and migrant hummingbirds. In the grasslands, birds such as Montezuma quails, Cassin's sparrows, and Botteri's sparrows wait for the summer rains to begin nesting. Couch's and plains spadefoot toads breed, the males giving their bleating or snoring calls to attract females. Saguaros quickly soak up massive amounts of water so they'll have enough stored to last through the coming dry period. Plants that bloomed in spring set seeds, which the rains carry to new locations and nourish.

Travelers need to use caution in the monsoon season. So powerful are these rainstorms that it may be better to pull well off the highway and park rather than try to continue driving. Most last only a short time, and it's better to lose a few minutes than to have an accident. Dry desert washes can turn into raging rivers with frightening speed; don't get trapped in a steep-sided canyon, and never try to drive through a flooded wash. Even after the storm, normally dry roads can turn into mudpits, so take care when you're off the pavement.

The oddest feature of the monsoon rains is their highly localized nature. A storm may drench an area as small as a couple of city blocks, while all around is dry land. The edge of the rain is so sharply defined that it's almost like a huge showerhead was pouring water down on a precisely outlined spot.

Buenos Aires National Wildlife Refuge

- 117,000 acres ■ South-central Arizona, 50 miles southwest of Tucson off Ariz. 286 ■ Best seasons winter and spring ■ Camping, hiking, mountain biking, bird-watching, wildlife viewing ■ Contact the refuge, P.O. Box 109, Sasabe, AZ 85633; phone 520-823-4251

THERE'S A DE FACTO conservation champion hiding in the grasslands of the Altar Valley, along the Mexican border in south-central Arizona. It takes the form of a chunky, cinnamon-colored bird that almost vanished from the Earth, and whose future remains far from secure.

The bird is the masked bobwhite, a subspecies of the northern bobwhite quail familiar throughout the eastern United States. Confined to grassland in Arizona and Sonora, Mexico, the masked bobwhite was thought to be extinct by the mid-20th century, a victim of the degradation of its habitat through overgrazing. In 1964 a small population was found in Mexico, and though biologists tried to reintroduce the quail to its former range and increase its numbers, they eventually realized the only way to save it was to set aside a large tract of land that could be managed specifically for its benefit. As a result, in 1985 the U.S. Fish and Wildlife Service bought 102,000 acres of ranchland west of Arivaca, and then set about trying to restore the grassland's ecological health.

That tract, plus later additions, composes Buenos Aires National Wildlife Refuge, one of southern Arizona's most varied and appealing wildlife-viewing sites. The masked bobwhite is far from the only story here; in fact, the odds of seeing a covey of these quail are fairly slim. But as refuge habitats recover, a whole range of plants and animals benefit, from native grasses to the rare Chiricahua leopard frog.

What to See and Do

As you drive to the refuge **visitor center,** 8 miles north of Sasabe off Ariz. 286, keep alert for mule deer and pronghorn; both are frequently seen along the entrance road. Pronghorn were brought here from Texas in 1987, with additional animals introduced in 2000 from near Flagstaff, Arizona, where development had destroyed their habitat.

Helpful staff members and volunteers at the visitor center can provide maps, species lists, and advice about roads and trails. An exhibit identifies native grasses, which the refuge is trying to encourage in place of the introduced Lehmann's lovegrass, an African plant with poor wildlife value. If nearby **Aguirre Lake** has water, you might want to walk its half-mile access trail to look for waterfowl or shorebirds.

Running south from the visitor center for 10 miles, **Antelope Drive** offers fine grassland birding and, with some luck, looks at other refuge wildlife as well. Pronghorn might be seen as you drive this dirt road (check on its condition after rain), and in winter the roadsides teem with sparrows of a dozen or more species.

The rolling grassland along the drive is perfect habitat for red-tailed hawks and northern harriers, which can be common in winter. The pleasure of seeing these raptors is tempered here by the knowledge that they're among the main predators of masked bobwhite. The captive-raised quail seem to lack natural awareness of predators; in the summer of 1999, refuge biologists introduced wild masked bobwhite captured in Mexico in the hope that better survival skills might be passed on to new generations of quail.

You might see (or at least hear) a masked bobwhite along the drive, but the chances are better for spotting a Gambel's or scaled quail, both common. The secretive Montezuma quail is also found here, which makes this refuge the only place in the United States with four species of quail present.

Both black-tailed and antelope jackrabbits are found on the refuge grasslands; the former is widespread in the West, while the latter's U.S. range is confined to small areas near the Mexican border. To differentiate them, look for the antelope jackrabbit's whiter pelage and lack of black on the tips of its huge ears.

Antelope Drive is the designated wildlife route on the refuge, but more than 100 miles of dirt roads are open for driving (many requiring four-wheel drive), mountain-biking, or walking. High spots along the roads offer beautiful panoramas of a vast patchwork of mesquite-dotted grassland, with the striking granite tower of **Baboquivari Peak,** sacred to the Tohono O'odham Indians, rising to the west.

Though grassland makes up the majority of Buenos Aires, other habitats offer a variety that no visitor should miss. On the eastern edge of the refuge, a 1-mile trail winds alongside **Arivaca Creek** under velvet mesquites, Arizona walnuts, and huge Fremont cottonwoods. You might find a troop of coatimundis here, or the prints of javelinas, bobcats, or raccoons when rains have left the trail soft and muddy.

A couple of miles east, just outside the small town of Arivaca (where a second refuge visitor center is open on weekends and possibly at other times), you'll find **Arivaca Cienega,** a disjunct area of the refuge well worth a visit. "Cienega" is a word you'll see often in these parts; from the Spanish *cien aguas,* or one hundred waters, it refers to a marsh or wetland. Here, a 2-mile loop trail circles a marsh fed by seven springs, creating a rare permanent body of water. Green and great blue herons frequent the area in summer, and in winter ducks cruise open water, while marsh wrens and Virginia rail skulk in the cattails.

Ask at either of the refuge visitor centers about visiting **Brown Canyon** in the Baboquivari Mountains, a beautiful area with a 47-foot natural bridge at its upper end. The canyon, which is open only to guided tours, is home to zone-tailed hawks, golden eagles, and mountain lions, among other species. ■

The Shy Monster

Gila monsters elicit a mixture of wonder and fear in most people. The wonder comes from this lizard's impressive size (20 inches or more) and the beauty of its skin, which resembles orange-and-black beadwork. Fear is felt by those who've heard that it's the only poisonous lizard in the United States, and think of it as they'd think of a rattlesnake. But the Gila monster is in truth a shy, slow-moving creature, and poses practically no threat to anyone except those who try to capture or harass it. This "monster" can't inject its poison as many snakes do. Instead, it must bite its prey—mostly small mammals and

Gila monster

other lizards—and chew, giving time for poison to run along grooved teeth in the rear of its mouth. The Gila monster is a fascinating part of the desert ecosystem. If you spot one, admire it from a distance, and let it be.

Pajarita Wilderness

■ 7,420 acres ■ South-central Arizona, 20 miles west of Nogales off FR 39
■ Best seasons fall-spring ■ Hiking, bird-watching, wildlife viewing ■ Remote
and rugged terrain; FR 39 (Ruby Rd.) is rough but usually passable ■ Contact
Nogales Ranger District, Coronado National Forest, 303 Old Tucson Rd.,
Nogales, AZ 85621; phone 520-281-2296. www.fs.fed.us/r3/coronado

RUGGEDLY SCENIC **Sycamore Canyon,** the centerpiece of this small wilderness, has long been a renowned birding destination. It's one of the very few spots in the United States where there's a good chance to find the five-striped sparrow, a species whose range in this country is confined to extreme southern Arizona. T-shirts read "I hiked Sycamore Canyon— Birding's Bataan," comparing the strenuous route that runs 5 miles along Sycamore Creek to World War II's infamous march. Bring plenty of water and caution if you want to enjoy this rewarding outing, which offers much of interest to birders and nonbirders alike.

The "trail"—often just the streambed—begins at **Hank and Yank Spring** (named for two 19th-century ranchers), off Forest Road 39, 9 miles west of Peña Blanca Lake. Arizona sycamores give the canyon its name; scanning them, Fremont cottonwoods, and other streamside vegetation might bring sightings of elegant trogons, thick-billed kingbirds, sulphur-bellied flycatchers, rose-throated becards, and a number of other sought-after birds. The five-striped sparrow nests in thick brush on hillsides, and the little bird is easiest to find when males perch conspicuously to sing in spring and summer.

Look on slopes for the rare Goodding's ash, named for Leslie Goodding, a biologist who discovered several new species while doing research in Arizona beginning in the 1930s; velvet ash is more common in the canyon. A species of spleenwort (a type of fern) that grows in the canyon is, mystifyingly, found only here, in Mexico, and in the Himalaya. The very rare Tarahumara frog once occurred here and nowhere else in the United States, but the last Arizona specimen was seen in the 1980s; biologists hope to reintroduce this amphibian, which is thought to have been extirpated in part by poisonous mining wastes that polluted waterways. (You'll see evidence of mining all along Forest Road 39 between Nogales and Arivaca, and people still pan for gold in streams in the area.)

With luck you'll spot a mule deer or a troop of coatimundis on your hike, which at times passes through narrow passages where the tall rock walls converge closely. In summer (when you probably shouldn't be here anyway), flash floods caused by monsoon rains (see p. 258) can pose a serious danger, with the water level rising with terrifying swiftness.

In places, small waterfalls add to the beauty of the canyon. Here and there the creek forms pools, and it may be easier simply to get your feet wet than to try to scramble around them. If you continue far enough along this trail, you'll reach a fence marking the Mexican border, the hike's turnaround point. ■

Senita cactus at sunset, Organ Pipe Cactus National Monument

Organ Pipe Cactus National Monument

■ 330,690 acres ■ Southwest Arizona, 75 miles south of Gila Bend off Ariz. 85
■ Best months mid-Nov.–mid-April ■ Camping, hiking, bird-watching, wildlife
viewing ■ Adm. fee ■ Intensely hot in summer ■ Contact the monument,
Route 1, Box 100, Ajo, AZ 85321; phone 520-387-6849. www.nps.gov/orpi

LOCATED AWAY FROM THE URBAN CENTERS of Phoenix and Tucson, and far
from the glamour destination of the Grand Canyon, on a lonely road that
leads only to Mexico, Organ Pipe Cactus National Monument is sometimes overlooked by travelers in the Southwest. That's a shame, because
as a showcase of Sonoran Desert environment this park is unsurpassed.
You'll find no skyscraping peaks here, no dramatic canyons—the main
attraction is a beautiful expanse of native plants and their associated
wildlife, set amid rugged volcanic hills.

Beauty is in the eye of the beholder, of course. Few would argue with
applying that word to the display of wildflowers in Organ Pipe after a wet
winter, when Mexican poppies, brittlebushes, globemallows, lupines, Ajo
lilies, owl's clover, penstemons, and many other species dot the desert
with color, joined by ocotillos, prickly pears, hedgehog cactuses, and

chollas. Wildflowers aside, the more you learn about the ways plants and animals have adapted to an arid, hot environment, the more beauty you see in even the humblest things: the "spade" on the hind foot of a spade-foot toad, which allows it to burrow into the ground, where it remains until summer monsoon rains bring it forth in a breeding frenzy; the long nose of a lesser long-nosed bat, which can reach into cactus flowers for nectar; the huge ears of the jackrabbit and the kit fox, which help dissipate heat; even the resinous coating on creosotebush leaves, which cuts down on transpiration of precious water.

You can see all these things at Organ Pipe Cactus National Monument, and countless other fascinating natural machinations large and small—protected here as an intact, or nearly so, ecosystem. Recognizing the environmental significance of this site, the United Nations listed it as a World Biosphere Reserve in 1976, putting it in the same category as Amazonia and the Everglades.

The national monument is named for the organ pipe cactus, a common species farther south in Mexico, but in the United States confined to a small area along Arizona's southern border. Named for its tall, closely spaced columns resembling the rows of sounding tubes of a pipe organ, it's just one of many notable species here, among them senita (another columnar cactus) and the distinctive-looking elephant tree. Mexican leaf-cutter ants are found in the United States only here, and there's even a butterfly, Howarth's white, that's a specialty of the park.

Two scenic drives facilitate explorations of Organ Pipe, but to appreciate it best you should get out and explore on foot. That doesn't have to mean long backcountry hikes (though camping in the desert is an excellent way to get to know it). Short and medium-length trails offer a chance to see flora and fauna; do your best to be out at dawn and dusk, when wildlife is most active. (Bear in mind that rattlesnakes, of which Organ Pipe hosts six types, can be active then, too. This is no reason to stay off trails, but it is a reason to be cautious.) Walk slowly and quietly. Stop often to simply stand and listen. Carry a hand lens to examine cactus spines, leaves, or a quail feather in the path. See how many of the park's 26 species of cactus you can identify. Look for animal tracks. Smell things. Take your time and enjoy the beauty of it all.

What to See and Do

As you drive into the national monument along Ariz. 85, you're bound to note the striking peak standing above the ridgeline to the east. Called **Montezumas Head** today, it was known to Native Americans as "Old Woman With a Basket." Like much of the Ajo Range, the peak is composed of rhyolite, rock formed by lava cooling on the surface of the earth (rather than by underground cooling of magma, which produces granite and related material). In many places within the national monument you'll see cliffs with distinct bands of dark rhyolite paralleling lighter bands of tuff,

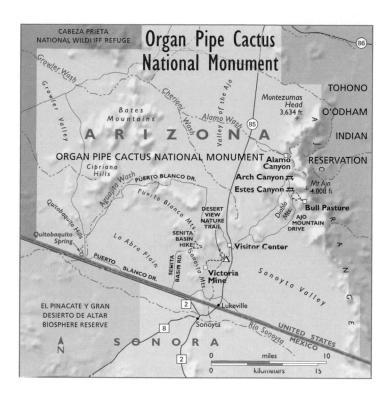

Organ Pipe Cactus National Monument

CABEZA PRIETA NATIONAL WILDLIFE REFUGE

86

Growler Wash

Growler Valley

TOHONO

Bates Mountains

Cherioni Wash

Valley of the Ajo

Montezumas Head 3,634 ft +

Alamo Wash

O'ODHAM

85

ARIZONA

INDIAN

ORGAN PIPE CACTUS NATIONAL MONUMENT

Cipriano Hills

Agajita Wash

PUERTO BLANCO DR.

Alamo Canyon

RESERVATION

Arch Canyon

Estes Canyon

Mt Ajo 4,808 ft +

Quitobaquito Hills

Puerto Blanco Mts.

DESERT VIEW NATURE TRAIL

Diablo Mts.

Bull Pasture

AJO MOUNTAIN DRIVE

Quitobaquito Spring

La Abra Plain

SENITA BASIN HIKE

SENITA BASIN RD.

Sonoyta Mts.

Visitor Center

PUERTO BLANCO DR.

Victoria Mine

Sonoyta Valley

EL PINACATE Y GRAN DESIERTO DE ALTAR BIOSPHERE RESERVE

2

Lukeville

UNITED STATES MEXICO

8

Sonoyta

Rio Sonoyta

N

SONORA

2

0   miles   10

0   kilometers   15

volcanic ash compressed into rock.

There's a fine and informative audiovisual presentation at the park visitor center that introduces the Sonoran Desert and explains why the park you've just entered is so exceptional. As always, a few minutes chatting with a ranger or naturalist about your particular interests can increase your enjoyment of the park tremendously. Just outside, a short wheelchair-accessible nature trail identifies a few common desert plants.

Drive south to the monument's campground to hike either the **Victoria Mine Trail,** 4.5 miles round-trip into granite hills to an abandoned gold and silver mine, or the **Desert View Nature Trail,** a 1.2-mile loop with vistas over the

Sonoyta Valley in the southeastern part of the monument.

Ajo Range Drive

Across Ariz. 85 from the visitor center is the start of the 21-mile **Ajo Range Drive,** an unpaved but well-graded loop around the **Diablo Mountains** to the edge of the Ajos. (Be sure to buy the road guide at the visitor center.) As soon as you begin the drive, heading northeast, you'll observe organ pipe cactus in abundance. These cold-sensitive plants live here at the northern edge of their range, and so favor south-facing slopes; they weren't nearly so noticeable as you drove south into the park.

Organ pipe, saguaro, and cholla cactuses favor the looser, gravelly soils of the alluvial foothills known as *bajadas* over the flat low ground, where the soil is more tightly packed. Creosote bush and bursage, a shrub related to ragweed, dominate the flats. Along washes grow mesquite, foothills paloverde (the Arizona state tree), and ironwood, among other water-dependent plants.

Nine miles into the loop, watch for a natural rock arch 90 feet wide on a cliff far above the road. Less than 2 miles farther, you'll reach the **Estes Canyon picnic area,** where a fairly strenuous loop trail ascends a canyon in the foothills of the Ajo Range. A spur leads to **Bull Pasture,** where early ranchers grazed their cattle, making a round trip of 4.1 miles. In the higher elevation, you'll leave the desert environment and enter a zone of oaks, junipers, and jojobas, shrubs favored by bighorn sheep—which, with luck, you might spot here. Those with stamina can continue 3 more hard miles to the top of 4,808-foot **Mount Ajo.**

Puerto Blanco Drive

Back at the visitor center, you'll find the entrance to the **Puerto Blanco Drive,** named for the mountains it encircles on its 53-mile loop. (Plan on at least a half day to travel this unpaved route.) At its southwestern corner, the drive passes **Quitobaquito Spring,** an oasis bordered by cattail, cottonwood, and mesquite located practically on the Mexican border. Birding can be excellent here from fall through spring. The pond is best known as the home of an endangered subspecies of the desert pupfish. Just over an inch long, the pupfish has evolved to tolerate great fluctuations in water temperature, oxygen content, and salinity—necessities for survival in confined desert water holes.

As the drive heads back east toward Ariz. 85, watch for the north spur to **Senita Basin,** one of the park's highlights. Look along the road for senita cactus and elephant tree, both specialties of the national monument. The former looks something like organ pipe cactus but has deeper fluting and a dense growth of spines at the top of its columns; the latter is named for the resemblance of its thick trunk to the leg of an elephant.

Guided Hike: Senita Basin

This 2.9-mile loop begins at the parking lot at the end of Senita Basin Road, a spur near the end of the Puerto Blanco Drive. It's an easy route with little elevation change, but like the rest of Organ Pipe it can be brutally hot at midday in the warm months. Morning and late afternoon are best, not only for temperature but to increase your chances of seeing wildlife. Keep an eye out for rattlesnakes and scorpions, but don't let their potential presence keep you from enjoying the walk.

The hills that surround you as you start the hike are formed of pinkish granite, volcanic magma that cooled beneath the surface, unlike the rhyolite seen commonly in the Ajo Range. All around are typical desert plants including ocotillos, creosote bushes, organ pipe cactuses, paloverdes, and ironwoods. This last tree, which blooms with purplish flowers in late May, is named for its

Aerial view of the Ajo Range, Organ Pipe Cactus National Monument

extremely hard wood, among the heaviest of any tree in the world.

Soon you'll cross a small rise with lots of white quartz scattered over the ground. Old-time miners saw this mineral as an indication that gold and silver might be present; you'll see evidence of mining in many places along the trail.

Where the trail splits in 0.2 mile, bear right. You'll pass several saguaro cactuses growing up through the branches of the "nurse" trees that sheltered them in their infancy; later, the cactus roots may take so much water from the soil that the nurse can be killed. (So much for gratitude...) One of the common shrubs along the way is limberbush, with small leaves clustered along its branches. Gently bend a branch and you'll understand the name; a small amount of rubber can be extracted from this plant.

At a junction a mile along the trail, turn left onto what was once a wagon road. In less than a half mile you'll descend slightly to cross a wash, a good spot for desert birds. In another few hundred yards you should reach another junction; turn left for the last mile back to the parking lot. ■

Cabeza Prieta National Wildlife Refuge

■ 860,010 acres ■ Southwest Arizona, southwest of Ajo off Ariz. 85 ■ Best
months Nov.-April ■ Primitive camping, hiking, wildlife viewing ■ Very remote,
rugged, and undeveloped; extreme heat makes summer visits inadvisable
■ Contact the refuge, 1611 N. 2nd Ave., Ajo, AZ 85321; phone 520-387-6483.
southwest.fws.gov/refuges/arizona/cabeza.html

FOR THE GREAT MAJORITY of nature-oriented travelers headed south from
Gila Bend, the preferred destination is Organ Pipe Cactus National Monument (see pp. 263-67), which offers developed trails and scenic drives
through superb Sonoran Desert landscape. A few intrepid folks, though,
possessed of a high-clearance vehicle, adequate water, and emergency
equipment, may want to explore Cabeza Prieta National Wildlife Refuge,
one of Arizona's wildest natural areas.

Visitors should stop at the refuge office in Ajo to obtain a permit to
enter; military activities make certain areas dangerous at times. Talk to
staff members about these activities, road conditions, and ask for other
advice about seeing this remote wilderness area, encompassing more than
1,300 square miles along the Mexican border.

Charlie Bell Road provides a practical introduction to the refuge,
running west from Ajo across **Daniels Arroyo** for 18 miles into the
Growler Mountains, one of seven ranges in this immense area. (A lava-
topped granite peak in the southwestern section gave the refuge its name:
cabeza prieta, or dark head.) Two-wheel-drive vehicles with high clearance can traverse this route, which near its end enters the wilderness area
that comprises more than 90 percent of the refuge.

Reptiles are abundant at Cabeza Prieta, though many are rarely seen.
Careful observation might turn up a chuckwalla (the refuge's largest
lizard), a side-blotched lizard, a Great Basin whiptail, or one of two
species of horned lizard. Look for the striking, 4-inch-long zebra-tailed
lizard, too; its scientific name, *Callisaurus,* means "beautiful lizard"—an
apt description. Bear in mind that Cabeza Prieta is home to six species of
rattlesnakes, including the Mojave rattlesnake, which possesses an especially dangerous venom.

Desert bighorn sheep and the endangered Sonoran subspecies of
pronghorn are among the mammals at Cabeza Prieta; the refuge office
can provide advice about possible viewing sites, but neither of these
species is easily seen.

Four-wheel-drive vehicles are required to travel **El Camino del Diablo,** the primitive road that crosses the southern part of the wildlife
refuge. This route was used by both Native Americans and Spanish military expeditions; early travelers reported that the bones of cattle and
horses lined its length, along with human graves. Stretching more than
120 miles between paved highways, this historic route remains a journey
to be undertaken only with serious planning—the "Devil's Road" is still a
dangerous one for the unprepared traveler. ■

Hassayampa River Preserve

■ 333 acres ■ West-central Arizona, 3 miles southeast of Wickenburg off
US 60 ■ Best months mid-Sept.–mid-May. Closed Mon.-Tues. ■ Hiking, bird-
watching, wildlife viewing ■ Contact the preserve, 49614 Hwy. 60, Wickenburg,
AZ 85390; phone 520-684-2772

ONCE UPON A TIME, this property
along the lovely Hassayampa River
was a guest ranch whose owners
called it the Garden of Allah. The
name may have been fanciful, but
in fact it remains a kind of paradise today—a sanctuary for rare
species and, more importantly, for
an ecosystem fast disappearing
from Arizona.

Rising in the Bradshaw Mountains south of Prescott, the Hassayampa runs south to join the
Gila River, flowing underground
for most of its 100-mile path.
(Hassayampa is a Native American
word that means "river that runs
upside down.") Near Wickenburg,
though, bedrock forces the river
up, and for 5 miles its clear waters
travel along the surface. The
resulting lush riparian habitat supports a superb variety of wildlife,
from common species such as rac-

Bird-watching, Hassayampa River Preserve

coons and mule deer to yellow-billed cuckoos and willow flycatchers,
both regionally declining birds.

Most experts believe that only 5 to 10 percent of Arizona's original
riparian habitat remains intact today, the rest lost to dams, agricultural
clearing, groundwater pumping, and water-diversion projects. Dismay-
ingly, studies also show that 80 to 90 percent of desert wildlife species
depend on streams and their associated flora for survival.

As you walk trails on the Hassayampa River Preserve's 333 acres you
might see a zone-tailed hawk soaring overhead or spot the brilliant crimson flash of a vermilion flycatcher. A skittering in the leaves might be a
Gilbert's skink, a rare lizard that finds a home at the preserve. Though it's
present, you probably won't see a longfin dace, a small desert fish that
survives drought by living in shrinking riverine pools until rains return.
The dace is one of 33 fish that were native to Arizona when Europeans
arrived, most of which have suffered from ensuing environmental
changes. One species is extinct, five others have been extirpated from the

state, and many others are threatened or endangered. Bullfrogs and mosquito fish, both non-native introductions, eat some diminutive species of fish, adding to the woes of habitat loss.

The preserve office, located in a restored 1860 adobe ranch house, offers exhibits on riparian ecology, and message boards list recent wildlife sightings. Outside, spend a few quiet minutes at the butterfly and hummingbird gardens. In winter, Anna's hummingbirds swarm feeders; they also nest on the preserve, along with black-chinned and Costa's hummingbirds.

Take the **Lake Trail** around four-acre **Palm Lake,** lined with marsh vegetation and always offering something to see. Pied-billed grebes swim calmly along the surface but dive quickly when threatened. Coots, somber in black and white, are easily seen; their more colorful cousins, common moorhens, show a yellow-tipped red bill and seldom stray from the reeds. Look carefully to spot a sora rail, a skulking bird that walks haltingly along the bank as if carefully considering each step.

The **River Ramble** and **Mesquite Meander Trails,** both half-mile routes, wind through the bosque (the Spanish word for "woodland") along the Hassayampa, among cottonwoods, willows, and mesquites. Here's where you might hear the *kuk-kuk-kuk* call of the yellow-billed cuckoo, a common bird in the eastern United States but threatened in the Southwest by loss of nesting areas. A herd of javelinas—pig-like mammals—might appear, rooting for mesquite beans, insects, or lizards, but you're more likely to see their tracks along the river.

Mesquite-dominated bosques once were common along Arizona rivers, but have declined along with other riparian vegetation. Related to peas and beans, mesquites produce important wildlife food as they provide homes for birds and other creatures. These hardy trees send down roots as far as 175 feet, allowing them to endure periods of drought—just one of countless adaptations to life in an arid world.

Arizona leopard frogs live in the river here, preferring stretches of swift riffles; males have a guttural chuckling call. Introduced bullfrogs like calm water, where courting males give their roaring *jug-o-rum* call. In spring, the riverside forest can be loud with birdsong from species including yellow warblers, summer tanagers, and Abert's towhees. ∎

Tammy-whacking

As if the loss of native vegetation weren't enough, many riparian areas have been invaded by saltcedar, or tamarisk. A shrub or small tree, this exotic was introduced from the Mediterranean region for its pink flower spikes and as a windbreak. Tamarisks produce seeds that germinate more easily than native trees, and their extensive root systems steal water from surrounding vegetation. In many parks, staff members go out "tammy-whacking," cutting down the aliens. It's an arduous process, but it can make a difference in restoring native habitat.

Palm Canyon, Kofa National Wildlife Refuge

Kofa National Wildlife Refuge

■ 665,400 acres ■ Southwest Arizona, 60 miles north of Yuma off US 95
■ Best months Oct.-April ■ Primitive camping, hiking, wildlife viewing ■ Very
hot in summer ■ Contact the refuge, 356 W. 1st St., Yuma, AZ 85364; phone
520-783-7861. southwest.fws.gov/refuges/arizona/kofa.html

"KOFA" STANDS FOR KING OF ARIZONA, a gold mine that gave its name to
a mountain range, and to the wildlife refuge that encompasses both of
them. Old mine shafts and pits dot this area, evidence of valuable minerals taken out of the ground.

For naturalists, though, Kofa's greatest treasure is the habitat it provides for the desert bighorn sheep, about 600 to 900 of which roam the
rugged mountains. Your best chance for seeing bighorns is to drive one
of the dirt roads leading east from US 95 around and into the mountains
early in the morning, scanning ridgetops with binoculars.

Kofa is also known for a small grove of California fan palms, one of
only two or three areas of naturally occurring palms in Arizona. **Palm
Canyon** is by far the most visited spot in the refuge, and, unlike the
refuge's remote backcountry, it's easily accessible. From US 95 south of
Quartzsite by 18 miles, a dirt road leaves the highway just north of Milepost 85 and leads 7 miles east to the mouth of the canyon. (A road that
splits off north leads to **Kofa Queen Canyon,** a good area for bighorn
observation.) From the parking area a half-mile trail ascends to a viewpoint from which the palms can be seen in a narrow crevice on the north
wall, providing an exotic scene in these rugged, arid mountains. ■

Bill Williams River National Wildlife Refuge

Lower Colorado River National Wildlife Refuges

■ Western Arizona, along the Arizona-California border ■ Hiking, boating, kayaking, canoeing, bird-watching, wildlife viewing ■ Contact the refuges (see following pages)

TOURIST BROCHURES FOR Arizona's Colorado River region—its "West Coast"—tend to show the same images time after time: water-skiers cutting across blue water, bikini-clad women waving from speedboats, colorful sailboats leaning in the wind, fancy waterside resorts. They tell how water from the river provides for the needs of Phoenix and other cities, how it irrigates agricultural land, and how huge reservoirs have created "paradise" in the desert.

This is all accurate, up to a point. Waterskiing is fun, and city people need water. But a price was paid for recreation, for urban growth, for raising crops in a land of scant rain, for turning a desert into a coast.

It was paid by the Colorado River. It was paid by unglamorous creatures like the bonytail chub, the Colorado pikeminnow, the Yuma clapper rail, the leopard frog, the beaver, and by vanished marshes and woodlands of cottonwood and willow.

Once, the Colorado ran wild on its 1,450-mile course through the West to the Gulf of California. Its water rose and fell in natural cycles: at times rushing along, scouring vegetation from canyons and overtopping its banks to spread silt and seeds, at times subsiding to create calm backwaters where fish laid eggs. Broad belts of trees lined its banks in many places, while elsewhere cattails and other marsh plants grew in profusion.

As European settlers arrived, they and their descendants wanted a different kind of river, one whose waters were impounded to provide greater and more predictable water supplies, to generate electricity, to stop flooding, and to create recreational lakes. A series of dams—beginning with Hoover in 1935 and including Glen Canyon, Davis, Parker, and Imperial —transformed the lower Colorado. Exotic species that competed with natives were introduced into its ecosystem, intentionally or accidentally.

Now, of the state's 33 native fish, more than half are listed as threatened or endangered. Populations of the southwestern variety of willow flycatcher and Yuma clapper rail have dropped precipitously. These changes are signs of the regional disappearance of riparian-associated plants and animals, from wildflowers and insects to hawks and trees.

Nothing can bring back the lower Colorado River as the naturally functioning ecosystem it was. However, in four national wildlife refuges scattered along the river between Yuma and Bullhead City you can experience a sampling of the wild Colorado as it has survived into the 21st century. You can see waterfowl and pelicans (and even, perhaps, a willow flycatcher); you can walk under cottonwoods; you can hear the honking call of the Sonoran Desert toad; you can glimpse a beaver swimming across an opening in a marsh.

None of the four have extensive trails or driving tours compared to some refuges, and it helps to have (or rent) a canoe to get the most out of a couple. But all have worthwhile natural attractions, and all are worth a visit to gain an understanding of the once and future Colorado River.

Imperial National Wildlife Refuge

It's a fascinating experience, at the **Imperial National Wildlife Refuge** *(Off US 95, 40 miles N of Yuma. 520-783-3371. southwest.fws.gov/ refuges/arizona/imperial/html. Open only weekends in winter)*, to stand on an overlook enjoying ducks, egrets, and other waterbirds in a green Colorado River marsh, and within five minutes set out on a trail through a desert that receives, on average, less than 4 inches of rain a year. As well as providing an entertaining natural contrast, the hike brings home the importance of riparian areas in an arid environment. How many critters live in an acre of the marsh? How many live on an acre of the desert?

The answer to the second question is: more than it seems, but still not a lot. The marsh and the river serve as oases here, sustaining much of the wildlife that dwells in the adjoining desert as well as its own inhabitants.

To begin your discoveries at Imperial, the southernmost of the four lower Colorado refuges, stop at the visitor center just north of Martinez Lake. After you've picked up a map and talked to a staff member, walk to the nearby observation tower to scan the fields below. Depending on the season you might see great blue herons, great egrets, sandhill cranes, Canada geese, or snow geese feeding in or near the cropland. From here you can appreciate the fact that the refuge protects the last unchanneled section of the Colorado River before it enters Mexico. In all, Imperial stretches along 30 miles of the river, which spreads out to form ponds, backwaters, and marshes on both the Arizona and California sides.

Drive north on Red Cloud Mine Road, which crosses desert washes as it leads to three lookout points from which you can inspect the river and its bordering wetlands. Early or late in the day you could, if you're lucky, spot a mule deer heading toward the river for water—or if you're very lucky, a desert bighorn sheep. From the lookouts you'll have a chance to observe a wide variety of birds, including more than a dozen species of ducks, white pelicans, double-crested cormorants, pied-billed grebes, ring-billed gulls, swallows, vermilion flycatchers, marsh wrens (more easily heard than seen), and red-winged and yellow-headed blackbirds.

Red Cloud Mine Road also passes the parking area for the **Painted Desert Trail,** a 1-mile loop through multicolored volcanic rock formations. Before beginning the trail, be aware of how much water you need to walk through the desert (one gallon per person per day), and understand that rattlesnakes prefer rocky habitats. Early morning is the best time to be here, when wildlife is most active. Black-tailed jackrabbits, desert cottontails, Gambel's quails, phainopeplas, desert iguanas, and chuckwallas are just a few of the animals that live here. As you pass along washes, note the mesquite, ironwood, and paloverde; all these trees have adapted to a dry environment, but they grow best along watercourses.

Cibola National Wildlife Refuge

Though much of **Cibola National Wildlife Refuge** (*17 miles S of Blythe, CA, off I-10 via Neighbour's Blvd. 520-857-3253. southwest.fws.gov/ refuges/arizona/cibola.html*) lies in Arizona, the refuge is usually reached by driving south from Blythe, California, on a road that crosses the Colorado River a few miles before reaching the wildlife refuge's headquarters. Here the 4-mile **Canada Goose Drive** loops through cropland where large flocks of Canada and snow geese and sandhill cranes rest and feed in winter. Accustomed to traffic nearby, these birds often remain near the road, allowing close-up views and, with a telephoto lens, excellent photos. (Stay inside your vehicle to avoid disturbing them.) As you make the one-way circle, watch for other open-country birds such as red-tailed hawks, burrowing owls, Say's phoebes, Gambel's quail, roadrunners, loggerhead shrikes, and western meadowlarks.

Located just north of the Imperial refuge, Cibola covers 13 miles of the Colorado River, encompassing extensive marshes where a healthy population of the endangered Yuma clapper rails nests. Your chances of seeing this shy bird are slim, though its *kek-kek-kek* call is heard often at dawn and dusk in spring. Rails skulk through marsh vegetation and occasionally show themselves in the reeds at the edge of open water.

From fall through spring, you'll have no trouble seeing ducks in refuge marshes and lakes. Ask at the refuge office about roads leading through **Hart Mine Marsh** in Cibola's southern section, continuing south to a lookout over **Cibola Lake,** where wading birds, white pelicans, and

waterfowl occur seasonally. Lands surrounding the refuge are also home to
feral burros, hardy creatures whose
ancestors toted supplies for miners
and homesteaders before the era of
sport-utility vehicles.

Here as in many places throughout
the Southwest, the introduced
tamarisk (salt cedar) has taken over
large areas, crowding out the original
vegetation; refuge personnel work
hard to eliminate it where possible,
re-creating the native cottonwood and
willow habitat. Work progresses, too,
on restoring former channels of the
Colorado, to provide more water to
Hart Mine Marsh and the wildlife that
depends on it.

The Big Minnow

The Colorado pikeminnow
once was considered the best
food fish in the lower Colorado. The largest minnow in
the United States (up to 6
feet long and weighing as
much as 80 pounds), it feeds
on other fish and was once
the top predator in the river,
playing the same role that the
mountain lion does in forests.
Dams and other changes in
the Colorado led to the
pikeminnow's listing as endangered in 1967. The bonytail
chub, the woundfin, and the
razorback sucker are among
other Colorado River natives
imperiled by habitat loss.

Bill Williams River National Wildlife Refuge

The best remaining native riparian
habitat on the lower Colorado River
lies within this refuge *(19 miles N of Parker on Ariz. 95. 520-667-4144.
southwest.fws.gov/refuges/arizona/billwill.html)*, located where the **Bill
Williams River** enters the artificial expanse of **Lake Havasu.** Named for
a river named for a 19th-century mountain man, the refuge essentially
offers two ways to experience its environment.

The marsh at the river's mouth is best seen by canoe or other small
nonmotorized boat, which can be launched at the shoreline behind
refuge headquarters on Ariz. 95 or at one of the lake's commercial mari-
nas. Paddle upstream along the river (actually a backwater area of the
lake) to explore cattails that are home to clapper rails and possibly spot
a beaver or muskrat. The marsh is often alive with various wetland birds
such as grebes, coots, ducks, belted kingfishers, herons, gulls, and common moorhens. You can travel upstream as much as 2.5 miles, seeing a
woodland of Fremont cottonwoods, Goodding willows, and mesquites
like the ones that once bordered nearly the entire lower Colorado. The
endangered bonytail chub and razorback sucker have been reintroduced
into the lake here.

If you don't have access to a canoe, you can walk to various lookout
points around the Ariz. 95 bridge over the river to scan for waterbirds.
This is a good place to learn to separate Clark's and western grebes, two
lookalike species that are common breeders here.

The Bill Williams River refuge extends for 9 miles upriver, east from
Lake Havasu. Just south of the river bridge, **Planet Ranch Road** parallels
the river on the south bank, providing another way to see the area. The

first 3.5 miles of this dirt road are usually passable by passenger car, but four-wheel drive is required for the exceptionally soft sand route beyond. Take special care on this narrow, winding road, where a joyrider could be around the next bend.

Get out and walk the road or explore the riparian zone (choked in many places by exotic tamarisk) and you'll have a chance of finding the endangered southwestern willow flycatcher, though the population of this bird has declined and it has become very rare here. Several of its flycatcher relatives are seen far more often, including black phoebes, ash-throated flycatchers, and the beautiful vermilion flycatcher. Listen for the call of the yellow-billed cuckoo, another species hurt by destruction of riparian areas in the Southwest. In spring, the slopes above the road are bright with the yellow flowers of brittlebush. Scan the cliffs above occasionally and you could spot a desert bighorn sheep looking back at you.

Havasu National Wildlife Refuge

Havasu National Wildlife Refuge *(N of Lake Havasu City on Ariz. 95. 760-326-3853. southwest.fws.gov/refuges/arizona/havasu.html)* ranges from Lake Havasu City along 30 miles of the Colorado River and upper Lake Havasu. Its southern part is not of the greatest interest to wildlife-watchers, although by taking London Bridge Road north from Lake Havasu City you can stop at **Mesquite Bay,** where a fishing pier provides a lookout from which you can scan for wintering ducks and other water-birds on the open water.

More productive is the expansive **Topock Marsh,** an area of drowned trees and wetland vegetation north of I-40. Many people enjoy putting a canoe in the water here to explore backwaters, but even lacking a boat you can see a good variety of birds from lookouts such as **New South Dike** *(1.5 miles N of I-40 off Ariz. 95),* or **Pintail Slough,** 8 miles farther north. Herons, egrets, ducks, grebes, double-crested cormorants, and common moorhens all breed in the area. The endangered Yuma clapper rail nests here, too, but here as elsewhere patience and luck are needed actually to see one; scan muddy banks at the edges of reeds and you might spot a normally shy rail briefly showing itself in the open.

For most people, the highlight of a trip to the refuge is the 16-mile boat trip through **Topock Gorge,** where tall sandstone cliffs squeeze the Colorado River through narrow canyons and desert bighorn sheep scamper across the cliffs above. Along the way you'll find beautiful beaches for relaxing and impromptu picnics (but not for camping, which is prohibited in the gorge). Nature-oriented visitors will want to take a canoe or kayak (easily rented from local outfitters, which will also arrange to pick you up at the south end of the gorge), the better to explore shallow backwaters off the main river. Winter is by far the best time for the trip, since waterbirds are more common and motorized boat traffic is much lighter. In summer, recreational boaters make Lake Havasu and the gorge a zoo—and not the wildlife kind, either. ■

Kayakers in Topock Gorge, Havasu National Wildlife Refuge

Other Sites

The following is a select list of other sites of interest located in the Southwest.

Colorado Plateau

Agua Fria National Monument

Forty miles north of Phoenix, off I-17, this 71,000-acre new national monument (established by President Bill Clinton in January 2000) contains more than 400 prehistoric sites with petroglyphs and extensive agricultural terracing. Contact Phoenix Field Office, Bureau of Land Management, 2015 W. Deer Valley Rd., Phoenix, AZ 85027; phone 623-580-5500. phoenix.az.blm.gov

Southern Rocky Mountains

Edward Sargent State Wildlife Area

This wildlife preserve borders the Chama River, just south of the New Mexico-Colorado state line. The area, which comprises a major portion of the Chamita River Valley, consists of a broad basin of grasslands and wildflowers, providing excellent habitat for deer and elk. It's located near Chama off N. Mex. 17. Contact New Mexico Game and Fish, P.O. Box 25112, Santa Fe, NM 87504; phone 505-827-7911 or 800-862-9310. www.gmfsh.state.nm.us

Chihuahuan Desert and Grasslands

Las Vegas National Wildlife Refuge

Although hiking in the refuge is limited to a half-mile trail, the marshes, ponds, and canyons you'll find here offer excellent bird-watching. In winter, hawks, eagles, and waterfowl are commonly seen. The refuge lies 6 miles southeast of Las Vegas on N. Mex 281. Contact the refuge, Rte. 1, Box 399, Las Vegas, NM 87701; phone 505-425-3581.

Mescalero Sands

Located 45 miles east of Roswell off US 380, this peaceful preserve of white sand dunes and native grasses offers an opportunity to encounter an endangered sand dune lizard and see prairie chickens performing their entertaining courtship dance. Contact Roswell Field Office, Bureau of Land Management, 2909 W. 2nd St., Roswell, NM 88201; phone 505-627-0272. www.gmfsh.state.nm.us/pagemill_text/publication/mescalero.html

Randall Davey Audubon Center

Exhibits of regional wildlife are featured here along with the half-mile El Temporal Trail, leading through a meadow of grasses, juniper, and pinyon and ponderosa pine. The center is a great resource for information on the nearby trails, birding sites, and wildlife viewing. Natural history workshops are offered throughout the year. Contact the center, 1800 Upper Canyon Rd., Santa Fe, NM 87501; phone 505-983-4609. www.trail.com/~rdac

Sugarite Canyon State Park

Wooded trails lead through the canyon, where you can see the park's distinctive basaltic rock columns, known as caprock; rock climbing is permitted. The visitor center features historical exhibits on the coal-mining camp located here in the early 1900s. The park is located 10 miles northeast of Raton, off N. Mex 72. Contact the park, HCR 63, P.O. Box 386, Raton, NM 87740; phone 505-445-5607. www.emnrd.state.nm.us/nmparks

Valley of Fires Recreation Area

Extensive lava flows as old as 2,000 years are the highlight of this Bureau of Land Management site, located 4 miles west of Carrizozo on US 380. The area also offers camping and hiking. Contact Roswell Field Office, 2909 W. 2nd St., Roswell, NM 88201; phone 505-627-0272. www.gmfsh.state.nm.us/pagemill_text/publication/mescalero.html

New Mexico Highlands and Rio Grande Valley

Dripping Springs Preserve

Located near Las Cruces, east of I-25 on University Blvd., the preserve's centerpiece is its sheer canyons ever wet by spring-fed streams. A diversity of plants thrive here including velvet ash, netleaf, hackberry, and evening primrose. Among the birds you can see are red-naped sapsuckers, prairie falcons, and canyon wrens. A small visitor center provides interpretive brochures. Contact the Nature Conservancy, 212 E. Marcy St., Santa Fe, NM 87501; phone 505-988-3867.

Gila Riparian Preserve

One-third of all native North American bird species have been seen in the area of this preserve, a property of the Nature Conservancy. Adjacent to Gila National Forest, the preserve protects the fragile riparian habitat along the Gila River. It is located northwest of Silver City via US 180 and N. Mex. 293. Contact the Nature Conservancy, 212 E. Marcy St., Santa Fe, NM 87501; phone 505-988-3867.

Holloman Lakes

This undeveloped bird-watching site, located west of Alamagordo on US 70 near Holloman Air Force Base, is centered around several artificial salt ponds. The area is a haven for wading birds, shorebirds, and waterfowl. Contact Las Cruces Field Office, Bureau of Land Management, 1800 Marquess St., Las Cruces, NM 88005; phone 505-525-4300.

Mimbres River Preserve

This small, 160-acre nature preserve protects a stretch of the Mimbres River that serves as a refuge for the endangered Chihuahua chub. Thought to be extinct for more than 100 years, this unique fish was rediscovered here in the 1970s. The site is located 35 miles northeast of Silver City via N. Mex. 152 and N. Mex. 35. Contact the Nature Conservancy,

212 E. Marcy St., Santa Fe, NM 87501; phone 505-988-3867.

Rock Hound State Park

Set on the rugged west slope of the Little Florida Mountains, the park's abundant agates, geodes, quartzes, opals, perlites, and pitchstone make it a favorite among rock hounds. Park officials allow visitors to collect rocks (up to 15 pounds). Trails provide spectacular views of the surrounding landscape. Contact the park, P.O. Box 1064, Deming, NM 88030; phone 505-546-6182. www.emnrd.state.nm.us/nmparks

Arizona Highlands

Desert Botanical Garden

This 145-acre facility is a showplace for desert plants from around the world. The third-mile Desert Discovery Trail introduces visitors to yuccas, agaves, euphorbias, and other plants from Madagascar, Australia, and elsewhere. Year-round classes highlight desert flora, fauna, and landscape. Contact the botanical garden, 1201 N. Galvin Pkwy.,

Phoenix, AZ 85008; phone 480-941-1225. www.dbg.org

Sky Islands and the Arizona Desert

Alamo Lake State Park

A reservoir of the Bill Williams River, Alamo Lake offers a combination of desert environs and excellent fishing, particularly largemouth bass and catfish. The marina provides equipment and boat rentals. Hikers will find excellent walking in the Rawhide and Buckskin Mountains. The park is located 36 miles north of Wenden via US 60 and the Alamo Lake Access Road. Contact the park, P.O. Box 38, Wenden, AZ 85357; phone 520-669-2088. www.pr.state.az.us

Picacho Peak State Park

A prominent landmark and a magnet for adventuresome hikers, Picacho Peak rises 1,500 feet above the desert floor. There's an easy trail around the base of the peak where in spring you'll find a spectacular show of wildflowers. The park is also a

popular spot for camping and picnicking. It's located 35 miles northwest of Tucson off I-10. Contact the park, P.O. Box 275, Picacho, AZ 85241; phone 520-466-3183. www.pr.state.az.us

Roper Lake State Park

Located 4 miles south of Safford off US 191, Roper Lake is a delightful desert oasis at the foot of Mount Graham. Activities include fishing, camping, picnicking, hiking, and swimming. Contact the park, Rte. 2, Box 712, Safford, AZ 85546; phone 520-428-6760. www.pr.state.az.us

South Mountain Park

Billed as the world's largest city park, South Mountain's historic 16,500 acres served as Hohokam Indian hunting ground and a Depression-era work camp. The park's 58 miles of multiple-use trails offer hiking, mountain biking, and horseback riding. Contact the park, 10919 S. Central Ave., Phoenix, AZ 85040; phone 602-495-0222. www.ci.phoenix.az.us/parks/hikesoth.html

Resources

The following is a select list of resources. Contact state and local associations for additional outfitter and lodging options. For chain hotels and motels in Arizona and New Mexico, see p. 283.

Current information about road conditions is available at 888-411-7623 or www.azfms.com (Arizona); 505-827-9300 or 800-432-4269 (New Mexico).

ARIZONA

Federal and State Agencies

Arizona Game & Fish Department
2221 W. Greenway Rd.,
Phoenix, AZ 85023
602-942-3000
www.gf.state.az.us
Hunting and fishing licenses, and site information.

Arizona Office of Tourism
2702 N. 3rd St., Ste. 4015
Phoenix, AZ 85004
800-842-8257
www.arizonaguide.com
General resource for travel in Arizona, including camping and lodging information.

Arizona State Parks
1300 W. Washington St.
Phoenix, AZ 85007
602-542-4174
www.pr.state.az.us
Information on Arizona parks, including camping.

Arizona Trail Association
P.O. Box 36/36
Phoenix, AZ 85067
602-252-4794
aztrail.org
Information source for the 750-mile trans-state trail.

Bureau of Land Management
222 N. Central Ave.
Phoenix, AZ 85004
602-417-9200
www.az.blm.gov

Rules and regulations for use and camping on BLM-managed lands.

Public Lands Information Center
222 N. Central Ave.
Phoenix, AZ 85004
602-417-9300
www.publiclands.org
Part of a national network which provides information and educational resources on state and federally managed public lands. Recreation permits may be obtained here.

U. S. D. A. Forest Service, Southwestern Region
517 Gold Ave. S.W.
Albuquerque, NM 87102
505-842-3292
www.fs.fed.us/r3/
Source for maps, as well as camping and trail information, for national forests and grasslands in Arizona and New Mexico.

Outfitters and Activities

Air Grand Canyon
Family Tours
P.O. Box 3399
Grand Canyon, AZ 86023
520-638-2686
www.airgrandcanyon.com
Aerial tours in high-wing
Cessna airplanes over
the Grand Canyon,
Lake Powell, and Glenn
Canyon Dam.

Arizona Raft Adventures
4050 E. Huntington Dr.
Flagstaff, AZ 86004
520-526-8200 or
   800-786-7238
www.azraft.com
Oar-raft, plus paddle- and
motor-raft and kayak trips,
on the Colorado River.

Arizona River Runners
P.O. Box 47788
Phoenix, AZ 85068
602-867-4866 or
   800-477-7238
www.raftarizona.com
Motorized and oar-raft
trips on the Colorado
River.

Blue Sky Whitewater
143 N. High St.
Globe, AZ 85501
520-425-5252 or
   800-425-5253
www.blueskyexpeditions.net
White-water rafting and
scenic float trips. Blue Sky
offers a spring run down
the Upper Salt River
through Salt River Canyon
Wilderness, and a summer
trip on the Gila River.

Cimarron River Company
7902 E. Pierce St.
Scottsdale, AZ 85257
480-994-1199
Features one- to five-day
trips on the Upper Verde
Wild and Scenic River,
and day trips on the
Lower Verde.

Colorado River and Trail
Expeditions
P.O. Box 57575
Salt Lake City, UT 84157
801-261-1789 or
   800-253-7328
www.crateinc.com
Motorized, kayak, oar,
and paddleboat trips.

De Chelly Tours
P.O. Box 2539
Chinle, AZ 86503
520-674-3772
www.gst.net/~rolandm/dct
Navajo-owned company
offers day and multiday Jeep
tours of Canyon de Chelly
National Monument.

Far Flung Adventures
P.O. Box 284
Globe, AZ 85502
800-231-7238
www.farflung.com
Features one- to five-day
trips on the Upper Salt
River, plus white-water
classes and swift-water
rescue training.

Grand Canyon Airlines
Hwy. 64, P.O. Box 3038
Grand Canyon National
   Park Airport
Grand Canyon, AZ 86023
520-638-2407 or
   800-528-2413
www.grandcanyonairlines
   .com
Operating since 1927,
GCA offers flights over
the canyon year-round.

Grand Canyon Expedition
Company
P.O. Box 0
Kanab, UT 84741
435-644-2691 or
   800-544-2691
www.gcex.com
Motorized and dory excur-
sions; history, ecology, geology, and photo tours.

Justin's Horse Rental
P.O. Box 881
Chinle, AZ 86503
520-674-5678
Two-hour to multiday rides
in Canyon de Chelly area.

Kenai Helicopters
Hwy. 64
Grand Canyon, AZ 86023
520-638-2764
www.flykenai.com
Tours of the Grand Canyon.

Outdoor Adventure
River Specialists
P.O. Box 67
2687 S. Hwy. 49
Angels Camp, CA 95222
209-736-4677 or
   800-346-6277
www.oars.com
Dory, kayak, and oar trips
on the Colorado River.

Papillon Grand Canyon
Helicopters
Hwy. 64
Grand Canyon, AZ 86023
520-573-6817
www.papillon.com
Aerial tours of the canyon,
plus day and overnight
excursions to Havasupai
Indian Village.

Thunderbird Lodge
P.O. Box 548
Chinle, AZ 86503
520-674-5841 or
   800-679-2473
www.tbirdlodge.com
Half- and full-day jeep
tours of Canyon de Chelly
National Monument.

Outdoor Education and Resources

Grand Canyon Field Institute
P.O. Box 399
Grand Canyon, AZ 86023
520-638-2485
www.grandcanyon.org/
   fieldinstitute
Hiking, backpacking, and
rafting excursions, plus
classes and workshops in
Grand Canyon National
Park. Topics include geology, archaeology, Native
American culture, photog-
raphy, and art. GCFI's
educational vacations
are suitable for individuals,
families, and groups.

Museum of Northern
Arizona
3101 N. Fort Valley Rd.
Flagstaff, AZ 86001
520-774-5213
www.musnaz.org
Educational field pro-
grams focus on the
natural history and cul-
tures of the Colorado
Plateau. Multiday excur-
sions include hiking, backpacking, camping, rafting,
kayaking, van tours, and
motel-to-motel trips.

Nature Conservancy
of Arizona
1510 E. Ft. Lowell St.
Tucson, AZ 85719
520-622-3861
www.tnc.org
Birding and natural history
tours of the Sonoran
Desert and southeastern
Arizona.

Southeastern Arizona Bird
Observatory
  1 Main St., P.O. Box 5521
  Bisbee, AZ 85603
  520-432-1388
  Dedicated to the study
  and preservation of the
  region's birds and other
  wildlife, and habitats, this
  nonprofit organization
  offers nature programs
  year-round.

Tucson Audubon Society
  300 E. University Blvd.
  Tucson, AZ 85705
  www.audubon.org/
  chapter/az/tucson
  Trips to San Pedro River,
  Madera Canyon, Mt. Lem-
  mon, and Aravaipa West.

Lodging

See Arizona Office of
Tourism (p. 279).

Arizona Dude Ranch
Association
  P. O. Box 603
  Cortaro, AZ 85652
  www.azdra.com
  Resource for rural to
  resort-style ranches.

Arizona Trails Bed and
Breakfast Reservation
Service
  P.O. Box 18998
  Fountain Hills, AZ 85269
  480-837-4284 or
  888-799-4284
  www.arizonatrails.com

Mi Casa Su Casa Bed and
Breakfast Reservation
Service
  P.O. Box 950
  Tempe, AZ 85280
  480-990-0682 or
  800-456-0682
  www.azres.com

**Canyon de Chelly, Petrified
National Forest, and vicinity**

Holbrook is a popular gateway to Canyon de Chelly and
the Petrified Forest. Contact
the Chamber of Commerce
(520-524-6558 or 800-524-
2459. www.arizonaguide.
com/cities/holbrook).

**Grand Canyon National
Park, and vicinity**

Grand Canyon National Park
Lodges runs El Tovar Hotel;
Bright Angel, Kachina, Thun-
derbird, Maswik, and Yavapai

Lodges; Phantom Ranch,
and Trailer Village. For
reservations (book well in
advance), contact the conces-
sionaire (303-297-2757. www
.grandcanyonlodges.com)
  Gateway towns including
Grand Canyon Village,
Williams, and Tusayan offer
a wide range of accommodations, from camping to
hotels. For information, visit
www.thecanyon.com/nps;
or contact Grand Canyon
Tourism at the Williams-
Grand Canyon Chamber of
Commerce (800-638-2052.
www.thecanyon.com).

**Saguaro National Park and
Santa Catalina Mountains**

Tucson is the launch for
exploring Saguaro National
Park and the Santa Catalina
Mountains. For lodging information, contact the Metro
Tucson Convention & Visitors
Bureau (520-624-1817
or 800-638-8350. www
.visittucson. org).

**Sedona and Oak Creek
Canyons, and vicinity**

For information on lodgings,
camping, or activities in
the Sedona area, contact
the Sedona-Oak Creek
Canyon Chamber of Com-
merce (520-282-7722
or 800-288-7336. www
.sedonachamber.com).

**White Mountains and
Mogollon Rim**

Show Low is a popular
gateway to this area. For
lodging and other tourist
information, contact the
Show Low Chamber of
Commerce (520-537-2326
or 888-SHOWLOW.
www. arizonaguide.com/
cities/showlow).

Camping

For a listing of private
campgrounds around the
state, contact the Arizona
Office of Tourism (see
p. 279). Arizona State Parks
(see p. 279), the U. S. D.A.
Forest Service (see p. 279),
and the Bureau of Land
Management (see p. 279)
also operate campgrounds
throughout Arizona. Addi-
tional information is available
at www.gorp.com

Happy Campers
  1111 10th St., No. 175
  Alamogordo, NM 88310
  505-925-0679
  www.happycampers.net
  Resource for RV camping
  in the Southwest.

NEW MEXICO

Federal and
State Agencies

Bureau of Land Management
  1474 Rodeo Rd.
  Santa Fe, NM 87505
  505-438-7400
  www.nm.blm.gov
  (see p. 279)

New Mexico Department
of Tourism
  491 Old Santa Fe Trail
  P.O. Box 20002
  Santa Fe, NM 87501
  505-827-7400 or
  800-733-6396
  www.newmexico.org
  General travel resource.

New Mexico Game and Fish
  P.O. Box 25112
  Santa Fe, NM 87504
  505-827-7911 or
  800-862-9310
  www.gmfsh.state.nm.us
  Information, proclamation
  requests, and fishing and
  hunting licenses.

New Mexico State Parks
  P.O. Box 1147
  Santa Fe, NM 87504
  888-667-2757
  www.emnrd.state.nm.us/
  nmparks
  General information source.
  Some parks accept reservations; call 877-664-7787 or
  visit www.icampnm.com

Public Lands Information
Centers (see p. 279)
  1474 Rodeo Rd.
  Santa Fe, NM 87505
  505-438-7542

  2909 W. 2nd St.
  Roswell, NM 88201
  505-627-0210

  6501 4th St. N.W., Ste. G
  Albuquerque, NM 87107
  505-345-9498 or
  877-851-8946

U. S. D.A. Forest Service
(see p. 279)

Outfitters and Activities

Derringer Outfitters
& Guides
P.O. Box 157
Quemado, NM 87829
www.wild-horse
-ranch.com
505-773-4860 or
  888-760-8131
Year-round wilderness
training, seminars, and
activities, including hiking,
camping, hunting, fly-
fishing, horseback riding,
backpacking, canoeing,
kayaking, white-water
rafting, river floats; horse,
goat, and llama pack trips;
and tours of Indian ruins.

Far Flung Adventures
P.O. Box 707
El Prado, NM 87529
505-758-2628
www.farflung.com
Since 1977, this company
has offered trips on the
Lower Gorge and Taos
Box of the Rio Grande,
and Rio Chama.

Great Southwest
Adventures
P.O. Box 31151
Santa Fe, NM 87594
505-455-2700
www.swadventures.com
Tours of Santa Fe, Taos,
Los Alamos, Chimayo,
Abiquiu, Bandelier
National Monument,
Jemez Mountains, and
other northern New
Mexico sites. Photography
and evening tours, hiking
and backpacking trips;
custom tours arranged.

Native Sons Adventures
1033-A Paseo del Pueblo
Sur
Taos, NM 87571
505-758-9342 or
  800-753-7559
www.newmex.com/nsa
Half- and multiday trips
on the Rio Grande and
Rio Chama, plus hiking
and mountain bike tours
in the Taos vicinity.

New Mexico Guides
Association
P.O. Box 2463
Santa Fe, NM 87504
505-988-8022
www.nmguides.com
Guide certification pro-
gram covers regional his-
tory, natural history, art,
culture, and architecture;
and tour management.

New Mexico Mountain Bike
Adventures
P.O. Box 443
Cerrillos, NM 87010
505-474-0074
www.gorp.com/nmmbadv/
Features rides in the
Jemez Mountains and
other wild places near
Santa Fe; women-only
rides offered.

New Mexico Touring
Society
P.O. Box 1261
Albuquerque, NM 87103
505-237-9700
www.swcp.com/~russells/
nmts
Caters to recreational
riders of all ages and abilities. Day and multiday
road and mountain bike
rides around the state.

Santa Fe Rafting Company
P.O. Box 23525
Santa Fe, NM 87502
505-988-4914 or
  800-467-RAFT
www.santaferafting.com
Half- to three-day trips
on the Lower Gorge and
Taos Box of the Rio
Grande, and Rio Chama.

Southwest Wilderness
Adventures
P.O. Box 9380
Santa Fe, NM 87504
505-983-7262 or
  800-869-RAFT
Day and overnight raft
trips on the Rio Grande.

Sun Mountain Bike
Company.
107 Washington Ave.
Santa Fe, NM 87501
505-820-2902
www.sunmountainbikeco
.com
Focus on excursions
around the Santa Fe area,
including tours of the
Tesuque Valley and Santa
Fe National Forest.

Lodging

See New Mexico Dept. of
Tourism (p. 281)

New Mexico Bed &
Breakfast Association
P.O. Box 2925
Santa Fe, NM 87504
505-766-5380 or
  800-661-6649
www.nmbba.org
Central source for bed-
and-breakfast lodgings.

New Mexico Central
Reservations
20 First Plaza, Ste. 25
Albuquerque, NM 87102
505-766-9770 or
  800-466-7829
www.nmtravel.com
Arranges lodging as well
as airline reservations and
rental cars. Custom travel
packages offered.

New Mexico Hotel &
Motel Association
811 St. Michaels Dr.
Santa Fe, NM 87505
505-983-4554
www.nmhotels.com
For reservations at lodg-
ings, including bed and
breakfasts and resorts,
throughout the state.

Taos Valley Resort
Association
P.O. Box 85
Taos Ski Valley, NM 87525
505-776-2233 or
  800-776-1111
visitnewmexico.com
Central reservation agent
for northern New Mexico.

**Bitter Lake National
Wildlife Refuge, and
vicinity**

Roswell serves as the
gateway to Bitter Lake
Wildlife Refuge. For
lodging and other tourist
information, contact the
Roswell Chamber of
Commerce (505-623-5695
or 877-849-7679.
www.roswellnm.org).

**Carlsbad Caverns NP,
Guadalupe Mountains NP,
and vicinity**

Carlsbad is the main gateway to Carlsbad Caverns
and Guadalupe Mountains
National Parks. For information on lodging and
activities, contact the Carlsbad Chamber of Com-
merce (505-887-6516 or
800-221-1224. www
.caverns.com/~chamber).

Manzano and Sandia Mountains

Albuquerque is the base from which to embark on a trip into the Manzano and Sandia Mountains. For lodging and other tourist information, contact the Albuquerque Convention & Visitors Bureau (505-842-9918 or 800-284-2282. www.abqcvb.org).

Pecos Wilderness

A popular gateway to the Pecos Wilderness is nearby Santa Fe. For information on lodging, contact the Santa Fe Convention & Visitors Bureau (505-955-6200 or 800-877-2489. www.santafe.org).

Rio Grande Wild and Scenic River, and vicinity

Situated along the river, Taos is a popular access for recreational activities on the Rio Grande. For information on lodging and outfitters, contact the Taos County Chamber of Commerce (800-732-TAOS. www.taoschamber.org).

White Sands National Monument, and vicinity

Alamogordo, the gateway to White Sands, offers a wide range of accommodations. For information, contact the Chamber of Commerce (505-437-6120 or 800-826-0294. www.alamogordo.com).

Camping

For a listing of private campgrounds around the state, contact the New Mexico Department of Tourism (see p. 281). New Mexico State Parks (see p. 281), the U. S. D. A. Forest Service (see p. 279), and the Bureau of Land Management (see p. 281) also operate campgrounds throughout New Mexico. Additional information is available at www.gorp.com.

Happy Campers
1111 10th St., No. 175
Alamogordo, NM 88310
505-925-0679
www.happycampers.net
Resource for RV camping in the Southwest.

Hotel & Motel Chains in Arizona & New Mexico

Accommodations are available in both states unless otherwise noted.

Best Western International
800-528-1234

Choice Hotels
800-4-CHOICE

Clarion Hotel
800-CLARION

Comfort Inn and Suites
800-221-2222

Days Inn
800-325-2525

Double Tree Hotels and Guest Suites
800-222-TREE

Econo Lodge
800-446-6900

Embassy Suites
800-EMBASSY

Fairfield Inn by Marriott
800-228-2800

Friendship Inns Hotel
800-453-5411

Hampton Inn
800-HAMPTON

Hilton Hotels
800-HILTONS

Holiday Inns
800-HOLIDAY

Howard Johnson
800-654-2000

Independent Motels of America
800-841-0255

LaQuinta Motor Inns
800-531-5900

Lowes Hotels
800-112-0888 (Ariz. only)

Motel 6
800-466-8356

Quality Inns-Hotels-Suites
800-228-5151

Radisson Hotels International
800-333-3333

Ramada Inns
800-2-RAMADA

Red Lion
800-547-8010 (Ariz. only)

Red Roof Inns
800-843-7663 (Ariz. only)

About the Author and the Photographer

Mel White, a former newspaper reporter and magazine editor, has for the past decade been a free-lance writer specializing in travel and natural history. He has written or contributed to a dozen National Geographic books, including the two-volume *National Geographic Guide to Birdwatching Sites* and *Exploring the Great Rivers of North America*. His work as a contributing editor to National Geographic **Traveler** has taken him from Amazonia to the Seychelles to New Zealand's Milford Track, but his appreciation of America's diverse environments remains undiminished. He lives in Little Rock, Arkansas.

A travel and natural history photographer based in Arizona, **George H. H. Huey**'s passion is visual interpretation of remaining wildlands. His subjects range from western landscapes to natural details to international destinations. Huey's work has appeared in dozens of magazines, including *Audubon*, Conde Nast *Traveler*, *Islands*, *National Geographic*, *Outside*, *Time*, and *Travel& Leisure*. Books include *The Smithsonian Guide to Natural America: The Southwest*, *California's Channel Islands*, and *Grand Views of Canyon Country*.

Illustrations Credits

Photographs in this book are by George H. H. Huey except for the following:
pp. 88-89 - Michael S. Quinton

Index

National Geographic Guide to America's Outdoors: Southwest
by Mel White
Photographed by George H. H. Huey

Published by the National Geographic Society
John M. Fahey, Jr., *President and Chief Executive Officer*
Gilbert M. Grosvenor, *Chairman of the Board*
Nina D. Hoffman, *Senior Vice President*

Prepared by the Book Division
William R. Gray, *Vice President and Director*
Charles Kogod, *Assistant Director*
Barbara A. Payne, *Editorial Director and Managing Editor*

Guides to America's Outdoors
Elizabeth L. Newhouse, *Director of Travel Books*
Cinda Rose, *Art Director*
Barbara A. Noe, *Associate Editor*
Caroline Hickey, *Senior Researcher*
Carl Mehler, *Director of Maps*
Roberta Conlan, *Project Director*

Staff for this Book
Patricia Daniels, Alison J. Kahn, *Editors*
Dorrit Green, *Art Director*
Molly Roberts, *Illustrations Editor*
Victoria Garrett Jones, Keith R. Moore, Jane Sunderland, *Researchers*
Lise Sajewski, *Editorial Consultant*
Thomas L. Gray, Nicholas P. Rosenbach, *Map Editors*
Thomas L. Gray, Nicholas P. Rosenbach, Mapping Specialists, *Map Research*
Matt Chwastyk, Jerome N. Cookson, Mapping Specialists, *Map Production*
Tibor G. Tóth, *Map Relief*
R. Gary Colbert, *Production Director*
Meredith Wilcox, *Illustrations Assistant*
Julia Marshall, *Indexer*
Angela George, *Project Assistant*
Deb Antonini, *Contributor*
Gary Bell and Rici Peterson, *Consultants*

Manufacturing and Quality Control
George V. White, *Director;* John T. Dunn, *Associate Director;* Vincent P. Ryan, *Manager;*
Phillip L. Schlosser, *Financial Analyst*

Library of Congress Cataloging-in-Publication Data

White, Mel, 1950-
    Guide to America's great outdoors. Southwest/by Mel White; photography by George H. H. Huey.
      p. cm.—(National Geographic guides to America's outdoors)
    Includes index.
    ISBN 0-7922-7950-6
  1. Southwest, New—Guidebooks. 2. National parks and
reserves—Southwest, New—Guidebooks. 3. Outdoor recreation—Southwest,
New—Guidebooks. I. Title: Southwest. II. Huey, George H. H. III.
National Geographic Society (U.S.) IV. Title. V. Series.

  F785.3 .W47 2000
  917.904'33—dc21

                                                                    00-056237
                                                                    CIP

The information in this book has been carefully checked and is accurate as of press date.
However, details are subject to change, and the National Geographic Society cannot be
responsible for such changes, or for errors or omissions. Assessments of sites are based on
the authors' subjective opinions, which do not necessarily reflect the publisher's opinion.
The publisher cannot be responsible for any consequences arising from the use of this book.